The Spurgeon Collection

PARABLES

The
CH SPURGEON
collection

The
CH SPURGEON
collection

Parables

EMERALD HOUSE

BELFAST **GREENVILLE**
NORTHERN IRELAND **SOUTH CAROLINA**

The CH Spurgeon Collection
VOLUME 4: PARABLES
Copyright © 1998 Emerald House Group

Published by
Emerald House Group, Inc.
1 Chick Springs Road, Suite 206
Greenville, SC 29609 USA

and

Ambassador Productions
16 Hillview Avenue
Belfast, Northern Ireland
BT5 6JR

Cover design and illustration by Matt Donovan

Handwriting in background on cover from actual sermon notes written by C.H.
Spurgeon. Used by permission. Courtesy of the Bob Jones University Mack Library.

CONTENTS

I

THE SOWER

"Behold, a sower went forth to sow."—Matt. 13: 3.

THIS was a very important event. I do not say that it was important if you took the individual case alone; but, if you took the multitudes of cases in which it was also true, it was overwhelmingly important in the aggregate: "A sower went forth to sow." Yes, Christ thinks it worth while to mention that a single sower went forth to sow, that a Christian man went out to address a meeting on a village green, or to conduct a Bible Class, or to speak anywhere for the Lord. But when you think of the hundreds of preachers of the Gospel who go out to sow every Lord's Day, and the myriads of teachers who go to instruct the children in our Sabbath Schools, it is, surely, in the aggregate, the most important event under heaven.

You may omit, O recording angel, the fact that a warrior went forth to fight; it is far more important that you should record that "a sower went forth to sow." You may even forget that a man of science went into his laboratory, and made a discovery, for no discovery can equal in importance the usual processes of husbandry. Do you hear the song of the harvest home? Do you see the loaded wagons follow one another in a long line to the farmer's barn? If so, remember that there would be no harvest home if the sower went not forth to sow. As the flail is falling upon the wheat, or the threshing machine is making the grain to leap from among the chaff, and the miller's wheels are grinding merrily, and the women are kneading the dough, and the bread is set upon the table, and parents and children are fed to the full, do not forget that all this could never happen unless "a sower went forth to sow." On this action hinges the very life of man. Bread, which is the staff of his life, would be broken, and taken from him, and his life could not continue did not a sower still go forth to sow.

And the spiritual sowing stands in the same relation to the spiritual world that the natural sowing occupies in the natural world. It is a most important thing that we should continually go forth to preach the Gospel. It may seem, to some people, a small matter that I should occupy this pulpit, and I shall not lay any undue importance upon that fact; yet eternity may not exhaust all that shall result from the preaching of the Gospel here; there may be souls, plucked like brands from the burning, saved with an everlasting salvation, lamps lit by the Holy Spirit that shall shine like stars in the firmament of God for ever and ever. Who knoweth, O teacher, when thou labourest even among the infants, what the result of thy teaching may be? Good corn may grow in very small fields. God may bless thy simple words to the babes that listen to them. How knowest thou, O my unlettered brother, when thou standest up in the cottage meeting to talk to a few poor folk about Christ, what may follow from that effort of thine? Life or death, heaven or hell, may depend upon the sowing of the good seed of the Gospel.

It is, it must be, the most important event that can ever happen, if the Lord goeth forth with thee when thou goest forth as the sower went forth to sow. Hark to the songs of the angels; see the overflowing brightness and excessive glory of thy Heavenly Father's face. He rejoices because souls are born to Christ; but how could there be this joy, in the ordinary course, and speaking after the manner of men, without the preaching of the Word? For it still pleases God, by the foolishness of preaching, to save them that believe.

I am going to try to answer three questions concerning this sower. First, *who was he?* Secondly, *what did he do?* And, thirdly, *what was he at?*

First, WHO WAS HE? We do not know anything at all about him except that he was a sower. His individuality seems to be swallowed up in his office. We do not know who his father was, or his mother, or his sister, or his brother; all we know is that he was a sower, and I do like to see a man who is so much a minister that he is nothing else but a minister. It does not matter who he is, or what he has, or what else he can do, if he does this one thing. He has lost his identity in his service, though he has also gained it over again in another way. He has lost his selfhood, and has become, once for all, a sower, and nothing but a sower.

Observe that *there are many personal matters which are quite unimportant.* It is not mentioned here whether he was a refined sower, or a rustic sower; and it does not matter which he was. So is it with the workers for Christ; God blesses all sorts of men. William Huntington, the coal-heaver, brought many souls to Christ. Some have doubted this; but, in my early Christian days, I knew some of the excellent of the earth who were the spiritual children of the coal-heaver. Chalmers stood at the very opposite pole, a master of cultured gracious speech, a learned, well-trained man; and what multitudes Chalmers brought to Christ! So, whether it was Huntington or Chalmers, does not matter: "A sower went forth to sow." One preacher talks like Rowland Hill, in very plain Saxon with a touch of humour; another, like Robert Hall, uses a grand style of speech, full of brilliant rhetoric, and scarcely ever condescending to men of low degree, yet God blessed both of them. What mattered it whether the speech was of the colloquial or of the oratorical order so long as God blessed it? The man preached the Gospel; exactly how he preached it need not be declared. He was a sower, he went forth to sow, and there came a glorious harvest from his sowing.

Now you have begun earnestly to speak for Christ, but you are troubled because you cannot speak like Mr. So-and-so. Do not try to speak like Mr. So-and-so. You say, "I heard a man preach, the other night; and when he had done, I thought I could never preach again." Well, it was very naughty, on your part, to think that. You ought rather to have said, "I will try to preach all the better now that I have heard one who preaches so much better than I can." Just feel that you have to sow the good seed of the kingdom; and, if you have not so big a hand as some sowers have and cannot sow quite so much at a time, go and sow with your smaller hand, only mind that you sow the same seed, for so God will accept what you do. You are grieved that you do not know so much as some do, and that you have not the same amount of learning that they have. You regret that you have not the poetical faculty of some, or the holy ingenuity of others. Why do you speak about all these things? Our Lord Jesus Christ does not do so; he simply says, "A sower went forth to sow." He does not tell us how he was dressed; he mentions nothing about whether he was a black man, or a white man, or what kind of man he was; he tells us nothing about him except that he was a sower. Will you try to be nothing but a soul-winner?

Next notice that, as the various personal matters relating to the man are too unimportant to be recorded, *his name and his fame are not written in this Book.* Do you want to have your name put to everything that you do? Mind that God does not let you have your desire, and then say to you, "There, you have done that unto yourself, so you can reward yourself for it." As far as ever you can, keep your own name out of all the work you do for the Lord. I used to notice, in Paris, that there was not a bridge, or a public building, without the letter "N" somewhere on it. Now, go through all the city, and find an "N" if you can. Napoleon hoped his fame would live in imperishable marble, but he had written his name in sand after all; and if any one of us shall, in our ministry, think it the all-important matter to make our own name prominent, we are on the wrong tack altogether. When George Whitefield was asked to start a new sect, he said, "I do not condemn my brother Wesley for what he has done, but I cannot do the same; let my name perish, but let Christ's name endure for ever and ever."

We have no record of the name and the fame of this man, yet *we do know something about him.* We know that he must have been, first of all, an eater, or he never would have been a sower. The Gospel is seed for the sower, and bread for the eater; and every man, who really goes out to sow for God, must first have been an eater. There is not a man, on the face of the earth, who treads the furrows of the field and sows the seed, but must first have been an eater of bread; and there is not a true servant of God, beneath the cope of heaven, but has first fed on the Gospel before he has preached it. If there be any who pretend to sow, but who have never themselves eaten, God have mercy upon them! What a desecration of the pulpit it is for a man to attempt to preach what he does not himself know! What a desecration it is of even a Sunday School class for an unconverted young man, or young woman, to be a teacher of others! I do not think such a thing ought to be allowed. Wherever it has been permitted, I charge any, who have been trying to teach what they do not themselves know, to cry to God to teach them, that they may not go and pretend to speak in the name of the Lord, to the children, till, first of all, Christ has spoken peace and pardon to their own hearts, and he has been formed in them the hope of glory. May every worker put to himself the question, "Have I fed upon and enjoyed that good Word which I am professing to teach to others?"

Next, having been an eater, he must also have been a receiver. A sower cannot sow if he has not any seed. It is a mere mockery to go up and down a field, and to pretend to scatter seed out of an empty hand. Is there not a great deal of so-called Christian work that is just like that? Those who engage in it have not anything to give; and, therefore, they can give nothing. We must receive the Gospel seed from God before we can sow it. The sower went to his master's granary and received so many bushels of wheat, and he then went out and sowed it. I am afraid that some would-be sowers fail in this matter of being receivers. They are in a great hurry to take a class, or to preach here, or there, or somewhere else, but there is nothing in it all. What can there be in thy speech but sounding brass, and a tinkling cymbal, unless thou hast received the living Word from the living God, and art sent forth to proclaim it to men?

A true sower, also, is a disseminator of the Word of God. No man is a sower unless he scatters the truth. If he does not preach truth, he is not a sower in the true meaning of that term. A man may go whistling up and down the furrows, and people may mistake him for a sower, but he is not really one; and if there is not, in what we preach, the real, solid truth of God's Word, however prettily we may put our sweet nothings, we have not been serving the Lord.

We seem to know a little about this sower now, and we further know that *he was one of a noble line*. What our Lord really said was, "THE SOWER went forth to sow;" and I think I see him coming forth out of the ivory palaces, from the lone glory of his own eternal nature, going down to Bethlehem, becoming a babe, waiting a while till the seed was ready, and then standing by the Jordan, and by the hill-side, and at Capernaum, and Nazareth, and everywhere scattering those great seeds that have made the wilderness and the solitary place to be glad, and the desert to rejoice and blossom as the rose. See how all Christendom has sprung from the sowing of that Man; and our glorious Lord has long been reaping, and this day is reaping still, the harvest of the seed-sowing on the hill-sides of Galilee. "The Sower went forth to sow." Are you not glad to be in that noble line?

But who are the sowers who came next? Men "of whom the world was not worthy," men who suffered for their Lord and Master, his apostles, and those who received their word, and who were faithful even unto death, a goodly army of all sorts of people, old and young, rich and poor, wise and unlettered. And there has always continued a band of sowers going forth to sow, men who could not help doing it, like the tinker of Bedford. They commanded him not to sow any more of the seed, and they cast him into prison because he would still do it; but, through the window of that prison he kept on sowing great handfuls of seed which are, even now, falling upon the broad acres of our own and other lands. When they bade him be quiet, he said, "If you let me out of prison to-day, I will preach again to-morrow, by the grace of God." "Oh, then!" they answered, "go back to your cell, sir." "Yes," he said, "and I will lie there till the moss grows on my eyelids, before I will make you any promise that I will be silent." He must sow, he could not help it. Well, now, to-day, it is imagined by some that the new theology is to put an end to our sowing of the good seed of the Kingdom; but will it? I believe that the sowers will still go to every lane and alley of the city, and to every hamlet and village of our country, when God wills it, for the Gospel is as everlasting as the God who gave it, and, therefore, it cannot die out; and, when they think that they have killed the plant, it will spring up everywhere more vigorous than before.

The sower is not only a man of an honourable line, but he is also a worker together with God. It is God's design that every plant should propagate and reproduce its like; and especially is it his design that wheat, and other cereals so useful to men, should be continued and multiplied on the face of the earth. Who is to do it? God will see that it is done; and, usually, he employs men to be his agents. There are some seeds that never can be sown by men, but only by birds. But as to wheat, man must sow that; you cannot go into any part of the world, and find a field of wheat unless a man has sown the seed to produce it. You may find fields full of thistles, but wheat must be sown. It is not a wild thing, it must have a man to care for it; and God, therefore, links himself with man in the continuance of wheat on the face of the earth; and he has so arranged that, while he could spread the Gospel by his Spirit without human voices, while he could bring untold myriads to himself without any instrumentality, yet he does not do so; and, as means to the end he has in view, he intends YOU to speak, that he may speak through you, and that, in the speaking, the seed may be scattered, which he shall make to bring forth an abundant harvest.

Now, secondly, WHAT DID THIS SOWER DO? He "went forth." I think this means, first, that *he bestirred himself*. He said, "It is time that I went forth to sow. I have waited quite long enough for favourable weather; but I remember that Solomon said, 'He that observeth the wind shall not sow.' I feel that the sowing time has come for me, and I must set about it." Can I look upon some here, who have been members of the church for years, but who have never yet done anything for the Lord? If you have been a servant of God for many years, and have never yet really worked for the salvation of souls, I want you now just to say to yourself, "Come now, I must really get at this work." You will be going home soon; and when your Master says to you, "Did you do any sowing for me?" you will have to reply, "No, Lord; I did plenty of eating. I went to the Tabernacle, and I enjoyed the Services." "But did you do any sowing?" "No, Lord; I did a great deal of hoarding; I laid up a large quantity of the good seed." "But did you do any sowing?" he will still ask, and that will be a terrible question for those who never went forth to sow.

You are very comfortable at home, are you not? In the long winter evenings that are coming on, it will be so pleasant to enjoy yourselves at home of an evening. There, stir the fire, and draw the curtain close, and let us sit down, and spend a happy time. Yes, but is it not time for you, Mr. Sower, to go forth? The millions of London are perishing; asylums for the insane are filling, jails are filling, poverty is abounding, and drunkenness at every street-corner. Harlotry is making good men and women to blush. It is time to set about work for the Lord if I am ever to do it. What are some of you doing for God? Oh, that you would begin to take stock of your capacity and say, "I must get to work for the Master. I must do it at once, or I may be called home, and my day be over before I have sown a single handful of wheat."

Next, *the sower quitted his privacy*. He came out from his solitude, and began to sow. This is what I mean. At first, a Christian man very wisely lives indoors. There is a lot of cleaning and scrubbing to be done there. When the bees come out of their cells, they always spend the first few days of their life in the hive cleaning and getting everything tidy. They do not go out to gather honey till they have first of all done the housework at home. I wish that all Christian people would get their housework done as soon as they can. It needs to be done. I mean, acquaintance with experimental matters of indwelling sin, and overcoming grace. But, after that, then the sower went forth to sow. He was not content with his own private experience, but he went forth to sow. There are numbers of people who are miserable because they are always at home. Go out, brother; go out, sister. Important as your experience is, it is only important as a platform for real usefulness. Get all right within, in order that you may get to work without.

The sower, when he went forth to sow, also *quitted his occupation of a learner and an enjoyer of the truth*. He was in the Bible Class for a year or two, and he gained a deal of Scriptural knowledge there. He was also a regular hearer of the Word. You could see him regularly sitting in his pew, and drinking in the Word; but, after a while, he said to himself, "I have no right to remain in this Bible Class; I ought to be in the Sunday School, and take a class myself." Then he said to himself, on a Sabbath evening, "I have been to one service to-day, and have been spiritually fed, so I think I ought to go to one of the lodging-houses in the Mint, and speak to the people there, or find some other holy occupation in which I can be doing some good to others."

"A sower went forth to sow." Where did he come from? I do not know what house he came from, but I can tell you the place from which he last came. *He came out of the granary*. He must have been to the granary to get the seed. At least, if he did not go there before he went to sow, he did not have anything that was worth sowing. We must always go to the granary, must we not? Without the diligent and constant study of Scripture, of what use will our preaching be? "I went into the pulpit," said one, "and I preached straight off just what came into my mind, and thought nothing of it." "Yes," said another, "and your people thought nothing of it, too." That is sure to be the case. You teachers, who go to your classes quite unprepared, and open your Bible, and say just what comes first, should remember that God does not want your nonsense. "Oh, but!" says one, "it is not by human wisdom that souls are saved." No, nor is it by human ignorance. He can never be a teacher who is not first a learner.

I wonder whether this sower did what I recommend every Christian sower to do; namely, to come forth from *the place where he had steeped his seed.* One farmer complained that his wheat did not grow, and another asked him, "Do you steep your seed?" "No," he replied, "I never heard of such a thing." The first one said, "I steep mine in prayer, and God prospers me." If we always steep our heavenly seed in prayer, God will prosper us also. For one solitary man to stand up, and preach, is poor work; but for two of us to be here, is grand work.

You have heard the story of the Welsh preacher who had not arrived when the Service ought to have been begun, and his host sent a boy to the room to tell him that it was time to go to preach. The boy came hurrying back, and said, "Sir, he is in his room, but I do not think he is coming. There is somebody in there with him. I heard him speaking very loudly, and very earnestly, and I heard him say that if that other person did not come with him, he would not come at all, and the other one never answered him, so I do not think he will come." "Ah!" said the host, who understood the case, "he will come, and the Other One will come with him." Oh! it is good sowing when the sower goes forth to sow, and the Other comes with him! Then we go forth with steeped seed, seed that is sprouting in our hands as we go forth. This does not happen naturally, but it does happen spiritually. It seems to grow while we are handling it, for there is life in it; and, when it is sown, there will be life in it to our hearers.

Further, this sower *went forth into the open field.* Wherever there was a field ready for the sowing, there he came. We must always try to do good where there is the greatest likelihood of doing good. If it is so in your little chapel, if the people do not come, I do not desire that the chapel should be burnt down, but it might be a very mitigated calamity if you had to turn out into the street to preach, or if you had to go to some hall or barn, for some people might come and hear you there who will never hear you now. You must go forth to sow. You cannot sit at your parlour window, and sow wheat; and you cannot stand on one little plot of ground, and keep on sowing there. If you have done your work in that place, go forth to sow elsewhere. Oh, that the Church of Christ would go forth into heathen lands! Oh, that there might be, among Christians, a general feeling that they must go forth to sow! What a vast acreage there still is upon which not a grain of God's wheat has ever yet fallen! Oh, for a great increase of the missionary spirit! May God send it upon the entire Church until everywhere it shall be said, "Behold, a sower went forth to sow."

When did this man go forth to sow? Our farming friends begin to sow very soon after harvest. That is the time to sow for Christ. As soon as ever you have won one soul for him, try and win another by God's grace. Say to yourself what the general said to his troops when some of them came riding up and said, "Sir, we have captured a gun from the enemy." "Then," said he, "go and capture another." After the reaping, let the sowing follow as speedily as possible. In season, this sower sowed. It is a great thing to observe the proper season for sowing, but it is a greater thing to sow in improper seasons also, for out of season is sometimes the best season for God's sowers to sow. "Be instant in season, out of season," was Paul's exhortation to Timothy. Oh, for grace to be always sowing! I have known good men to go about, and never to be without tracts to give away, and suitable tracts, too. They seem to have picked them out, and God has given them an occasion suitable for the tracts; or, if they have not given tracts, they have been ready with a good word, a choice word, a loving word, a tender word. There is a way of getting the Gospel in edgewise, when you cannot get it in at the front. Wise sowers sow their seed broadcast, yet I have generally noticed that they never sow against the wind, for that would blow the dust into their eyes; and there is nothing like sowing with the wind. Whichever way the Holy Spirit seems to be moving, and providence is also moving, scatter your seed, that the wind may carry it as far as possible, and that it may fall where God shall make it grow.

Thus I have told you what the man did: "A sower went forth to sow." I must answer briefly the last of the three questions I mentioned,—WHAT WAS THIS SOWER AT?

On this occasion, he did not go forth *to keep the seed to himself.* He went forth to throw it to the wind; he threw it away from himself, scattered it far and wide. He did not go out to defend it; but he threw it about, and left it to take its chance. He did not go, at this time, to examine it, to see whether it was good wheat or not. No doubt he had done that before; but he just scattered it. He did not go out to winnow it, and blow away the chaff, or pick out any darnel that might be in it. That was all done at home. Now he has nothing to do but to sow it, *to sow it,* TO SOW IT; and he sows it with all his might. He did not even come to push others out of the field who might be sowing bad seed, but he took occasion, at this particular time, to go forth to sow and to do nothing else.

One thing at a time, and that done well,
Is a very good rule, as many can tell;

and it is especially so in the service of God. Do not try to do twenty things at once: "A sower went forth TO SOW." *His object was a limited one.* He did not go forth to make the seed grow. No, that was beyond his power; he went forth to sow. If we were responsible for the effect of the Gospel upon the hearts of men, we should be in a sorry plight indeed: but we are only responsible for the sowing of the good seed. If you hear the Gospel and reject it, that is your act, and not ours. If you are saved by it, give God the glory; but if it proves to be a savour of death unto death to you, yours is the sin, the shame, and the sorrow.

This man's one object was positively before him, and we are to impart the truth, to make known to men the whole of the Gospel. You are lost, God is gracious, Christ has come to seek and to save that which is lost. Whosoever believeth in him shall not perish, but shall have everlasting life. On the Cross he offered the sacrifice by which sin is put away. Believe in him, and you live by his death. This sowing, you see, is simply telling out the truth; and this is the main thing that we have to do, to keep on telling the same truth over, and over, and over, and over again, till we get it into the minds and hearts of men, and they receive it through God's blessing. If the sower had sat down at the corner of the field, and played the harp all day, he would not have done his duty; and if, instead of preaching the simple Gospel, we talk of the high or deep mysteries of God, we shall not have done our duty. The sower's one business is to sow; so, stick to your sowing.

Now let me remind you that *sowing is an act of faith*. If a man had not great faith in God, he would not take the little wheat he has, and go and bury it. His good wife might say to him, "John, we shall want that corn for the children, so don't you go and throw it out where the birds may eat it, or the worms destroy it." And you must preach the Gospel, and you must teach the Gospel, as an act of faith. You must believe that God will bless it. If not, you are not likely to get a blessing upon it. If it is done merely as a natural act, or a hopeful act, that will not be enough; it must be done as an act of confidence in the living God.

This sowing was also *an act of concentrated energy*. The sower "went forth TO sow." He went forth, not with two aims or objects, but with this one; not dividing his life into a multitude of channels, but making all run in one strong, deep current, along this one river-bed.

I know not how far you may be going, but let it be written of you to-day, "The sowers went forth to sow," they went forth with one resolve that, by the power of the living Spirit of God, they who are redeemed with the precious blood of Jesus would make known his Gospel to the sons of men, sowing that good seed in every place wherever they have the opportunity, trusting in God to make the seed increase and multiply.

As for you who have never received the living seed, oh, that you would receive it at once! May God, the Holy Spirit, make you to be like well-prepared ground that opens a thousand mouths to take in the seed, and then encloses the seed within itself, and makes it fructify!

II

THE MUSTARD SEED
(For Sunday School Teachers)

"Then said he, Unto what is the kingdom of God like? and whereunto shall I resemble it? It is like a grain of mustard seed, which a man took, and cast into his garden; and it grew, and waxed a great tree; and the fowls of the air lodged in the branches of it."—Luke 13 : 18, 19.

THIS parable may be understood to relate to our Lord himself, who is the living seed. You know also how his church is the tree that springs from him, and how greatly it grows and spreads its branches until it covers the earth. From the one man Christ Jesus, despised and rejected of men, slain and buried, and so hidden away from among men—from him, I say, there ariseth a multitude which no man can number. These spread themselves, like some tree which grows by the rivers of waters, and they yielded both gracious shelter and spiritual food.

But at this time of the year, Sabbath School teachers come together specially to pray for a blessing on their work; and pastors are invited to say a word to cheer them in their self-denying service. This request I cheerfully fulfil. My discourse will not be a full explanation of the parable, but an adaptation of it to the cheering of those who are engaged in the admirable work of teaching the young the fear of the Lord.

In this parable light is thrown upon the work of those who teach the Gospel. First, *notice a very simple work:* "a grain of mustard seed, which a man took, and cast into his garden." Secondly, *observe what came of it:* "it grew, and waxed a great tree; and the fowls of the air lodged in the branches of it."

First, NOTICE A VERY SIMPLE WORK. The work of teaching the Gospel is as the casting of a grain of mustard seed into a garden.

Note, first, *what the nameless man did.* "It is like a grain of mustard seed, which a man took." *He took it;* that is to say, picked it out from the bulk. It was only one grain, and a grain of a very insignificant seed. A grain of mustard seed is too small a thing for public exhibition; but the man set it before his own mind as a distinct object to be dealt with. It is well for the teacher to know what he is going to teach; to have that truth distinctly in his mind's eye, as the man had the grain of mustard seed between his fingers. Depend upon it, unless a truth is clearly seen and distinctly recognised by the teacher, little will come of it to the taught. It may be a very simple truth; but if a man takes it, understands it, grasps it, and loves it, he will do something with it. Beloved, first and foremost let us ourselves take the Gospel, let us believe it, let us appreciate it, let us prize it beyond all things; for truth lives as it is loved, and no hand is so fit for its sowing as the hand which grasps it well.

Further, in this little parable we notice that this man *had a garden:* "Like a grain of mustard seed, which a man took, and cast into his garden." Some Christian people have no garden— no personal sphere of service. They belong to the whole clan of Christians, and they pine to see the entire band go out to cultivate the whole world; but they do not come to personal particulars. It is delightful to be warmed up by missionary addresses and to feel a zeal for the salvation of all the nations; but, after all, the net result of a general theoretic earnestness for all the world does not amount to much.

It is the duty of every believer in Christ, like the first man, Adam, to have a garden to dress and to till. Children are in the Sunday Schools by millions: thank God for that! But have *you* a class of your own? All the church at work for Christ! Glorious theory! Are *you* up and doing for your Lord? It will be a grand time when every believer has his allotment and is sowing it with the seed of truth. The wilderness and the solitary place will blossom as the rose when each Christian cultivates his own plot of roses. Teach your own children, speak to your neighbours, seek the conversion of those whom God has especially entrusted to you.

Having a garden, and having this seed, *the man sowed it:* and simple as this is, it is the hinge of the instruction. You have a number of seeds in a pill-box. There they are: look at them!

Take that box down this day twelve months, and the seeds will be just the same. Lay them by in that dry box for seven years, and nothing will happen. Truth is not to be kept to ourselves: it is to be published and advocated. If you put truth away and leave it without a voice, it won't prevail; it will not even contend. When have great truths prevailed? Why, when brave men have persisted in declaring them. Daring spirits have taken up a cause which has been, at the first, unpopular, and they have spoken about it so earnestly, and so often, that at length the cause has commanded attention: they have pressed on and on till the cause has triumphed altogether. Not even the Gospel itself, if it be not taught, will prevail. If revealed truth be laid on one side and kept in silence, it will not grow. Mark how, through the dark ages, the Gospel lay asleep in old books in the libraries of monasteries, till Luther and his fellow reformers fetched it out and sowed it in the minds of men.

This man simply cast it into his garden. He did not wrap it round with gold leaf, or otherwise adorn it; but he put it into the ground. The naked seed came into contact with the naked soil. O teachers, do not try to make the Gospel look fine; do not overlay it with your fine words, or elaborate explanations. The Gospel seed is to be put into the young heart just as it is. Get the truth concerning the Lord Jesus into the children's minds. Make them know, not what you can say about the truth, but what the truth itself says. The Gospel is the thought of God: in and of itself it is the message which the soul needs. It is the Gospel itself which will grow. Take a truth, specially that great doctrine, that man is lost and that Christ is the only Saviour, and see to it that you place it in the mind. Teach plainly the great truth that whosoever believeth in him hath everlasting life; and that the Lord Jesus bare our sins in his own body on the tree, and suffered for us, the just for the un-just—I say take these truths and set them forth to the mind, and see what will come of it. Sow the very truth; not your reflections on the truth, not your embellishments of the truth, but the truth itself.

That which is described in the parable was an insignificant business: the man took the tiny seed and put it into his garden. It is a very commonplace affair to sit down with a dozen children around you and open your Bible and tell them the well-worn tale of how Jesus Christ came into the world to save sinners. No Pharisee is likely to stand and blow a trumpet when he is going to teach children: he is more likely to point to the children in the temple, and sneeringly say, "Hearest thou what these say?" It is a lowly business altogether. Dear Sunday School teacher, do not become weary of your humble work, for none can measure its importance. Tell the boys and girls of the Son of God, who lived and loved and died that the ungodly might be saved. Urge them to immediate faith in the mighty Saviour, that they may be saved at once. Tell of the new birth, and how the souls of men are renewed by the Holy Spirit, without whose divine working none can enter the kingdom of heaven. Teach the Gospel of grace, and nothing but the Gospel of grace, if you would see grace growing in the hearts of your young people.

Secondly, let us consider *what it was that the man sowed*. We have seen that he sowed: what did he sow? It was one single seed, and that seed a very small one; so very, very small, that the Jews were accustomed to say, "As small as mustard seed." Hence the Saviour speaks of it as the smallest among seeds; which it may not have been absolutely, but which it was according to common parlance; and our Lord was not teaching botany, but speaking a popular parable. Yes, the Gospel seems a very simple thing: Believe and live! Look to Jesus dying in the sinner's stead! Look to Jesus crucified, even as Israel looked to the brazen serpent lifted up upon a pole. It is simplicity itself: in fact, the Gospel is so plain a matter that our superior people are weary of it, and look out for something more difficult of comprehension. People nowadays are like the negro who liked to hear the Scriptures "properly confounded"; or like the other who said, "You should hear our minister dispense with the truth!" Sowing seed is work too ordinary for the moderns: they demand new methods. But we must not run after vain inventions: our one business is to sow the Word of God in the mind of children. It is yours and mine to teach everybody the simple truth, that Jesus Christ came into the world to save sinners, and that whosoever believeth in him shall not perish, but have everlasting life. We know nothing else among men or among children. Men sneeringly say, "What can be the moral result of preaching such a Gospel? Surely it would be better to discourse upon morals, social economics and the sciences?" Ah, if you can do any good in those ways, we will not hinder you; but our belief is that a hundred times more can be done with the Gospel; for it is the power of God unto salvation unto every one that believeth. The Gospel is not the enemy of any good thing; say, rather, it is the force by which good things are to be carried out. Whatsoever things are pure and honest and of good repute are all nurtured by that spirit which is begotten by the simple Gospel of Christ. Yet conversions do not come by essays upon morals, but by the teaching of salvation by Christ. The cleansing and raising of our race will not be effected by politics or science, but by the Word of the Lord, which liveth and abideth for ever.

But the seed, though very small, was *a living thing*. There is a great difference between a mustard seed and a piece of wax of the same size. Life slumbers in that seed. What life is, we cannot tell. Even if you take a microscope you cannot spy it out. It is a mystery: but it is essential to a seed. The Gospel has a something in it not readily discoverable by the philosophical enquirer, if, indeed, he can perceive it at all. Take a maxim of Socrates or of Plato, and enquire whether a nation or a tribe has ever been transformed by it from barbarism to culture. A maxim of a philosopher may have measurably influenced a man in some right direction; but who has ever heard of a man's whole character being transformed by any observation of Confucius or Socrates? I confess I never have. Human teachings are barren. But within the Gospel, with all its triteness and simplicity, there is a divine life, and that life makes all the difference. The human can never rival the divine, for it lacks the life-fire. Within God's Word, however simple it may be, there dwells an omnipotence like that of God, from whose lips it came.

Truth to tell, a seed is *a very comprehensive thing*. Within the mustard seed what is to be found? Why, there is all in it that ever comes out of it. It must be so. Every branch, and every leaf, and every flower, and every seed that is to be, is, in its essence, all within the seed: it needs to be developed; but it is all there. And so, within the simple Gospel, how much lies concentrated? Look at it! Within that truth lie regeneration, repentance, faith, holiness, zeal, consecration, perfection. Heaven hides itself away within the Gospel. We may not at first see all its results, nor, indeed, shall we see them at all, till we sow the seed and it grows; but yet it is all there. Do you believe it, young teacher? Have you realized what you have in your hold when you grasp the Gospel of the grace of God? It is the most wonderful thing beneath the skies. Do you discern that within its apparently narrow lines the Eternal, the Infinite, the Perfect, and the Divine are all enclosed? As in the Babe of Bethlehem there was the Eternal God, so within the simple teaching of "Believe and live" there are all the elements of eternal blessedness for men, and boundless glory for God.

And for this reason it is so wonderful: *it is a divine creation.* Summon your chemists: bring them together with all their vessels and their fires. Select a jury of the greatest chemists now alive, analytical or otherwise, as you will. Learned sirs, will you kindly make us a mustard seed? You may take a mustard seed, and pound it and analyse it, and you may thus ascertain all its ingredients. So far so good. Is not your work well begun? Now make a single mustard seed. We will give you a week. It is a very small affair. You have all the elements of mustard in yonder mortar. Make us one living grain: we do not ask for a ton weight. One grain of mustard seed will suffice us. Great chemists, have you not made so small a thing? A month has gone by. Only one grain of mustard seed we asked of you, and where is it? Have you not made one in a month? What are you at? Shall we allow you seven years? Yes, with all the laboratories in the kingdom at your service, and all known substances for your material, and all the world's coal-beds for your fuel, get to your work.

This baffles the wise men: they cannot make a living seed. No; and nobody can make a Gospel, or even a new Gospel text. The thinkers of the age could not even concoct another life of Christ to match with the four Gospels which we have already. I go further: they could not create a new incident which would be congruous with the facts we already know. Who will write a new Psalm, or even a new promise? Clever chemists prove their wisdom by saying at once, "No, we cannot make a mustard seed"; and wise thinkers will equally confess that they cannot make another Gospel. My learned brethren are trying very hard to make a new Gospel for this nineteenth century; but you teachers had better go on with the old one. The advanced men cannot put life into their theory. The Gospel of Sunday School teachers, that Gospel of "Believe and live," however men may despise it, has God-given life in it. Go on and use the one living truth with your children, for nothing else has God's life in it.

To sow a mustard seed is *a very inexpensive act*. Only one grain of mustard: nobody can find me a coin small enough to express its value. I do not know how much mustard seed the man had; certainly it is not a rare thing; but he only took one grain of it, and cast it into his garden. He emptied no exchequer by that expenditure; and this is one of the excellencies of Sabbath School work, that it neither exhausts the church of men nor of money. However much of it is done, it does not lessen the resources of our Zion: it is done freely, quietly, without excitement, without sacrifice of life; and yet what a fountain of blessing it is!

Still, it was *an act of faith*. It is always an act of faith to sow seed; because you have, for the time, to give it up, and receive nothing in return. The farmer takes his choice seed-corn and throws it into the soil of his field. He might have made many a loaf of bread with it; but he casts it away. Only his faith saves him from being judged a maniac: he expects it to return to him fifty-fold. If you had never seen a harvest, you would think that a man burying good wheat under the clods had gone mad; and, if you had never seen conversions, it might seem an absurd thing to be constantly teaching to boys and girls the story of the Man who was nailed to the tree. We preach and teach as a work of faith; and, remember, it is only as an act of faith that it will answer its purpose. The rule of the harvest is, "According to thy faith, be it unto thee." Believe, dear teacher, believe in the Gospel. Believe in what you are doing when you tell it. Believe that great results from slender causes spring.

It was an act which brought the sower no honour. The Saviour has chronicled the fact that the man took a grain of mustard seed and sowed it; but thousands of men had gone on sowing mustard seed for half a lifetime without a word. Dear teacher, go on sowing, though nobody should observe your diligence, or praise your faithfulness.

It seems to me that our Lord selected the mustard seed in this parable, not because its results are the greatest possible from a seed—for an oak or a cedar are much greater growths than a mustard tree—but he selected it because it is the greatest result as compared with the size of the seed. Follow out the analogy. Come to yonder school and see! That earnest young man is teaching a boy, one of those wild creatures of the street; they swarm in every quarter. A dozen young turks are before him, or say young arabs of the street; he is teaching them the Gospel. Small affair, is it not? Yes, very; but what may come of it? Think of how joyfully much may grow out of this little! What is that young man teaching? Only one elementary truth. Do not sneer; it is truth, but it is the mere alphabet of it. He touches upon nothing deep in theology: he only says, "Christ Jesus came into the world to save sinners. Dear boy, believe in the Lord Jesus, and live." That is all he says. Can any good thing come out of Nazareth? The teacher himself is teaching the one truth in a very poor way; at least, *he* thinks so. Ask him, when he has done, what he thinks of his own teaching; and he replies, "I do not feel fit to teach." Yes, that young man's teaching is sighed over; and in his own judgment it is poor and weak; but there is life in the truth he imparts, and eternal results will follow—results of which I have now to speak in the second part of my sermon.

Secondly, let us enquire, WHAT CAME OF IT?

First, "*it grew.*" That was what the sower hoped would come of it: he placed the seed in the ground, hoping that it would grow. It is not reasonable to suppose that he would have sown it if he had not hoped that it would spring up. Dear teacher, do you always sow in hope, do you trust that the Word will live and grow? Expect the truth to take root, and expand and grow up.

But though the sower expected growth, he could not himself have made it grow. After he had placed the seed in the ground, he could water it, he could pray God to make the sun shine on it; but he could not directly produce growth. Only he that made the seed could cause it to grow. Growth is a continuance of that almighty act by which life is at first given. The putting of life into the seed is God's work, and the bringing forth of the

life from the seed is God's work too. This is a matter within
your hope, but far beyond your power.

A very wonderful thing it is, that the seed should grow. If
we did not see it every day, we should be more astonished at
the growth of seed than at all the wonders of magicians. A
growing seed is God's abiding miracle. You see a piece of ground
near London covered with a market-garden, and after a few
months you go by the place, and you see streets, and a public
square, and a church, and a great population. You say to yourself, "It is remarkable that all these houses should have sprung
up in a few months." Yet that is not at all so wonderful as
for a ploughed field to become covered four feet high with
corn. Wonder at the growth of grace. See how it increases,
deepens, strengthens! Growth in grace is a marvel of divine
love. That a man should repent through the Gospel, that he
should believe in Jesus, that he should be totally changed,
that he should have a hope of heaven, that he should receive
power to become a child of God—these are all marvellous
things; and yet they are going on under our eyes, and we fail
to admire them as we should.

To the sower this growth was very pleasing. How pleasant
it is to see the seed of grace grow in children! Do you not
remember when you first sowed mustard-and-cress as a boy,
how the very next morning you went and turned the ground
up to see how much it had grown. How pleased you were when
you saw the little yellow shoot, and afterwards a green leaf or
two! So is it with the true teacher: he is anxious to see growth,
and he makes eager enquiry for it. An unsympathetic person
cries, "Oh, I do not think anything of that child's emotions.
It is merely a passing impression: he will soon forget it." The
teacher does not think so. The cold critic says, "I don't think
much of a child's weeping. Children's tears lie very near the
surface." But the teacher is full of hope that he sees in these
tears a real sorrow for sin, and an earnest seeking after the Lord.

People talk thus because they do not love children and live
with the desire to save them. If you sympathize with children,
you are pleased with every hopeful token and are on the watch
for every mark of divine life within them. Think, then, of what
my text says: "It grew." Oh, for a prayer just now, from all of
you: "Lord, make the Gospel grow wherever it falls! Whether

the preacher scatters it, or the teacher sows it; whether it falls among the aged people, or the young; Lord, make the Gospel grow!" Pray hard for it.

Next, having started growing, *it became a tree;* Luke says, "It waxed a great tree." The greatness was seen mainly in comparison with the size of the seed. Here is the wonder: not that it became a tree, but that, being a mustard seed, it should become "a great tree." Do you see the point of the parable? I have already brought it before you. Listen! It was only a word spoken—"Dear boy, look to Jesus." Only such a word, and a soul was saved, its sin was forgiven, its whole being was changed, a new heir of heaven was born. Do you see the growth? A word produces salvation! A grain of mustard seed becomes a great tree! A little teaching brings eternal life. That is not all: the teacher, with many prayers and tears, took her girl home, and pleaded with her for Christ, and the girl was led to yield her heart to the dominion of Christ Jesus—a holy, heavenly life came out of that pleading. See! she becomes a thoughtful girl, a loving wife, a gracious mother, a matron in Israel, such a one as Dorcas among the poor, or Hannah with her Samuel. What a great result from a little cause!

A boy was about as wild as any roamer of our streets: a teacher knelt by his side, with his arm about the lad's neck. He pleaded with God for the boy, and with the boy for God. That boy was converted, and as a youth in business he was an example to the workroom; as a father, he was a guide to his household; as a man of God, he was a light to all around; as a preacher of righteousness, he adorned the doctrine of God his Saviour in all things. A mustard seed becomes a great tree; a few words of holy admonition may produce a noble life.

But is that all? Our teaching may preserve souls from the deep darkness of the abode of the lost. A soul left to itself might hurry down from folly to vice, from vice to obduracy, from obduracy to fixed resolve to perish; but by the means of loving teaching all this is changed. Rescued from the power of sin, like a lamb snatched from between the jaws of the lion, the youth is now no longer the victim of vice, but seeks holy and heavenly things. Hell has lost its prey; and see up yonder, heaven's wide gate has received a precious soul. "Sweeping through the gates of the New Jerusalem" many have come who were led there from the Sunday School. They who once were foul are now white-robed, washed in the blood of the Lamb. Hark to their songs of praise! All this was brought about through a brief address of a trembling brother who stood up one Sunday afternoon to close the school and talk a little about the Cross of Jesus. Or all this came of a gentle sister who could never have spoken in public, but yet was enabled to warn a young girl who was growing giddy and seemed likely to go sadly astray. Wonderful that a soul's taking the road to heaven or to hell should be made, in the purpose of God, to hinge upon the humble endeavours of a weak but faithful teacher!

This great tree became a shelter: "the fowls of the air lodged in the branches of it." Mustard in the East does grow very large indeed. The commonest kind of it may be found eight or ten feet high; but there is a kind which will grow almost like a forest tree, and there probably were some of these latter trees in the sheltered region wherein our Lord was speaking. A mustard which grew here and there in Palestine was of surprising dimensions. When the tree grew, the birds came to it. Here we have *unexpected influences*. Think of it. You do not know all you are doing when you are teaching a child the way of salvation by Jesus Christ.

There seems no link between sowing a grain of mustard seed and birds of the air; but the winged wanderers soon made a happy connection. There may seem no connection between teaching that boy and the reclaiming of cannibals in New Guinea; but I can see a very possible connection. Tribes in Central Africa may have their destiny shaped by your instruction of a tiny child. When John Pounds bribed an urchin with a hot potato to come and learn to read the Bible, I am sure John Pounds had no idea of all the Ragged-schools in London; but there is a clear line of cause and effect in the whole matter. When Nasmyth went about from house to house visiting in the slums of London, I do not suppose that he saw in his act the founding of the London City Mission and all the Country Town Missions. No man can tell the end of his beginnings, the growth of his sowings. Do the next thing that lies before you. Do it well. Do it unto the Lord. Leave results with his unbounded liberality of love; but hope to reap at least a hundred-fold.

When one person is converted, how many may receive a blessing out of him none can tell. Now is the day for romances: our literature is drenched with tales religious or irreligious. What stories might be written concerning benefits bestowed, directly and indirectly, by a single godly man or woman! I now close with these three practical observations. *Are we not highly honoured to be entrusted with such a marvellous thing as the Gospel?* If it be a seed comprehending so much within it, which will come to so much if it be properly used, blessed and happy are we to have such good news to proclaim! Well now, beloved teacher, next Sunday, when you leave your bed, and say, "I have had a hard week's work, and I could half wish that I had not to go to my class"; answer yourself thus: "But I am a happy person to have to talk to children about Christ Jesus. If I had to teach them arithmetic or carpentering, I might get tired of it; but to talk about Jesus, whom I love, why, it is a joy for ever."

Let us be encouraged to sow the seed in evil times. If we do not see the Gospel prospering elsewhere, let us not despair; if there were no more mustard seed in the world, and I had only one grain of it, I should be all the more anxious to sow it. You can produce any quantity if only one seed will grow. I have often thought to myself: Other men may teach Socialism, deliver lectures, or collect a band of fiddlers, that they may gather a congregation; but I will preach the Gospel. I will preach more Gospel than ever if I can; I will stick more to the one cardinal point. The other brethren can attend to the odds and ends, but I will keep to Christ crucified. To the men of vast ability, who are looking to the events of the day, I would say, "Allow one poor fool to keep to preaching the Gospel." Beloved teachers, be fools for Christ, and keep to the Gospel. Don't you be afraid: it has life in it, and it will grow.

And, lastly, *we are bound to do it.* If so much will come out of so little, we are bound to go in for it. Nowadays people are readily caught by any scheme, or speculation, or limited liability company, that promises to give them immense dividends! I should like to make you wise by inviting you to an investment which is sure. Sow a mustard seed and grow a tree. Talk of Christ, and save a soul: that soul saved will be a blessing for ages, and a joy to God throughout eternity.

III

A GREAT BARGAIN

"Again, the kingdom of heaven is like unto a merchant man, seeking goodly pearls: Who, when he had found one pearl of great price, went and sold all that he had, and bought it."—Matt. 13: 45, 46.

A MERCHANTMAN endeavours to trade so as to make a profit. Whether he deals in pearls or in grain, he does not hope to obtain riches by labour. He leaves that to those who eat their bread in the sweat of their face. He tries to get his by the sweat of his brain. He is dependent not so much upon labour as upon knowledge, upon skill, upon the advantage which superior acquaintance with the article which he deals in gives to him. Now, this merchantman is, at the very commencement, in some measure a picture of the seeker after Christ. Christ and his salvation are not to be earned; they are not to be procured as the result of labour. But Christ is to be had by knowledge. What saith the Scripture? "By his knowledge shall my righteous servant justify many" (Isa. 53: 11); that is, through their knowing Christ they become justified. This is, indeed, another way of putting the system of salvation which is stated thus: "How shall I hear without a preacher?" The work begins with hearing the preacher; then it goes on to believing what they hear, and through believing they are saved. This is virtually knowledge—the knowledge communicated by God's messenger or by God's word—the knowledge heard, the knowledge believed. So men come to the knowledge of him whom to know is life eternal, for when a man knows Christ and understands him, so that he gives his heart to him, then is he saved. Inasmuch, then, as the merchantman seeks his advantage by superior knowledge, he becomes a type of the man who gets saved through obtaining the knowledge of the glory of God in the face of Jesus Christ.

I shall not, however, enlarge upon this analogy, but proceed at once to speak of the merchantman in this parable; for here we have a fit emblem of many who lay hold on Christ and find him to be their all in all. Let us watch this merchantman while he is doing four things; first, *seeking;* then, *finding;* then *selling out*; and, fourthly, *buying again.*

First, then, we shall WATCH HIM WHILE HE IS SEEKING. "The kingdom of heaven is like unto a merchantman seeking goodly pearls." It is different from the man who, by accident, discovered a treasure while he was in the field. He was looking for something else, and came upon the treasure. That is the man whom God, in infinite sovereignty, saves, though he was heretofore indifferent and careless. This is a person of a nobler sort. He is of a higher grade of mind, of altogether different mental constitution. He is seeking goodly pearls, something good, not exactly seeking the one pearl of great price, for at first he does not know about it; but, still, he is seeking pearls, and he comes upon one pearl in consequence of his seeking.

Now, notice about him, as a seeker, that *he has his mind aroused and engaged.* He is thinking about pearls. His heart is occupied with his business. His energies are thrown into it. All his thoughts are in the direction of precious stones. Oh that we could wake men up to exercise the faculty of thinking, and then to direct, to regulate, and to control their thoughts! But thinking is an occupation that a great many persons altogether dislike. They are frivolous. We cannot get them to think about anything. Why is it that people are so passionately fond of reading novels, and so seldom read the true histories which are quite as interesting, and far more capable of affording pleasure and pastime? It is because the minds of men are frivolous. An idle tale—a silly story of a love-sick maid—will engross them by the hour together; but anything that is solid and worth the knowing seems to have small charm for their shallow brains.

Not a few men work so hard with their hands, and suffer such fatigue from bodily labour, that they are scarcely able to think much; while there are others who dissipate their time and consume their lives in idleness, till they are utterly disqualified for any vigorous thought. They are lazy and sluggish. They have the dry rot in their very souls. Their brains do not work. They seem to live in one everlasting lethargy and day-dream. Oh that men were wise, that they were thoughtful!

Happy were the preacher who knew that he was addressing himself to a thoroughly intelligent, thoughtful congregation. We should expect, then, that the handfuls of good seed would drop into the furrows readily, and bring forth an abundant harvest. This merchantman's mind was aroused. He had something before him.

Equally evident is it that *he had a fixed definite object.* He had given himself to pearl-hunting, and pearl-hunting was to be the one object of his life. If you had met him, and said, "What are you seeking?" he would have answered in a moment, "I am seeking good pearls: have you any to sell me?" He would have been sure to have the answer ready to hand. But ask many a man whom you meet with, "Sir, what are you living for?" he would, perhaps, tell you what his trade or what his profession might be; but if you pressed him with the question, "What is the main object of life?" he would not like to say that he was living only to enjoy himself—seeking his own pleasure. He would hardly like to say that he was living to grasp and grab and get a fortune. He would hardly know how to answer you. Many young men are in this condition: they have not a definite object. Now, you will not make a good captain if you do not know the port you are sailing for. You will make a poor life of it, young man, if you go out as an apprentice, and then afterwards out as a master, with no definite aim and end. Say to yourself, "I can only live for two things. I can live for God, or I can live for the devil; which now am I going to do?" Get your mind well fixed and firmly resolved as to which it shall be. I will put it to you as boldly and baldly as even Elijah did when he said, "If Baal be God, serve him; and if Jehovah be God, serve him." If the world, if the flesh, if the devil be worth serving, go follow out the career of a sensualist and say so. Let yourself know what you are at: but if God be worth serving, and your soul worth the saving, go in for that; but do not sneak through this world really seeking yourself, and yet not having the courage to say to yourself, "Self, you are living for yourself."

This merchantman had *an object which was not at all commonplace.* Other people might go in for bricks and stones, or for grain, or for timber. He was a merchantman seeking pearls, and those of the best he could pick up. He did not go in for common sea pearls, or pearls such as you may get in a Scotch river, but he went in for goodly pearls. He took a high aim, as far as that line of action was concerned. He went into a fine business.

Lives of great men all remind us
We may make our lives sublime.

It augurs well for a young man when he has such an aspiration as this within him, "My life, too, shall be sublime. I will not seek mean or menial objects, I will not cultivate any depraved or grovelling tastes. I will seek something that I can commend to my own conscience—something that will bear reflection when I come to die—something that will carry the sterling mark when I have to value it in another world." O young merchantman, if thou art about to start in business, I recommend thee this business of seeking goodly pearls. Seek truth, seek honour, seek temperance, seek peace, seek love, seek that which will make thee good and true and right.

He went to seek pearls, and *he sought them with diligence*. He did not open a shop, and say, "Pearls bought here if anybody likes to bring them;" but he went forth in quest of them. How far he travelled I do not know; but the Oriental trader frequently goes immense distances. You may meet at Nijni-Novgorod, in the south of Russia, with traders who have been all round the globe seeking what they want—men who do not always travel by railway, but who will walk any distance to obtain the very article on which they have set their minds, and in which they deal. Distance seems with them to be no object. Ah, and when a man has got a noble object before him, and says, "Before I die, I will accomplish something that shall be right and true and beneficial to my fellow men," he will face hardships that would baffle his fellows. I pray God that he may have the perseverance to carry that out, and that he may say, "Is there anything right to be learned? I will learn it, let it cost me what it may of care and toil, of headaches and heartaches, of buying experience and burning the midnight oil. If there is anything to be done that is good and true, I will do it at any hazard, for I am seeking goodly pearls."

And as the man was seeking, so he was *using discrimination at the same time*. When we are very diligent and full of desire we are in imminent danger of being easily deceived; but this man seeking goodly pearls was not like a lady unacquainted with the nature of pearls, but he was a merchantman who knew a pearl when he saw it. He knew the character of pearls and the value of pearls; he could tell which were cloudy, and which had a soft radiance, and which were of the first water. Indeed, he could tell a genuine pearl from an imitation one. Yes, and I pray God that if he put into the heart of any brother here to live for the right and for the true, he would give you great discrimination, for there are many shams in the world, and you may readily grasp that which appears to be substantial goodness, and it may turn out to be a shadow. Go in for the good; yea, cast your soul about to find the best.

Evidently this merchant *went into the business with comparatively moderate expectations.* He was seeking pearls. They must be of a tolerable size, and pure. He evidently expected to buy a good many of them. It was what he was seeking, seeking goodly "pearls" (in the plural). He had not reckoned that he should be fortunate enough to light upon one huge pearl that should be worth an emperor's ransom. That he had not looked for, though he did feel a desire that way. If anybody had said, "Would you like to find a big pearl?" he would have said, "That I would, infinitely better than to find a number of little ones." He hardly hoped for it, and therefore he did not seek it; but, still, he was ready enough to have it if it came in his way. And so, I am speaking of a class of persons who want everything they can get that is good and true. You want to be temperate in all things; you want to have an unsullied character. I recollect that was my own desire, when first I thought of the life that lay beyond me. Before I knew the Lord I used to think, "O that I might be kept from dishonesty, that I might be preserved from falsehood, that I might be kept from a malicious spirit, that I might be right-hearted and true." Those were the pearls that I wanted. I did not know just then that I could find something that would include all these minor pearls and a good deal more. Still, it is well when such a desire as that is in the heart especially of any young man. I wish it were in the heart of the old, if up till now they have never found the pearl of great price.

Thus have I shown you the man while he is seeking. Let us

go a stage farther, and look at this man's FINDING. He was buying pearls everywhere. Where he went he asked people if they had any pearls. He went down back streets, into the slums of big cities, and found out the Jews in those old days, living in the dirtiest corners of the city. He wanted to know whether they had any pearls. He was hard after pearls; and so it came to pass that he lit upon a pearl that he never hoped to see. It was more than he expected. Ah, I pray God that some here, whose hearts are honestly seeking after that which is right, may find Christ, who has in him more of the spirit of temperance, uprightness, truth, philanthropy than will be found anywhere else. Oh, that they might find him who is the truth, and whose doctrine is perfect holiness and everlasting life. "Being in the way, the Lord met with him," says one of old. Oh, if thou hast desires after that which is right and true and good, I trust that the Lord Jesus will manifest himself to you, and that you will say, "This is the very thing I sought for; I have longed and pined after it, and here it is."

This man *found all in one.* What the value of that pearl was I do not know. The estimate of its value is not given. We only know that he thought it worth all that he had; and he went away and sold all that he had that he might buy it. I warrant you that he thought it worth a great deal more than all that he possessed. Well, when a man finds Christ I cannot tell you how much he values him, but this I know, that all the world besides seems nothing to a Christian when he has once found his Lord and Master. "Oh what a Christ have I!" saith he.

We must mark next that the man having found it, was *resolved that he would have it.* He did not question whether he should buy it or not. If he had not gone out honestly to seek pearls he would have demurred at the price, but being intent upon pearl finding, he no sooner found this than he said, "I must have that. I can let the little pearls go if you like, but I must have that." And it is a grand thing when the Lord brings the human mind to this. "I see that in Christ there is everything I want—pardon for my sin, cleansing for my nature, grace to maintain my character and to make me perfectly fit for heaven. There is all in Christ that I want, and I must have him. I *must* have him. It comes to this, at any price, whatever it may cost me, I must and I will have him."

Now, although the parable does not say it in so many words, it is perfectly clear that the person with whom he was dealing was willing to sell. Albeit the Lord in his mercy does not sell his grace, but gives it freely, the manner in which he disposes of it is here described under the figure of selling. If you want Christ, you may have him, if you are willing to come to the terms which God lays down. If you desire this pearl of great price, there is no reason in the world why that pearl should not be yours now. If, having heard of Christ, your desire is toward him as all your soul can need, and you are ready to say, "I will not leave this house of prayer till Christ is mine," there is no obstacle to your possessing this priceless boon. Yea, God, even the Father, is willing that you should have his only begotten Son to be your pearl henceforth and for evermore.

Having thus described the seeker, and described the finder, we must go on to describe him SELLING OUT. He sold out all that he had. "Buy my farm," he says to one man. "Come buy it. I want money, and I must have money." And away went the furniture in the house, one article after another. They must all go, clear them all out. There was a rapid sale. Everything must go for that pearl. Away they shall go at the best price they will fetch, but go they must, for he must have the pearl. Well now, Jesus Christ is to be had, but there is a great deal that a man must give up if he is ever to call Christ his own.

"What, then," says one, "what am I to give up?" Well, there must be a selling off of a whole mass of *old prejudices*. Sometimes when the truth as it is in Jesus comes to a man's mind he repels it, because it is so different from what he has learnt ever since he was a child; and the notion is that you had better follow the religion of your parents. If you had been a Hottentot, you would have worshipped a fetish. If you had been born in Hindustan, you must have worshipped Juggernaut, according to that theory. But it is a great mercy when a man says, "Now, I understand that Jesus the Son of God has died in the room and place and stead of sinners that believe in him, and I am simply to believe in him, and I shall be saved. On my believing I shall receive a new nature and be born again by the Holy Spirit, and henceforth I shall become the disciple and the servant of Christ. Now," says the man, "I will do it.

It is contrary to what I have always been told. I have been led to think that it was my good works which would save me. I have heard that the grace was in the sacraments, but at length I perceive that God teaches in his Word that salvation is by faith in Jesus Christ, and I will have it. I will sell my prejudices off. Away they shall go."

Next to that you must sell off *your righteousness*. It will not fetch much, but I daresay you think it is a fine thing. Hitherto you have been very good, and your own esteem of yourself is that as touching the commandments—"all these have I kept from my youth up." And what with a good deal of church going, or attendance at the meeting house, and a few extra prayers on a Christmas Day and on Good Friday, and just a little dose of sacraments, you feel yourself in tolerably good case. Now, that old moth-eaten righteousness of yours that you are so proud of you must sell off and get rid of it, for no man can be saved by the righteousness of Christ while he puts any trust in his own. Sell it all off, every rag of it.

And everything else that you have heretofore thought fit to boast of—come, you must get rid of it. You know so much. Well, you had better sell off what you know, for except a man become as a little child he cannot enter the Kingdom of Heaven. You are somebody, you fancy you are not cast in a common mould, for you have a great strength of will and can force your own way to heaven. You will have to get rid of that little conceit, for that strength of yours will be your weakness. It is only when we are weak in ourselves that we can ever be strong in Christ. Are you contented so to do?

Ay, and there are some men that will have to give up a good deal of what they call pleasure, *sinful pleasure*. No pleasure which is honest, which is really beneficial to us, need ever be denied to us.

> *Religion never was designed*
> *To make our pleasures less.*

It makes them vastly more. But any pleasure that savours of sin is to be done away with. That mixing in loose company, anything approaching to lewdness, anything that has to do with the gratification of the vile passions of the flesh—come, for Christ's sake, can you give it up?

And, then, sometimes, in some cases, men have to give up a good deal of the honours and the satisfaction of life that arise from the esteem of their fellow-creatures. Has it come to this, "If I become a Christian they will ridicule me"? Well now, can you not put up with a little obloquy for Christ? "But if I am an earnest Christian then I shall have to encounter all sorts of slander." Be it so, and can you not give up the applause of men for the sake of Christ? "Ay, but I know what it is. I shall get the cold shoulder in society if I become a thoroughly earnest Christian. There is Lady So-and-so, for whom I have very great respect, whose good opinion I would not forfeit on any account, and she will not recognise me any more." Very well, can you put the whole lot of it into the scale and say, "I sell it all off; let it all go, that I may have the pearl"? Moses counted the reproach of Christ greater riches than all the treasures of Egypt.

You have got some prospects. If you become a Christian your old uncle will cut you out of his will. You know very well that if you shall go to hear the Gospel at such and such a place you are very likely to be turned out of your situation. "But we *must* live," says somebody. This is not at all clear to my mind. I do know that we must die, but as to "must living" I do not feel quite so certain about it. Infinitely better to die than ever to do a dishonourable thing. If Jesus Christ be our Master, we must be content to let the fairest prospect go, and all things that seem to tell for our success in this life must be secondary in our account. We must seek first the Kingdom of God and his righteousness. Ay, and sometimes love that has been longed for must go for Christ's sake. Company that has been delightful must be forsaken for Christ's sake, and if all this be done, yet still it is not enough. He that has Christ must give to Christ himself and all that he has. He has bought us with a price, and it is not surely meet for us to give him one arm, and one eye, and one foot, and half a heart. He that is a true Christian is a Christian through and through.

Now, the last thing is THE BUYING. He has sold all that he had, and then he pays the shekels over, pays them over that he may have the pearl, and he gets the pearl. It was a considerate purchase, a deliberate bargain. He said to himself, "That is a wonderful pearl. If I can get the money—my little stock won't fetch above five hundred pounds—but, if I can get it for that, I am a made man." It did not want much thinking over. Oh, if a soul did but know Christ, he would not think twice before he would have him. If men were not such fools—if they had but light from heaven to see the value of my Lord and Master, instead of our standing here and having to beg and persuade and find out new words of commendation, methinks they would only say, "Tell us about him. We will have him. What can we submit to so long as we may but make sure of him who forgives all sin, who gives immediate and perfect salvation to all who trust him? So long as we may have the Christ of whom it is written, 'He that believeth in him hath everlasting life,' we shall be content."

And it was *an immediate purchase.* He did not go home and say, "I shall think about this." No, but he knew that pearl and he said, "If I let that slip through my fingers I shall never see the like of it again. If anybody else gets that bargain, then I shall have lost the one opportunity of my life." And so he does but take time enough to go and sell his farm off, and the little land he had, and the little property he had. He was back quickly with his money, only afraid somebody might have slipped in between and offered another thousand or two more than he was able to raise, and that thus he might lose the pearl. So, he that cometh to Christ aright may well deliberate about it, but the end of his deliberation ought to be very speedy. "If he is to be had, let me have him. Oh, if I can know my sins forgiven, let me know it. Oh, if by any means I can have peace with God, if I can become a child of God and an heir of heaven, if my eternal happiness can be secured, oh, let it be secured! How is it done? Come, tell me at once."

And then it was a *joyful one.* I am sure his eyes twinkled as he paid over his money. I should like to have a picture of his face, when at last he had got his pearl. Ah, when a soul gets Christ it is—

> *Happy day, happy day,*
> *For he has washed my sins away.*

It is the beginning of delight to a soul when he can say, "Jesus is mine; I know he is. Grace has enabled me to lay hold upon him."

And, oh, what an *enriching purchase* it was which the man had made. When he had once got the pearl instead of his property he thought to himself, "Why, I have got a hundred times more property now than I had. Though I have given up that bit of land I can buy half a province now, if I like, with this pearl which I have obtained." So, if you have ever given up anything for Christ I am sure that the Lord Jesus Christ has made you very ample amends. "But," say some, "the martyrs were losers, were they not?" Well, they are up there, ask them. They will tell you as you look at them with their ruby crowns, all brilliant in the light of God, that they counted it their honour that they should be permitted to lay down their lives for Jesus' sake. Oh, there is no losing when you deal with him. "No man," says he, "shall lose house and lands for my sake that shall not receive in this world a hundredfold, and in the world to come, life everlasting."

This was a *final purchase*. The merchantman, according to the parable, never went buying pearls any more. "No," said he, "no; I have bought a pearl of great price, and now I will go out of the business." And when a man once finds Christ, then he seeks nothing more. If Jesus Christ be mine, "more than all in him I find."

And it was *a purchase he never regretted*. The parable does not say that he came back to the seller and said, "There, take your pearl, and let me have my house and lands again." No, it was done. The great transaction was done. He never wished to have it undone. With his pearl of immense worth he was a rich man, worthy to be the rival of princes, and he felt that it was enough. Oh, blessed are they who can say "It is enough," and can rejoice and bless and magnify the Lord.

Let me, however, just put in one word of caveat. Take care, dear merchant brothers, that when you buy a pearl you buy a good one—that it is the pearl of great price, because I have known noble spirits whom I have admired and felt ready to weep over; men that have been heroic in the pursuit of that which seemed to them perfectly true, and have made a sacrifice of all that they have for it, and yet they have been deceived. They have grasped antichrist instead of Christ, and welcomed the lie of hell which came to them in the garb of the angel of light. Mind, mind that you get Christ and his truth as you find it revealed in Scripture, and revealed a second time in your own heart by the Holy Ghost, for whatever is short of Christ will prove a cheat and deceive you.

If you get the Son of God, you have a hope divine which never can fail you; but, if you get a hope in priests or a hope connected with sacramentarianism, or any other hope but that of which Christ is top and bottom, beginning and end, you may make what sacrifice you will, but your brightest prospects will end in bitterest disappointment. The Lord grant that none of us may ever be thus balked of our life-confidence, that no such blank bewilderment may ever fall on our spirits.

IV

EARLY AND LATE

"For the kingdom of heaven is like unto a man that is an house-holder, which went out early in the morning to hire labourers into his vineyard. . . . And he went out about the third hour, and saw others standing idle in the market-place. . . . Again he went out, about the sixth and ninth hour, and did likewise. And about the eleventh hour he went out, and found others standing idle, and saith unto them, Why stand ye here all the day idle?"—Matt. 20: 1, 3, 5, 6.

WE have no right to tear passages of Scripture from their context and make them to mean what they were not intended to teach; and therefore I have in the reading (Matt. 19: 27; 20: 29) given you what I think to be the immediate design of the present parable. It is a rebuke to those who fall into a legal spirit and begin calculating as to what their reward ought to be in a Kingdom where the legal spirit is entirely out of place, since its reward is not of debt but of grace. I think I may now, without any violation of propriety, dwell upon one very distinct fact in connection with the parable.

I intend to call your attention to the fact that the labourers were hired at different periods of the day, by which doubtless we are taught that God sends his servants into his vineyard at different times and seasons; that some are called in early youth; and others are not led to enter into the service of the Master until declining years have brought them almost to the eventide of life.

I must, however, ask you to remember that *they were all called:* by the mention of which the Saviour would teach us that no man comes into the Kingdom of Heaven of himself. Without exception, every labourer for Jesus has been called in one sense or another, and he would not have come without being so called. They are all called. Were a man what he should be he would need no pressing and invitation to come to the Gospel of Christ; but since human nature is perverted, and men put

43

bitter for sweet and sweet for bitter, darkness for light and light
for darkness, man needs to be called by the outward word;
he needs to be invited, persuaded, and entreated; he needs,
to use the strong expression of the apostle Paul, that as though
God did beseech him by us we should pray him in Christ's
stead to be reconciled to God. Nay, further than this, although
some men come to work in a legal spirit in the vineyard through
this common call of the Gospel, yet no man in spirit and in
truth comes to Christ without a further call, namely, the
effectual call of God's Holy Spirit. The general call is given by
the minister, it is all that he can give. If the preacher attempts
to give the particular call as some of my hyper-Calvinistic
brethren do, confining the Gospel command to a certain
character and trying to be themselves the discoverers of God's
elect, and to make that particular which is always universal;
if the preacher acts thus, and virtually endeavours to give the
particular call, he makes a sorry mess of it, and usually fails
altogether to preach the Gospel of glad tidings to the sons of
men.

But when man is content to do what he can do, namely,
preach the commandment "that we believe on the Lord Jesus
Christ," and that "God commandeth all men everywhere to
repent," then there comes with the general call to the chosen
of God a particular and special call which none but the Holy
Ghost can give, but which he gives so effectually that all who
hear it become willing in the day of God's power, and turn with
full purpose of heart unto the Lord.

I want you to notice another fact before I come to the subject
now in hand, and that is, that *all those who are called are said to
have been hired.* Of course in a parable no word is to be con-
strued harshly; we are to give the meaning according to the
drift; but still I think we may say that there is this likeness
between hiring a servant and the engagement of a soul to Christ,
that henceforth a man hired has no right to serve another, he
serves the master who has hired him. When a soul is called by
grace into the service of the Lord Jesus Christ, he cries, "O
Lord, other lords have had dominion over me, but now thee
only will I serve." He plucks off the yoke of sin, its pleasure, its
custom, and he puts upon him that yoke of which the Master
says it is easy, and he bears that burden which Jesus tells us is

light. A hired servant must not work for another, he is not his own master; and "ye are not your own, ye are bought with a price" (1 Cor. 6: 19, 20).

Now the word "hired" was used in order to bring in the idea of reward. It was used to suit Peter's view of the case; it was used in order that his legal question of "What shall we have therefore?" might be clearly brought out, and its folly shown in the light of that sovereign grace which does as it wills with his own. Yet for all that believers are hired in an evangelical sense, they do not serve God for nought, they shall not work without a reward. "The wages of sin is death, but the gift of God is eternal life" (Rom. 6: 23). We shall have our reward for what we do for the Master, and though it be not wages in the sense of debt, yet verily I say unto you, there shall not be a single true-hearted worker for God who shall not receive of his Master most blessed wages of grace in the day when he comes to take account of his servants.

ALL ARE NOT CALLED BY GRACE AT THE SAME TIME. Some, according to the parable, are called *early in the morning.* Thrice happy are these! The earliest period at which a child may be called by grace it would be difficult for us positively to define, because children are not all of the same age mentally when they are of the same age physically, and even in the matter of mental development we dare not limit the Holy One of Israel as to the chosen period of operation. As far as our observation goes, grace works upon some little ones at the very dawn of moral consciousness. There are, no doubt, precocious children, whose intellect and affections are very much developed, and very deeply sanctified even so early as two or three years of age. There are interesting biographies extant, which prove that holiness may bloom and ripen in the youngest heart, children whom I might call infants with strict propriety, out of whose mouth God ordained praise, and did, through them, still the enemy and the avenger.

"Early in the morning" would also include those who have passed the first hour of the day, but who have not yet wasted the second opening hour. I mean those hopeful lads and girls who perhaps would rather I should call them youths; those who have reached their teens, have overleaped infancy and childhood, and are growing up in the heyday and vigour of

youth. Youngsters still more at home in the playground than
in the work-field, fitter, as Satan tells them, to be sporting in
the market-place than busy in the vineyard; such as these,
to the praise of divine love, are often hired by the householder.
It is worth while to warn some of our brethren who seem to be
exceedingly dubious of boyish and girlish piety, to warn them
against indulging harsh and suspicious doubts. We have
remarked that among all the slips and falls which have caused
us sorrow, we have had but little sorrow from those who were
added to us as boys or girls. There are those preaching the
Gospel this day with acceptance and power whom these hands
baptized into Jesus Christ very early in their boyhood, and
there are among us honoured servants of God who have served
this Church well, who, while they were yet at school were joyful
followers of the Lord Jesus Christ. With our earliest gettings
some of us got an understanding of the things of the kingdom;
our Bible was our child's primer, our spelling-book, the guide
of our youth and the joy of our earliest years. We thank God
that there are Timothys still among us, and those not few and
far between; and young Samuels, who, being brought as infants
to the Lord's house, have from that day forth worn the linen
ephod and served after their fashion as priests unto God,
serving him with all their hearts. Happy those who are called
early in the morning! They have peculiar reasons for blessing
and praising God.

There is a beauty about early piety which is indescribably
charming, and unutterably lovely in freshness and radiance.
We remark in childhood an artless simplicity, a child-like confidence, which is seen nowhere else. There may be less of
knowing but there is more of loving; there may be less of
reasoning, but there is more of simply believing upon the
authority of revelation; there may be less of deep-rootedness,
but there is certainly more of perfume, beauty, and emerald
verdure.

Early in the morning, when we have just risen from slumber,
work is easy; our occupation in the vineyard is a cheerful
exercise rather than a toil such as those find it who bear the
burden and heat of the day. The young Christian is not
oppressed with the cares and troubles of the world as others
are; he has nothing else to do but to serve his God. He is

free from the embarrassments which surround so many of us, and prevent our doing good when we would consecrate ourselves wholly to it. The lad has nought to think of but his Lord. There are his books and his lessons, but he can be fervent of spirit in the midst of them. There are the companions of his childhood, but in guilelessness and simplicity he may be of service to them and to God through them. Give me, I say, if I would have an auspicious time to work for Jesus, give me the blessed morning hours, when my heart is bounding lightest and joy's pure sunbeams tremble on my path; when my glowing breast lacks no ardour, and my happy spirit wears no chain of care.

One would prefer early conversion because such persons have not learned to stand idle in the market-place. A fellow, you know, who has been for hours standing with his hands in his pocket, talking with drunken men and so on, is not worth much at the eleventh hour, nay even by the middle of the day it has become so natural to him to prop the walls, that he is not likely to take to work very readily. Begin early with your souls. There are no workers like those who commenced work while they were yet children. What a promise of a long day there is for young believers; the sun has just risen, and he has to travel to his zenith and to descend again. There is ample room and verge enough though none to spare. If God in his providence permit it so to happen, that youngster yonder has twelve hours' work before him—what may he not accomplish? For a grand and glorious life early piety, if not essential, is certainly a very great advantage. To give those first days to Jesus will spare us many sad regrets, prevent us acquiring many evil habits, and enable us to achieve good success through the Holy Spirit's blessing.

Let it be the desire of parents to have their children converted as children! And oh! may God cast that desire into the hearts of some of you young people that before you reach one-and-twenty, before you are called men, you may be perfect men in Christ Jesus, that while you are yet children you may be children of God. May you as "newborn babes receive the sincere milk of the Word," and the Lord grant that you may "grow thereby."

The householder went out again *at the third hour*. This may represent the period in which we have mounted above being children and youths and are entitled to be called men. Suppose we settle the first hour as extending over the earliest seven or eight years of age; then the second hour runs on from that to twenty-one or thereabouts; and then we have a good length of time between twenty and thirty and onwards to reckon as the third, and fourth, and fifth hours. There are some whom divine grace renews at the third hour. This is late! One-and-twenty is grievously late, when you consider how much of early joy is now impossible, how much of sinful habit has now been acquired, how many opportunities for usefulness are now gone past recall. A quarter of the day has flown away for ever when we reach the third hour. It is the best quarter of the day, too, that has gone past recall.

I have no doubt there are many who think that to be converted at one-and-twenty is very soon; but why one-and-twenty years given to Satan? Why a fourth of man's existence devoted to evil? Besides, it may not be a fourth, it may be one half, nay, in how many cases it is the whole of life. The sun goes down ere it is yet noon, and the idler in the market-place has no hope of ever being a worker in the vineyard. Death who comes when God wills, and gives us no notice, may cut down the flower before it has fully opened. It is a sad thing to have lost those bright days in which the mind was least engaged, in which it was the most susceptible of forming godly habits. It is a sad thing to have learned so much of sin as one may have learned by one-and-twenty, a sad thing to have seen so much of iniquity, to have treasured up in one's memory so much of defilement. Twenty years with God; one might have been in such a time a good scholar in the kingdom; but twenty years in the world one begins to be like scarlet that has been lying in the dye till it is stained through and through.

It is late, but we thank God that it is not too late. Nay, it is not too late even for the grandest of purposes. Not only is this period of life not too late for salvation, but it is not too late to do much for Jesus Christ. Some of us when we were one-and-twenty, had finished five years of Christian ministry, and had been the means of bringing many souls to the Cross of Christ; but if others are led by grace to begin then, why there is a good period still remaining if God in providence spares our lives.

The young man is now in all his strength and vigour, his bones are full of marrow, and his heart is full of fire. He ought to have a good degree of education, and be prepared to acquire more.

Now he is just in the time when he should work. His plans of life are not settled as yet; he is not married yet, probably; as yet there are no children about him to have been injured by his ill example; he has an opportunity of rearing up a household in the fear of God. He is commencing business, he has an opportunity of so conducting that business that there may never need to be a time when he shall have to tack about and steer another course.

There is abundance of work to do for us who are in this third, fourth, and fifth hour of the day. In fact, I suppose the Church must look to us for its most active work. After this period and the next, a man frequently becomes rather a recipient from the Church than a donor to it in the matter of activity. Its fresh blood, its energy, its warmth of heart, its ready action, must to a great extent come from the young men who are converted. Oh, you of one-and-twenty, I would to God that you were all born from heaven! You maidens, in your early beauty may the Master in his infinite mercy bring you in! Oh, could you know the sweetness of his love, you would not need persuading! Could you understand the joy of true religion, you would not want entreating! There is more hallowed mirth enjoyed in secret with the Lord Jesus Christ, than in all the merriment the world can yield. One ounce of Christ's love is better than a ton of the world's flatteries. There may be less glitter about the things of God, but there is a "solid joy and lasting pleasure," which "none but Zion's children know."

The Master's grace was not exhausted, and therefore *he went out at the sixth hour*. We find him going into the market at high noon. Half the day was over. Who is going to employ a man and give him a whole day's wages when twelve o'clock has come? He will not do too much if you hire him at six, what will he do if you engage him at twelve? Half a day's work! that is a poor thing to seek or to offer. The Master, however, seeks and accepts it. He promises, "Whatsoever is right, I will give you;" and there are some found who at the sixth hour enter into the vineyard and, being saved by grace, begin their work for Jesus. This may represent the period of life in which man is supposed to be in his prime—when he is past forty and onward. *This is sadly late, very sadly late.* Sadly late in a great many respects, not only because there is so little time left, but because so very much of energy, and zeal, and force, which should have been given to God, has been wasted; and has to some extent been used to fight against God.

Forty years of hardness of heart! That is a long time for divine patience. Forty years of sin! That is a long season for conscience to mourn over. "Forty years long was I grieved with this generation," said God (Ps. 95 : 10). In the wilderness they hardened their hearts all that time; and he sware in his wrath that they should not enter into his rest. What a blessing for you of forty and unconverted, that he has not sworn so terrible an oath concerning you, that still his long-suffering lingers, still his patience bears with you, still does he say to you, "Go, work, my son—go work this day in my vineyard." It is sadly late, because it has become so more than natural to you to walk in the way of sin. You will have so much to contend with in future, as the result of the past. You will need much grace to conquer those corruptions which have had forty years to take root in. To your dying day the recollection of evil things which you heard during these forty years of unregeneracy will stick by you; you will hear the echoes of an old song just when you are trying to pray, and some deed which you regret and mourn over, will come to check you just when you are about to say, "Abba Father," with an unstammering tongue. It is late, it is very, very late, this sixth hour, *but it is not too late.*

It is not too late for some of the richest enjoyments; you can yet dine with Jesus; he can yet manifest himself unto you, as he doth not unto the world; you can have yet much time to serve him in. It is not too late yet to be distinguished among his servants. Take John Newton's life; he was called in the middle of the day, but John Newton left his mark in God's vineyard, a mark that will never be forgotten. I suppose Paul could not have been much less than of that age when he was called by sovereign grace; nay, the most of the apostles were probably very little short of this age when mercy met with them; still they did a glorious day's work. If saved by grace in middle life, you must work harder, you must let the time past suffice you to have wrought the will of the flesh, and now you must redeem the time, because the days are evil. Why, a man converted at forty should go double quick march to heaven, there should not be a moment lost now. Seek in the divine strength to do twice as much in the time, since you have only half the time to do a life's work in. Crowns for Christ, I know you wish to win them; then be up and doing for him. You are saved by grace, and by grace alone. You pant to honour Christ, because of his free love to you; cannot you endeavour to honour him as much in the remnant which remains as others do in the whole length of their life?

The householder *went out at the ninth hour*, at three o'clock in the afternoon. Nobody thinks of engaging day-labourers at three o'clock in the afternoon. A day's work to be done from three till six! It shows you that this Gospel hiring is nothing like a legal hiring; it must be all of grace, or a man would not think of doing such a thing. Well now, three o'clock in the afternoon, that is from sixty to seventy. The prime of life has gone. *It is late, it is sadly late, very sadly late.* It is late because all the powers of the man are weak now. His memory begins to fail; he thinks his judgment better than ever it was, but probably that is only his own opinion. Most of the faculties lose their edge in old age. He has acquired experience, but still there is no fool like an old fool; and a man who has not been taught by divine grace learns very little of any value in the school of providence.

Now think of it, is it not late? Here is the man: if he be converted now, what is there left of him? He is just a candle end. He may give a little light, but it is almost like a snuff burning in the socket. All those sixty years, seventy years, have been spent, where? Cover it all up. Let us go backward as Noah's sons did, and cover it all up; and oh, may almighty grace cover it too! The fact is terribly appalling—sixty, seventy years spent in the service of Satan! Oh what good the man might have done! Had he but served his God as he served the world, what good he might have done! He has made a fortune, has he! How rich he might have been in faith by this time. He has built a house! Yes, but how he might have helped to build the Church. The tabernacle is beginning to crumble about the man, and the warning is loud which reminds him that he must soon be gone and leave his wealth and his house;

and so if this be all, in the end it will turn out that he has done nothing; he has piled up shadows, heaped together thick clay, and that is all he has done; when he might, if he had believed in Jesus, have done so much for God and for the souls of men.

What evil habits he has acquired! What can you ever make of this man? If he be saved, it will be so as by fire. He is called, and he shall enter heaven, but oh! how little can he do for the Master, and what strong corruptions will he have to wrestle with, and what an inward conflict even till he gets to heaven! It is late, it is very late, but oh! blessed be God! *it is not too late.* We have had persons who have long passed the prime of their days, who have come forward and said, "We will cast in our lot with you because the Lord is with you." We have heard their joyous story of how the old man has become a babe, and how he that was hoary with years has been born again into the kingdom of Christ. It is not too late. Did the devil say so? The gate is shutting; I can hear it grating on the hinges, but it is not shut!

The day is nearly over, *it has come to the eleventh hour,* five o'clock! The men have been looking at their watches to see whether it will not soon be six; they are longing to hear the clock strike; they hope the day's work will soon close. See; the Master goes out into the market-place among those hulking fellows who are still loitering there, and he pitches upon some and asks them, "Why stand ye here all the day idle? Go and work! and whatsoever is right I will give you." At the eleventh hour they come in—half-ashamed to come I will be bound, hardly liking the others to see them; ashamed to begin work so late. Still they did steal in somewhere; and there were generous labourers who looked over the tops of the vines, and said to them, "Glad to see you, friends! glad to see you, however late." There were a few, I dare say, among the labourers, at least there are if this be the vineyard, who would even stop their work and begin to sing and praise God to think that their fellows had been brought in at the eleventh hour.

Now the eleventh hour must be looked upon as any period of life which is past threescore years and ten; how late it may extend I cannot tell. There is an authentic instance of a man converted to God at the age of a hundred and four, during the last Irish revival, who walked some distance to make a confession of his faith in Jesus Christ; and I recollect a case of one converted in America by a sermon which he had heard, I think, eighty-one years previously. He was fifteen when he heard Mr. Flavell at the end of a discourse, instead of pronouncing the blessing, say, "I cannot bless you. How can I bless those who do not love the Lord Jesus Christ? 'If any man love not the Lord Jesus Christ let him be Anathema Maranatha;'" and eighty-one years or more afterwards that solemn sentence came to the man's recollection when he was living in America, and God blessed it to his conversion.

There have been some to whom the eleventh hour has been the very hour of death; some, I say, how many or how few is not for me to know. There is one instance we know in Scripture; it was the dying thief. There is but one; God, however, in his abundant mercy can do as he wills to the praise of the glory of his grace, and at the eleventh hour he can call his chosen. It is very late, it is very very, very late, it is sorrowfully late, *it is dolefully late, but it is not too late*, and if the Master call thee, come—though an hundred years of sin should make thy feet heavy to thee, so that thy steps are painfully limping.

Have you ever thought of how the thief worked for his Lord? It was not a fine place for working, hanging on a cross dying, just at the eleventh hour; but he did a deal of work in the few minutes. Observe what he did. First he confessed Christ; he acknowledged him to be Lord, confessed him before men. In the second place he justified Christ—"This man has done nothing amiss." In the next place he worshipped the Lord Jesus, calling him "Lord." He even began to preach, for he rebuked his fellow sinner; he told him that he should not revile one who was so unrighteously condemned. He offered a petition which has become a very model of prayer—"Lord, remember me when thou comest into thy kingdom."

I want to show you now that DISTINGUISHING GRACE SHONE RESPLENDENTLY IN EVERY INSTANCE. Those called in the early morning have delightful reason for admiring sovereign grace, for they are spared the ills and sins of life. What distinguishing grace is that which called us when we were young! Herein is electing love. "When Israel was a child, then I loved him, and called my son out of Egypt" (Hos. 11: 1). Some of us in time and in eternity will have to utter a special song of thankfulness to the love which took us in our days of folly and simplicity and conducted us into the family of God. It was not because we were better disposed children than others, or because there was naturally anything good about us; we were wilful, heady, and high-minded, proud, wayward, and disobedient as other children are, and yet mercy separated us from the rest, and we shall never cease to adore its sovereignty.

Look at the grace which calls the man at the age of twenty, when the passions are hot, when there is strong temptation to plunge into the vices and the so-called pleasures of life. To be delivered from the charms of sin, when the world's cheek is ruddy, when it wears its best attire, and to be taught to prefer the reproach of Christ to all the riches of Egypt, this is mighty grace for which God shall have our sweetest song.

To be called of the Lord at forty, in the prime of life; this is a wonderful instance of divine power, for worldliness is hard to overcome, and worldliness is the sin of middle age. With a family about you, with much business, with the world eating into you as doth a canker, it is a wonder that God should in his mercy have visited you then, and made you a regenerate soul. You are a miracle of grace, and you will have to feel it and to praise God for it in time and eternity.

Sixty again. "Can the Ethiopian change his skin, or the leopard his spots? If so, then ye who are accustomed to do evil may learn to do well" (Jer. 13 : 23). And yet you have learned, you have had a blessed schoolmaster who sweetly taught you, and you have learned to do well.

But what shall I say of you that are called when you are aged? Ah you will have to love much, for you have had much forgiven. I do not know that you may be in thankfulness a whit behind those of us who are called in our early youth; we have much to bless God for, and so have you. We are at one extreme and you are at the other; we would love much because we have been spared much sinning, and you must love much because you have been delivered from much sinning. Called early or called late, called at midday or called at early noon, let us together, since we have been called by grace alone, ascribe it all to the Lord Jesus, and moved by the mighty constraints of his love, let us work for him till we can work no longer, and then praise him in glory.

V

THE PLEADING OF THE LAST MESSENGER

"Having yet therefore one son, his wellbeloved, he sent him also last unto them, saying, They will reverence my son. But those husbandmen said among themselves, This is the heir; come, let us kill him, and the inheritance shall be ours. And they took him, and killed him, and cast him out of the vineyard. What shall therefore the lord of the vineyard do? he will come and destroy the husbandmen, and will give the vineyard unto others."—Mark 12: 6–9.

YOU know the story of God's dealing with Israel, and Israel's dealing with God. The Lord chose their fathers, Abraham, Isaac, and Jacob; he made them a race separated unto himself; he brought them out of Egypt from under the iron yoke; he led them through the Red Sea; he fed them for forty years in the wilderness; he led them about and tutored them, even as a man teacheth his son. In due time he brought them into the land which floweth with milk and honey; and he put them under a dispensation eminently gentle and full of tenderness, where as a nation they might enjoy unbroken prosperity, sitting "every man under his vine and under his fig tree," none making them afraid (1 Kings 4: 25).

All that he required of them was that he should be their God, that they should put no idols in his place, but should obey his statutes. Alas! from the first they copied the nations among whom they dwelt: they set up the gods of Egypt when they were in the wilderness, and in Canaan they went astray after the polluted deities of the nations. They worshiped defiled gods with rites obscene; they even passed their children through the fire to Moloch, and did horrible things which angered the Most High. In his longsuffering he sent to them prophets one after another—prophets who received unworthy treatment at their hands whenever they rebuked their sins. The prophets were derided, persecuted, and even slain with the sword. God in great patience sent them more of his messengers, some of them grandly eloquent, like Esaias and Ezekiel; others of them full of tears, like Jeremiah; or clothed with dignity, like Daniel. They warned the people, and ceased not to plead with them, whether they would hear or whether they would forbear. Cruel treatment awaited many of the servants of the Lord; they were stoned, they were sawn asunder.

Israel rejected the servants that came from the great House-holder asking for the rent of his vineyard. They repudiated the claims of God, and cast off allegiance to him with contempt and disdain; until at last the nation was led into captivity, and in the end only lingered on the chosen soil as a mere remnant. Judah wept upon the dunghill; whereas aforetime she was adorned with bridal ornaments, and sat upon the throne. The adversary ruled in the halls of David; for the days of Herod, the Idumean tyrant, had come. The Roman yoke was heavy upon the people: their sins had brought them low. God, in his infinite compassion, gave them one more opportunity. He had one Son, his Wellbeloved Son, and he sent him to his Israel. With lips that dropped mercy and with eyes that over-flowed with tenderness, he came. "Oh, that thou hadst known," said he, "even thou, in this thy day!" He wept over the city which would not be saved. But his warning and his weeping were lost upon the blinded people. Those who had rejected the prophets, also rejected the Lord: the fate of the servants was repeated in "the heir." "Let us kill him," said they; and they put him to the death of the Cross. You know the story: it is full of infinite mercy on God's part, and of immeasurable guilt on the part of man. God seemed to out-do himself in his long-suffering, and man seemed to out-do himself in his wanton defiance of the Most High. Sin culminated in the murder of the Son of God; it reached its utmost height of horror when the cry was heard, "Crucify him! Crucify him!" Yes, they crucified the Lord of Glory.

What has this to do with us? I am not going to preach merely to rehearse a piece of ancient history which has no bearing on to-day; I do not so regard the death of our Lord. My anxiety is to reach the consciences of living men, and, if possible, to win to the Blessed Heir of all things, who has risen from the dead, some of those who have had a share in his death. I would

bring to the Great Householder the fruits of the vineyard which
he himself has planted, and I would move many hearts to
relent towards him at the remembrance of the wicked injuries
which have been done to his servants and to his Son. May the
Spirit of God silently move over this audience at this time, as I
try to use this passage, not in its strictest application, but with
such an application as I am sure the Spirit of God will approve!

The fact is that, unless changed by divine grace, we have all
refused to pay to our great God the service which is due to him.
He has put us here and given us this life, like a vineyard, for
us to cultivate; but many have cultivated that vineyard
entirely for themselves—themselves or their families and
friends, and not for their God, their Maker. "God is not in all
their thoughts." Now, the Lord has sent to such many messengers. We have had no prophets in these days living among us;
but we have the Word of God and the record of the testimonies
of his inspired messengers, and these virtually speak to us. We
have Moses and the prophets: they are speaking to us even
now. Besides that, we have been surrounded by men of God,
and encompassed by holy women who have appealed to us on
God's behalf. They have been urged to speak by the love of
their hearts, and they have tried to bring us to repent of past
rebellion and to yield ourselves at once to God. Many are the
voices around us and within us which persuade to render unto
the great Householder his due; but in many cases none of these
have been successful. Last of all God has sent to each one of
us his Son, that he in his own Person may lovingly repeat with
greater emphasis the requirements of the Lord of love. The
incarnate wisdom now cries to us, "My son, give me thine
heart." Jesus warns us, "Except ye repent, ye shall all likewise perish." He sets before us the way of reconciliation, and
bids us believe in him and live. With many a charming parable
he would draw the far-off prodigal home to the bosom of for-
giving love. The very coming of the Son of God in human form,
as Emmanuel, God with us, is love's great plea for reconciliation.
Who can resist so powerful an argument? It is in the Person
of Jesus Christ that God makes his last and strongest appeal to
the human conscience. By the Christ of God, he virtually
saith, "Turn ye, turn ye: why will ye die, O house of Israel?"
And I would to God that the answer might be from many a

heart, "Come, let us return unto the Lord; for he hath torn, and he will heal us." Cause it to be so, O great Spirit!

Three things I shall speak of now, and the first will be *the amazing mission:* "Having yet therefore one son, his wellbeloved, he sent him also last unto them, saying, They will reverence my son." Secondly, *the astounding crime:* "They took him, and killed him, and cast him out of the vineyard." And, therefore, thirdly, *the appropriate punishment,* of which the text says, "What shall therefore the lord of the vineyard do?" What vengeance can be sufficient for so base a deed?

First, then, let us dwell upon THE AMAZING MISSION: "Having yet therefore one son, his wellbeloved, he sent him also."

Please remember concerning the Son of God, sent to us to reconcile us to the Father, that *he came after many rejections of divine love.* As to Israel he followed the prophets, so to us he comes after many others. There are none among us, I should think, who have been left without admonitions and expostulations from God. He began early with some of us, calling us, like Samuel, when as yet we were children. He repeated those calls to us all through the days of our youth. It was never cheap to some of us to sin; we never went astray but what there was a something within which plucked us by the sleeve and warned us of our wrong-doing. We have been called to God by most earnest entreaties of faithful men and affectionate women. Discourses have been addressed to us which might have moved hearts of stone; but yet, though stirred for the moment, we remain obstinate enemies to God, dishonest to his claims, careful of this world, and forgetful of the world to come. After all these refusals, if the Lord had closed the casket of mercy, and had opened the vials of vengeance and had poured them out upon us, who could have blamed him? Instead of which, he still, in his longsuffering pity, speaks to us by his Son. Jesus Christ, by whom he made the worlds, condescends to be the Messenger of the covenant of grace. He gently reminds us of our offences against the great Father, of our wilfulness in not returning to him, and of the tremendous peril which we incur by remaining in opposition to the great God. The very existence of our Saviour gives us warning of our sin, of our ruin, and of the only way of escape. If it be so, that we have rejected God's claims so often, will not the time past suffice us to have played this dreadful game? Have we not had enough of trifling with our souls? O Lord, how long shall men act the part of fools and risk their immortal souls? Oh, will they not at length yield to wisdom? Jesus himself, by the preaching of the Gospel, pleads with us: are we determined to persevere in our evil ways? Do we not feel some tender relentings? Does not a "still small voice" urge us to arise and go to our Father? After many provocations, will we not at length yield to the God of grace?

Remember that Jesus Christ when he comes to us to-day, as the messenger of the Father, *comes for no personal ends.* When the messengers were sent by the householder, it was to claim the householder's rent; when the heir came, it was for the same purpose. So it is in the human emblem; but in the divine this becomes less conspicuous. When Jesus pleads with us, although he urges us to render unto God our love and our obedience, yet God does not stand in need of these as the householder stood in need of his rents. What is it to the infinite Jehovah whether thou serve him or not? If thou rebel against God, will he be less glorious? If thou wilt not obey the Lord, what difference can it make to his boundless happiness? Will his crown shine the less brightly, or his heaven be less resplendent because thou choosest to be a rebel against him? It is for thine own sake that God would have thee yield to him; how can it be for his own? If he were hungry he would not tell thee, for the cattle on a thousand hills are his. He can crush whole worlds to dust, "or with his word or with his nod"; and dost thou think he has aught to gain from thee? Thou alone wilt be the gainer or the loser; therefore when Jesus prays thee to repent, believe thou in the disinterestedness of his heart; believe that it can be nothing but the tenderest regard for thy well-being which makes him warn thee. Hear how Jehovah puts it: "As I live, saith the Lord God, I have no pleasure in the death of the wicked; but that the wicked turn from his way and live" (Ezek. 33: 11).

Let us see for a minute who this messenger is. *He is one greatly beloved of his Father,* and in himself *he is of surpassing excellence.* The Lord Jesus Christ is so inconceivably glorious that I tremble at any attempt to describe his glory. Assuredly, he is very God of very God, co-equal and co-eternal with the Father, and yet he deigned to take upon himself a human form.

He was born an infant into our weakness, and he lived a carpenter to share our toil. When he quits the bench and the saw it is to follow still more laborious ways as a teacher and healer of the people. He was the lowly and suffering teacher of the blessed will of the Father. He took upon himself the form of a servant, and yet in him dwelleth all the fulness of the Godhead bodily. He is the Prince of the kings of the earth, and yet he took a towel and washed his disciples' feet. Such is he who pleads with you. So majestic and so compassionate, so great, and yet so good: will you refuse him? If I plead with you, I am but as you are, flesh of your flesh; but if Jesus speaks to you, I beseech you by the glory of his Godhead, as well as by the tenderness of his manhood, do not refuse him. Because of his Godhead you must not dare to harden your hearts. He is God's Well-beloved; and, if you are wise, he will be yours. Do not turn your back upon him whom all the angels worship. Beware, lest thou reject One whom God loves so well; for he will take it as an insult to himself: he that despises the anointed of God has blasphemed God himself. I beseech thee, then, by the love which God bears to his Son, to listen to this matchless messenger of mercy, who would fain persuade thee to repent.

I have already said that he is so glorious that I cannot describe him; I will therefore only say that *his graciousness is as conspicuous as his glory*. There was never such a one as he. None of us loves men as Christ loves them; and if the loves of all the tender-hearted in the world could be run together, they would make but a drop compared with the ocean of the compassion of Jesus. Of old his delights were with the sons of men; and though he might have been happy enough among the angels, yet he quitted their company that he might take up this inferior race. Yea, he espoused our nature and became bone of our bone and flesh of our flesh, for love of that chosen company whom he calls his Bride. He hid not his face from shame and spitting, nor his body from the shedding of blood, nor his soul from deadly agony; but he loved the Church, and gave himself for it. It is this lover of souls that becomes God's advocate with us and pleads with us that we would cease from our rebellion. Do not refuse him! If he were stern and unloving, I could imagine that all the obstinacy of your nature might be aroused; but his love, which passeth the love of women, deserves another treatment. If you reject him, he answers you with tears; if you wound him, he bleeds out cleansing; if you kill him, he dies to redeem ; if you bury him, he rises again to bring us Resurrection. Jesus is love made manifest.

Furthermore, *his manner is most winning.* When I have been pleading for men with God, and I have ceased my pleading, I have feared that something in my tone or in my manner would cause my pleading to fail. I am not, perhaps, so tender as I should be, nor is there sufficient pathos in my tones. If I could do better, I would go to any school to learn. God has put me often to the school of suffering to instruct me in this respect ; and yet I do confess my failings with deep regret. But when Jesus, my Lord, pleads with you, this charge cannot be laid against him. His pleading is perfect. When Jonah preaches, his tones are harsh, and his spirit forbidding ; but that can never be said of Jesus. When Jeremiah weeps, there is an undertone of bitter complaint within the sweet sorrow of his love ; but it is never so with Jesus. "Never man spake like this man."

If ever his words thunder—as they often do—even in that thunder there is heard the voice of love. When he flashes with the lightning of judgment against Scribes and Pharisees, yet soft mercy-drops follow every flame of fire. He is stern because he is tender : his utterances of terror are born of a love which dares not conceal the truth, even though it breaks its heart in the telling of it. God is love, and Christ is God's love incarnate among men.

Yet again, when God sends his Son to plead with men, remember he does not urge us to anything which will be for our loss and detriment : *obedience to him is happiness for ourselves.* He does not urge us to follow a life of misery, nor to begin a course which will end in our destruction. Far from it. They that repent and turn to God through Jesus Christ find such joy, such happiness, that earth becomes to them the vestibule of heaven. The joy-bells ring within the Father's house, when a soul returns to its home. To persuade you to be holy is to induce you to be happy ; to urge you to seek God is to urge you to seek your own best welfare ; to urge you to lay down the weapons of rebellion and be reconciled to the Most High is to set before you the wisest, safest and best course that you can follow. The Lord God out of heaven cries to you: "This is my beloved Son ; hear ye him."

Remember, once more, that, if you do not hear the well-beloved Son of God, you have refused your last hope. *He is God's ultimation.* Nothing remains when Christ is refused. No one else can be sent; heaven itself contains no further messenger. If Christ be rejected, hope is rejected. Neither would you be converted though one rose from the dead; for Jesus has risen from the dead, and you have refused him. I should like every person that is unconverted to recollect that there is no other Gospel, and no more sacrifice for sin. I have heard talk of "a larger hope" than the Gospel sets before us: it is a fable, with nothing in Scripture to warrant it. Rejecting Christ, you have rejected all; you have shut against yourself the one door of hope. Christ, who knows better than all pretenders, declares that, "He that believeth not shall be damned." "There is none other name under heaven given among men, whereby we must be saved" (Acts 4: 12). This is clear; for heaven's grandest effort has been made. What more can God do?

I beg your attention while I look, in the second place, to THE ASTOUNDING CRIME. It was nothing less than an astounding crime, that when this householder sent his wellbeloved son, the husbandmen said one to another, "This is the heir; come, let us kill him, and the inheritance shall be ours. And they took him, and cast him out of the vineyard." "No," says one, "we never killed the Son of God." I will not charge you with having done so *literally;* that were to make myself chargeable with exaggeration. But a man may do virtually what he cannot do actually. If a murder be committed, and I approve of it, if my own principles lead up to it, if I feel no indignation against it, but express myself very coolly about it, if there is reason to believe that if I had been there I should have done the same, then I may be in the sight of God a partaker in the crime. There are many among us who are guilty of the body and blood of Christ.

Yes, thy sins have done the deed,
Driven the nails that fix'd him there,
Crown'd with thorns his sacred head,
Plunged into his side the spear,
Made his soul a sacrifice,
While for sinful man he dies!

Now I say this, that all those who persistently deny the Deity of Christ virtually kill him; for the Son of God is not alive if his Godhead be not in existence. All those who deny his Atonement also slay him; for the blood of sacrifice is the life of the Christ of God. The very essence of his Christhood, the soul of his character as Jesus, lies in his having been appointed to be a Propitiation for sin.

"Well, we have not done that," cry some of you. "We have been no opposers of the Deity or Sacrifice of Jesus." But let me remind you that if you do not judge him to be worthy of your most careful thoughts, if you are indifferent to his claims and refuse to obey his Gospel, you have virtually put him away. To you it is the same as if there were no Christ.

Is it nothing to you, all ye that pass by?
Is it nothing to you that Jesus should die?

You have virtually answered "It is nothing." You have set Christ down as nothing compared with the business of daily life, and thus you have virtually slain him: you have put him out of existence so far as you are concerned. In the little world of your mind there is no living Saviour: he is dead and buried to you, and the claims of God which he pleads you will not think upon. You have been occupied all the week with trivial amusements, or unimportant discussions, but you have not deigned to think of him whose advent into the world is so great a wonder, that if you never thought of anything else, you might be justified in a life of devout meditation. He who deserves all your thoughts gets none of them. You have nothing to do with Christ, his Cross, his people, or his cause; and therefore— I say it with no harshness, but with much grief—you are kill-Christs, and are guilty of his blood. I charge you with making away with your Saviour. I press the accusation home and trust that it will strike you with horror.

I have still closer work with some of you, who are most assuredly guilty. You were once members of the Church; you came to the communion-table, where they gather who remember his precious body and blood; you used to glory in his name; but you have gone back, you have denied the faith, you have ceased to be followers of the Lamb. Now, these are no words of mine, but inspired words:—You have "crucified the Son of God afresh, and put him to an open shame." You are beyond all question among those who have cast the heir out of the vineyard and slain him, deliberately turning your backs upon his sacred cause. The Lord have mercy on you!

I must press this home upon a great many more who have heard of Christ, and believe him to be God, and assent to all the truth about him, but who yet have never yielded themselves to his authority. What have you done? You have preferred the world to Christ: you have chosen Barabbas and condemned the Saviour. You have said to the claims of Jesus, "Wait." Can you say that anything has a greater claim on you than the Son of God? Is there anything that has a greater right to your thoughts, to your consideration, to your love, than the great salvation which Jesus Christ has wrought out? If you have pushed the Lord Jesus Christ out of the first place, he will occupy no other, and therefore you have virtually un-Christed him, and you are guilty of his blood. You must either be justified by him or you must be condemned by him.

What was the reason why these husbandmen, these dressers of the vineyard, dared thus to treat the heir? The reason is one which presses upon those who have rejected Christ. They did it, first, because *they had enjoyed a long immunity from punishment.* They had not been at once punished for their defiance of their lord. They had rejected his messengers without provoking him to war; they had gone on to stone and slay others of his servants, and the householder had not come upon them to overthrow them. They grew at last to be very hardened. I know not what they said, but I conceive that certain of them propagated the theory that their lord took no notice of what they did, or that he was too loving to punish them severely. "See!" said they, "he only sends fresh messengers if we kill the old ones; and even if we kill his son he will bear it. Let us not imagine that he will take vengeance. He is love, and even should we murder his son, he will lay up in store for us a larger hope."

Ungrateful men abuse God's long-suffering to-day as they did of old. They say, "Well, I have refused the Gospel a long time; I have put aside many appeals; but I am not dead, nor struck with blindness, nor smitten down with a stroke. I can go on at least a little longer in safety. I may refuse Christ yet again, for God is merciful." "Certain teachers," say you, "tell us that God is so good, that if we even kill his Son he will take no account of it. We will kill his Son, and so we will reject the atonement and trample on the precious blood, and yet we doubt not all will come right in the long run, and the evil of our crime will prove to be only temporary."

You do not put your thoughts into those words; but you are saying as much by your actions. You dare not *say* it, and yet it lurks in your hearts and works itself out in your deeds. You are going to run the dreadful risk of trifling with the Son of God. To you this seems a little thing, but horror takes hold of me at the thought of it. I will be no partner in your crime. I will not cease to warn you that it must be of all risks the most tremendous. Gracious as he is—and God has proved his grace by sending his Son—yet God is not effeminate nor unjust. If you refuse the mercy which he so freely proffers you, he will deal with you in his justice. He is the Judge of all the earth, and he must do right. For as truly as he is love, so truly is he holiness. He is wondrous in his power to forgive; but he is also terrible out of his holy places. "If the sinner turn not, he will whet his sword; he hath bent his bow, and made it ready."

The great reason, however, why these husbandmen determined to kill the heir was this: they said, "*Then the inheritance shall be ours.*" This is what the heart of man vainly desires. It says, "Let us be rid of this troublesome talk of religion, and then we can live for ourselves, and study our own pleasure without remorse of conscience. Are we not our own? Who shall be lord over us? If we are rid of this Jesus, we shall not have this claim being always made upon us, that we are God's creatures and that we ought to live to him. We do not intend to serve God. We will pay no rent to this householder. We will be our own proprietors. Who is the Lord, that we should obey his voice? If we can get rid of this Christ business we can live as we list, and do as we please, and no one will call us to account. If we can persuade ourselves that religion is not true, we shall then care nothing for checks and warnings, but we shall take our full swing and enjoy ourselves without stint. A short life and a merry one will suit us. We might enjoy ourselves if this matter of God, and Christ, and eternity, could be disposed of."

Yes, young man, this is what your prototype thought when he said to his father, "Give me the portion of goods that falleth to me." Then he gathered all together, and went into a far country, and spent his "substance in riotous living." This is what you hanker after. But your folly is exceeding great. I grieve as I look into your young face and read the idle dream of your heart. You little know what a tyrant he serves who lives as he lists. May God grant that I may never live as my sinful lusts would make me live! The grace of God can make you as free in holiness as in sin. Grace can make you more free in the service of God than in the service of yourself.

Self lies at the bottom of all rejection of Christ—"Let us kill him, and the inheritance shall be ours." Ah, it will not be yours; and if it were yours for a little while, and you could do just as you pleased with it, yet remember that the inheritance which is so gained will soon pass away, and you yourself will soon have to stand before the judgment-seat of Christ to give an account of the deeds done in the body, whether they be good, or whether they be bad. And what will *you* do who have slain your Saviour? What will you do in that day, who have lived and died unsaved?

I must close with that third head, which is so dreadful to me: THE APPROPRIATE PUNISHMENT. I do not suppose that the thought of this subject will be half so dreadful to anybody who is unconverted as it is to me. I tremble as I meditate upon the wrath to come. How glad I would be if I had not to preach from such a theme! But I must preach from it, or be a traitor to God, and an enemy to you. If you perish, your blood will be required at my hands, if I do not warn you of the punishment of sin. This is how the Saviour put it: "When the lord therefore of the vineyard cometh, what will he do unto those husbandmen?" He leaves our conscience to award the penalty. He leaves our imagination to prescribe a doom sufficient for a crime so base, so daring, so cruel. They have killed the only son of their lord, what will he do unto those husbandmen?

At this present moment I am afraid that this parable is being written out again in the history of the Church of God. God has put into his vineyard, or allowed to come into his vineyard, a number of religious teachers who are not rendering to him the honour due. Those religious teachers to whom I refer are not teaching the Gospel as it is delivered in Holy Scripture, but they are adapting it to the age, and to the scientific knowledge of the period. They are described in the book of the prophet Jeremiah: "Thus saith the Lord of hosts, Hearken not unto the words of the prophets that prophesy unto you: they make you vain: they speak a vision of their own heart, and not out of the mouth of the Lord. They say still unto them that despise me, The Lord hath said, Ye shall have peace; and they say unto every one that walketh after the imagination of his own heart, No evil shall come upon you." The thoughts of their own minds are given instead of the revelation of God. Thus they set up another gospel, which is not another; but there be some that trouble you. The spirit of the age is the spirit of proud self-sufficiency; be it ours to sit at Jesus' feet. My Lord will one day say to me, "I gave thee a message, didst thou deliver it? I bade thee speak in my name, didst thou speak my words or thine own? I gave thee a revelation, didst thou deliver that revelation as best thou couldst? or didst thou invent a new thing out of thine own brain?" I know how I shall answer. Beware that none of us sin against the Holy Ghost by setting up our dreams in rivalry with his certainties. Pray for those who do so, lest God deal with them speedily in vengeance. The Lord have mercy upon all false prophets, and bring them humbly and tremblingly to his feet, lest they ensnare the people yet more, to the overthrow of this nation, and the taking away of the candlestick out of its place.

I return to you whom I have already addressed. You have crucified the Son of God by refusing to believe in him. What shall the Lord do unto you when he comes? The sentence cannot be too severe, for the crime is beyond measure horrible. They slew the servants, and they slew the heir; no temporary punishment can meet the case. Those who plead for a light doom for such a crime must, in their own hearts, be rebels. Those who are evermore making light of hell are probably doing it in the hope of making it easy for themselves.

In Matthew 21, our Lord, comparing himself to the stone which should be the foundation, but which the builders reject, says, "On whomsoever it shall fall, it will grind him to powder." Sinner, if you reject the Saviour, you will have to feel his full weight. Boundless in power, infinite in majesty, *the whole weight of him will fall on you.* Will you think that over? This foundation stone falling upon you shall grind you to powder. I will not dwell further upon this tremendous thought, but I will repeat it in set and solemn form : the full weight of the incarnate God, in the day of his wrath, you will have to bear. It is put in another way in that expression—"The wrath of the Lamb." Is not that a marvellous combination, "The wrath of the Lamb"? Love when it turns to jealousy is the fiercest of all passions; and when the love of Christ in infinite justice shall be turned into holy indignation against unrighteousness, then it will be something terrible to think of, and to bear it will be the second death. Are you prepared to bear the awful weight of a Saviour's anger? No: you are not. Come, then, to Jesus. "Kiss the Son, lest he be angry, and ye perish from the way, while his wrath is kindled but a little." Do not refuse the Lord Jesus, who now pleads with you. Will you lose your souls? Will you reject Christ? Will you refuse the Son of God? Can you be so mad as to live and die without the Saviour? Are you so far gone as this? Turn, I beseech you, turn you this day. Lord, turn them, for thy dear Son's sake!

VI

THE WEDDING FEAST

"The kingdom of heaven is like unto a certain king, which made a marriage for his son, and sent forth his servants to call them that were bidden to the wedding: and they would not come. Again, he sent forth other servants, saying, Tell them which are bidden, Behold, I have prepared my dinner: my oxen and my fatlings are killed, and all things are ready: come unto the marriage."—Matt. 22 : 2–4.

HOW tenderly condescending is God to devise similitudes, that his children may learn the mysteries of the kingdom! If it be sometimes marvelled at among men that great minds are ever ready to stoop, what a far greater marvel that God himself should bow the heavens and come down to meet our ignorance and slowness of comprehension! When the learned professor has been instructing his class in the hall in recondite matters of deep philosophy, and then goes home and takes his child upon his knee, and tries to bring down great truth to the grasp of his child's mind, then you see the great love of the man's heart: and when the eternal God, before whom seraphims are but insects of an hour, condescends to instruct our childishness and make us wise unto salvation, we may well say, "herein is love."

Just as we give our children pictures that we may win the attention, and may by pleasing means fix truth upon their memories, so the Lord with loving inventiveness has become the author of many a charming metaphor, type, and allegory, by which he may gain our interest, and through his Holy Spirit enlighten our minds. He who is willing to learn, in a childlike spirit, is already in a considerable measure taught of God. May we all so study this instructive parable as to be quickened by it to all that is well-pleasing in the sight of God, for after all true learning in godliness may be judged of by its results upon our lives.

A certain king of wide dominions and great power designed

to give a magnificent banquet, with a GRAND OBJECT IN VIEW. The crown prince, his wellbeloved heir, was about to take to himself a fair bride, and therefore the royal father desired to celebrate the event with extraordinary honours. From earth, look up to heaven. The great object of God the Father is to glorify his Son. It is his will "that all men should honour the Son, even as they honour the Father" (John 5: 23). Jesus Christ, the Son of God, is glorious already *in his divine person.* He is ineffably blessed and infinitely beyond needing honour. All the angels of God worship him, and his glory fills all heaven. He has appeared on the stage of action as *the Creator,* and as such his glory is perfect, "For by him were all things created, that are in heaven, and that are in earth, visible and invisible, whether they be thrones, or dominions, or principalities, or powers: all things were created by him, and for him" (Col. 1: 16).

He said, "Light be," and it flamed forth. He bade the mountains lift their heads, and their summits pierced the clouds. He created the water-floods, he bade them seek their channels, and he appointed their bounds. Nothing is lacking to the glory of the Word of God, who was in the beginning with God, who spake and it was done, who commanded, and it stood forth. He is highly exalted also as *the preserver,* for he is before all things, and by him all things consist. He is that nail fastened in a sure place, upon which all things hang. The keys of heaven, and death, and hell, are fastened to his girdle, and the government shall be upon his shoulders, and his name shall be called Wonderful. He hath a name which is above every name, before which all things shall bow, in heaven, and earth, and under the earth. He is God over all. He is blessed for ever. To him that is, and was, and is to come, the universal song goeth up.

But there is another relation in which the Son of God has graciously been pleased to stand towards us. He has undertaken to be *a Saviour,* in order that he might be *a Bridegroom.* He had enough glory before, but in the greatness of his heart, he would magnify his compassion even above his power, and he therefore condescended to take into union with himself the nature of man, in order that he might redeem the beloved objects of his choice from the penalty due to their sins and might enter into

the nearest conceivable union with them. It is as Saviour
that the Father seeks to honour the Son, and the Gospel feast
is not for the honour of his Person merely, but for the honour
of his Person in this new, yet anciently purposed relationship.
It is for the honour of Jesus as entering into spiritual union
with his Church, that the Gospel is prepared as a royal entertainment.

When I said that here was a grand occasion, it certainly is
so in God's esteem, and it should be so in ours; we should
delight to glorify the Son of God. To all loyal subjects in any
realm, the marriage of one of the royal family is a matter of
great interest, and it is usual and fitting to give expression to
congratulations and sympathies by suitable rejoicings. In the
instance before us the occasion calls for special joy from all the
subjects of the great King of kings. For the occasion in itself
is a subject for great delight and thankfulness to us *personally*.
The marriage is with whom? With angels? He took not up
angels. It is a marriage with our own nature, "he took up the
seed of Abraham." Shall we not rejoice when heaven's great
Lord is incarnate as a man and stoops to redeem humanity
from the ruin of the fall? Angels rejoice but they have no such
share in the joy as we have. It is the highest personal joy to
manhood that Jesus Christ who thought it not robbery to be
equal with God, was made in the likeness of men that he might
be one flesh with his chosen. Arise ye who slumber! If there
was ever an occasion when ye should bestir your spirits and cry
"wake up my glory, awake psaltery and harp" it is now, when
Jesus comes to be affianced to his church, to make himself
of one flesh with her, that he may redeem her, and afterwards
exalt her to sit with him upon his throne. Here were abundant
reasons why the invited guests should come with joyful steps
and count themselves thrice happy to be bidden to such a
banquet.

Beside that we must consider the *royal descent* of the Bridegroom. Remember that Jesus Christ our Saviour is very God
of very God. Are we asked to do him honour? It is right, for to
whom else should honour be given? Surely we should glorify
our Creator and Preserver! Wilful must be the disobedience
which will not pay reverence to one so highly exalted and so
worthy of all homage. O come let us worship and bow down,

let us cheerfully obey those commands of God which aim at the honour of his Son.

Remember also the *Person* of Immanuel, and you will desire his glory. This glorious Son, whose fame is to be spread abroad, is most certainly God—of that we have spoken, but he is also most assuredly man, our Brother, bone of our bone, and flesh of our flesh. Do we not delight to believe that he, tempted in all points as we are, has never yet submitted to be stained by sin? Never such a man as he, head of the race, the second Adam, the everlasting Father—who among us would not do him reverence? Will we not seek his honour, seeing that now he lifts our race to be next to the throne of God?

Remember, too, his *Character*. Was there ever such a life as his? I will not so much speak of his divine character, though that furnishes abundant reason for worship and adoration, but think of him even as a man. What tenderness, what compassion, yet what holy boldness; what love for sinners, and yet what love for truth! Men who have not loved him have nevertheless admired him, and hearts in which we least expected to see such recognition of his excellencies have nevertheless been deeply affected as they have studied his life. We must praise him, for He is "chief among ten thousand, and altogether lovely."

Think, too, of his *achievements*. We take into reckoning whenever we do honour to a prince all that he may have done for the nation over which he rules. What, then, has Jesus done for us? Rather let me say what has he not done? Upon his shoulders were laid our sins; he carried them into the wilderness, and they are gone for ever. Against him came forth our foes; he met them in shock of battle, and where are they now? They arc cast into the depths of the sea. As for death itself, that last of foes, he has virtually overcome it, and ere long the weakest of us through him shall say, "O death, where is thy sting? O grave, where is thy victory?" He is the Hero of heaven. He returned to his Father's throne amidst the acclamations of the universe. Do *we* not, for whom he fought, for whom he conquered, do *we* not desire to honour him? Bring forth the royal diadem and crown him! Is the King's Son to be married, is there a festival in his honour? O then let him be great, let him be glorious!

Secondly, here is a GENEROUS METHOD of accomplishing the design. A king's son is to be honoured on the day of his marriage; in what way shall it be done? Barbarous nations have their great festivals, and alas, that men should have sunk so low; on such occasions rivers of human blood are made to flow. No blood is poured forth to honour the Son of heaven's great King. I doubt not Jesus will have honour even in the destruction of men if they reject his mercy, but it is not so that God elects to glorify his Son. Jesus the Saviour, on his wedding-day with manhood, is glorified by mercy, not by wrath. If blood be mentioned on such a day, it is his own by which he is glorified. The slaughter of mankind would bring no joy to him, he is meek and lowly, a lover of the sons of men. It has been the custom of most kings to signalise a princely wedding by levying a fresh tax, or demanding an increased subsidy from their subjects; but the parable shows that the King of kings deals with us not after the manner of man. He asks no dowry for his Son; he makes the marriage memorable not by demands but by gifts. Nothing is sought for from the people, but much is prepared for them, gifts are lavishly bestowed, and all that is requested of the subjects is, that they for awhile merge the subject in the more honourable character of the guest, and willingly come to the palace, not to labour or serve at the table, but to feast and to rejoice.

Observe, then, the generous method by which God honours Christ is set forth here under the form of a banquet. I noted Matthew Henry's way of describing the objects of a feast, and with the alliteration of the Puritans, he says, "A feast is for love and for laughter, for fulness and for fellowship." It is even so with the Gospel. It is for *love;* in the Gospel, sinner, you are invited to be reconciled to God, you are assured that God forgives your sins, ceases to be angry, and would have you reconciled to him through his Son. Thus love is established between God and the soul. Then it is for *laughter,* for happiness, for joy. It is not to sorrow but to joy that the great King invites his subjects, when he glorifies his Son Jesus.

A feast, moreover, is for *fulness.* The hungry famished soul of man is satisfied with the blessings of grace. The Gospel fills the whole capacity of our manhood. There is not a faculty of our nature which is not made to feel its need supplied when the soul accepts the provisions of mercy; our whole manhood is satisfied with good things and our youth is renewed like the eagles.

To crown all, the Gospel brings us into *fellowship* with the Father and his Son Jesus Christ. In Christ Jesus we commune with the sacred Trinity. God becomes our Father and reveals his paternal heart. Jesus manifests himself unto us as he doth not unto the world, and the communion of the Holy Ghost abides with us. Our fellowship is like that of Jonathan with David, or Jesus with John. We are brought into the heavenly banqueting house where the secret of the Lord is revealed to us, and our heart pours itself out before the Lord. Very near is our communion with God; most intimate love and condescension does he show to us. What say you to this? Is there not here a rich repast worthy of him who prepares it? Here all your capacious powers can wish, O sinner, shall be given to you; all you want for time and for eternity God prepares in the Person of his dear Son.

It was a very sumptuous festival, there were oxen, and there were fatlings, but none of these were taken from the pastures, or stalls of the guests. The Gospel is an expensive business; the very heart of Christ was drained to find the price for this great festival; but it costs the sinner nothing, nothing of money, nothing of merit, nothing of preparation. Just as you are, you are bidden to believe in Jesus. You are not asked to contribute to the provision, but to be a feaster at the divine banquet of infinite compassion.

How *honourable*, too, is the Gospel to those who receive it. An invitation to a regal marriage was a high honour to those who were bidden. I do not suppose that many of us are likely to be invited to a royal wedding, and, if we were, we should probably be greatly elated, for we should most of us feel it to be one of the great events of our lives. So was it with these people. A king's son is not married every day, and it is not everybody that is bidden to the monarch's entertainment. All their lives long they would say, "I was at his wedding and saw all the splendour of the marriage festival." Probably some of them had never before enjoyed such a feast as the luxurious potentate had prepared for that day and had never before been in such good company. Nothing so honours a man as for him to accept the Gospel. While his faith honours Christ, Christ honours him. It is no mean thing to be a king's son, but those who come to the marriage feast of God's own Son shall become King's sons themselves—themselves participators in the glory of the great heir of all things.

Surely here is an illustration of the folly of the unrenewed heart, and a proof of the deep depravity which sin has caused. If men turn their backs on Moses with his stony tables, I do not marvel, but to despise the loaded tables of grace, heaped up with oxen and fatlings—this is strange. To resist the justice of God is a crime, but to repel the generosity of heaven, what is this? We must invent a term of infamy with which to brand the base ingratitude. To resist God in majesty of terror is insanity but to spurn him in the majesty of his mercy is something more than madness. Sin reaches its climax when it resolves to starve sooner than owe anything to divine goodness. Come, guilty sinner, as you are, and take the mercy Jesus freely presents to you, and accept the pardon which his blood secures to those who believe in him.

Methinks when the messenger went out from the King and first of all marked signs of neglect among those who were bidden and saw that they would not come, he must have been mute with astonishment. He had seen the oxen, and seen the fatlings, and all the goodly preparations; he knew the King, he knew his Son, he knew what joy it was to be at such a feast; and, when the bidden ones began to turn their backs on him, and go their way to their farms, the messenger repeated his message over and over again with eagerness, wondering all the while at the treason which dared insult so good a King. He mourned that his fellow-citizens whom he loved should be such fools as to reject so good an offer and spurn so blessed a proclamation. I, too, am tossed to and fro in soul, with mingled but vehement feelings. O, my God, thou hast provided the Gospel, let none reject it, and so slight thy Son and dishonour thee, but may all rejoice in thy generous way of glorifying Jesus Christ, the Bridegroom of his Church, and may they come, and willingly grace the festival of thy love.

We now advance to our third point, and regretfully remember THE SERIOUS HINDRANCE which for awhile interfered with the joyful event.

The king had thought in his mind, "I will make a great feast; I will invite a large number. They shall enjoy all my kingdom can afford, and I shall thus show how much I love my son, and moreover all the guests will have sweet memories in connection with his marriage." When his messengers went out to intimate to those who had received previously an express invitation that the time was come, it is written, "They would not come;" not they *could* not, but they "*would* not come." Some for one reason, some for another, but without exception they would not come. Here was a very serious hindrance to the grand business. Cannot the king drag his guests to the table? Yes, but then it would not accomplish his purpose. He wants not slaves to grace his throne. Persons compelled to sit at a marriage-feast would not adorn it. What credit could it be to a king to force his subjects to feast at his table? No, for once, as I have said before, the subject must be merged in the guest. It was essential to the dignity of the festival that the guests should come with cheerfulness to the festival, but they would not come. Why? Why would they not come? The answer shall be such as to answer another question—Why do not you come and believe in Jesus? With many of them it was an indifference to the whole affair. They did not see what concern they had in the king or his son. Royal marriages were high things and concerned high people; they were plain-speaking men, farmers who went hedging and ditching, or tradesmen who made out bills and sold by the yard or pound. What cared they for the court, the palace, the king, the prince, his bride, or his dinner! They did not say quite that, but such was their feeling; it might be a fine thing, but it was altogether out of their line. How many run in the same groove at this hour? We have heard it said, "What has a working man to do with religion?" and we have heard others of another grade in life affirm that persons who are in business cannot afford time for religion, but had better mind the main chance. The Lord have mercy upon your folly!

At the bottom the real reason for the refusal of those in the parable was that they were disloyal, they would not come to the supper because they saw an opportunity for the loyal to be glad, and not being loyal they did not wish to hear the songs and acclamations of others who were. By staying away they insulted the king and declared that they cared not whether he was a king or not, whether his son was a prince or not. They determined to disavow their allegiance by refusing the invitation. Ah, ye who believe not in Jesus, at the bottom of it your unbelief is enmity to your Maker, sedition against the great Ruler of the universe, who deserves your homage. "The ox knoweth his owner, and the ass his master's crib," but ye know not, neither do ye consider; ye are rebels against the Majesty of heaven.

Moreover, the refusal was a slight to the prince as well as to his father, and in some cases the Gospel is refused mainly with this intent, because the unbeliever rejects the Deity of Christ, or despises his Atonement. Beware of this, I know of no rock more fatal than to dishonour Christ by denying his Sonship and his Deity. Split not upon it, I beseech you; "Kiss the Son, lest he be angry, and ye perish from the way when his wrath is kindled but a little." Indifference covered the refusal in the text, "they made light of it," but if you take off the film you will see that at the bottom there was treason against the majesty of the king, and distaste to the dignity of his son.

No doubt some of them despised the feast itself. They must have known that with such a king it could not be a starveling meal, but they pretended to despise the feast. How many there are who despise the Gospel which they do not understand, for almost invariably if you hear a man depreciate the Gospel, you will find that he has scarcely even read the New Testament and is an utter stranger to the doctrines of grace. Listen to a man who is voluble in condemnation of the Gospel, and you may rest assured that he is loud because he is empty. If he understood the subject better he would find, if he were indeed a man of candour, that he would be led at least to be silent in admiration if he did not become loyal in acceptance.

The feast is such as you greatly need; let me tell you what it is. It is pardon for the past, renewal of nature for the present, and glory for the future. Here is God to be our Helper, his Son to be our Shepherd, the Spirit to be our Instructor. Here is the love of the Father to be our delight, the blood of the Son to be our cleansing, the energy of the Holy Spirit to be life from the dead to us. You cannot want anything that you ought to want, but what is provided in the Gospel, and Jesus Christ will be glorified if you accept it by faith. But here is the hindrance, men do not accept it, "they would not come." Still will the cry go up, "Who hath believed our report?" Still will those who serve their Master best, have reason to mourn that they sow on stony ground, and cast their bread on thankless waters. Even the prince of preachers had to say, "Search the scriptures, for in them ye think ye have eternal life: . . . and ye will not come to me, that ye might have life" (John 5: 39, 40). Alas, alas, that mercy should be rejected and heaven spurned.

So now we must close with the most practical matter of consideration, THE GRACIOUS REJOINDER of the king to the impertinence which interfered with his plans. What did he say? You will observe that they had been bidden, and then called; after the Oriental custom, the call intimated that the festival was now approaching, so that they were not taken unawares, but knew what they did. The second invitation they rejected in cold blood, deliberately, and with intent. What did the monarch do? Set their city in a blaze, and at once root out the rebels? No, but in the first place, he winked at their former insolent refusal. He said in himself, "Peradventure they mistook my servants, peradventure they did not understand that the hour was come. Perhaps the message that was delivered to them was too brief, and they missed its meaning. Or, if perchance they had fallen into some temporary enmity against me, on reconsideration, they will wish that they had not been so rude and ungenerous to me. What have I done that they should refuse my dinner? What has my son done that they should not be willing to honour him by feasting at my table? Men love feasting, my son deserves their honour—why should they not come? I will pass over the past and begin again." There are many of you who have rejected Christ after many invitations, and my Lord forgets your former unkindnesses, and sends me again with the same message, again to bid you "come to the wedding." It is no small patience which overlooks the past and perseveres in kindness, honestly desiring your good.

The king sent another invitation—"all things are ready, come ye to the marriage," but you will please to observe that he changed the messenger. "Again he sent forth other servants." Yes, and I will say it, for my soul feels it, if a change of messengers will win you, much as I love the task of speaking in my Master's name, I would gladly die now, where I am, that some other preacher might occupy this platform, if thereby you might be saved. I know my speech to some of you must be monotonous. I seek out images fresh and many, and try to vary my voice and manner, but for all that one man must grow stale to you when heard so often. Perhaps my modes are not the sort to touch your peculiarities of temperament—well, good Master, set thy servant aside, and consider him not. Send other messengers if perchance they may succeed.

You notice, too, that the message was a little changed. At first it was very short. Surely if men's hearts were right, short sermons would be enough. A very brief invitation might suffice if the heart were right, but since hearts are wrong God bids his servants enlarge, expand, and expound. "Come, for all things are ready. I have prepared my dinner, my oxen and my fatlings are killed, all things are ready, come to the marriage." One of the best ways of bringing sinners to Christ is to explain the Gospel to them. If we dwell upon its preparations, if we speak of its richness and freeness, some may be attracted whom the short message which merely tells the plan of salvation might not attract. To some it is enough to say, "Believe in the Lord Jesus Christ and thou shalt be saved," for they are asking, "Sirs, what must I do to be saved?" but others need to be attracted to the wedding feast by the description of the sumptuousness of the repast. We must try to preach the Gospel more fully to you, but we shall never tell you of all the richness of the grace of God. Forsake your sins and your thoughts and turn to the Lord, for he will abundantly pardon you. He will receive you to his heart of love, and give you the kiss of his affection at this hour, if, like prodigal children, you come back and seek your Father's face. The Gospel is a river of love, it is a sea of love, it is a heaven of love, it is a universe of love, it is all love. Words there are none, fully to set forth the amazing love of God to sinners, no sin too big or too black, no crime too crimson or too cursed for pardon. If you do but look to his dear crucified Son all manner of sin and of blasphemy shall be forgiven you.

In this last message the guests were pressed very delicately, but still in a way which if they had possessed any generosity of heart at all, must have touched them. You see how the evangelist puts it, he does not say, "Come, or else you will miss the feast; come, or else the king will be angry; come, come, or else you will be the losers." No, but he puts it, as I read it, in a very remarkable way. I venture to say—if I be wrong, the Master forgive me so saying—the king makes himself the object of sympathy, as though he were an embarrassed host. See here, "My dinner is ready, but there is no one to eat it; my oxen and fatlings are all killed, but there are no guests." "Come, come," he seems to say, "for I am a host without guests." So sometimes in the Gospel you will see God speaks as if he would represent himself as getting an advantage by our being saved. Now we know that herein he condescends in love to speak after the manner of men. What can he gain by us? If we perish what is he the loser? But he makes himself often in the Gospel to be like a father who yearns over his child, longing for him to come home. He makes himself, the infinite God, turn beggar to his own creatures and beseeches them to be reconciled. Wondrous stoop; for, like a chapman who sells his wares, he cries, " Ho, every one that thirsteth, come ye to the waters; and he that hath no money, let him come." Do you observe how Christ, as he wept over Jerusalem, seems to weep for himself as well as for them. "How often would I have gathered thy children together" (Luke 13: 34). And God, in the prophets, puts it as his own sorrow, "How can I set thee as Admah, how can I make thee as Zeboim," as if it were not the child's loss alone, but the father's loss also, if the sinner died. Do you not feel, as it were, a sympathy with God when you see his Gospel rejected? Shall the Cross be lifted high, and none look to it? Shall Jesus die, and men not be saved by his death? O blessed Lord, we feel, if nothing else should draw us, we must come when we see, as it were, thyself represented as a host under our embarrassment, for lack of guests. Great God, we come, we come right gladly, we come to participate of the bounties which thou hast provided and to glorify Jesus Christ by receiving as needy sinners that which thy mercy has provided.

VII

ENTRANCE AND EXCLUSION

"And they that were ready went in with him to the marriage: and the door was shut."—Matt. 25: 10.

DURING the waiting period, the wise and foolish virgins seemed much alike, even as at this day one can hardly discern the false professor from the true. Everything turned upon the coming of the Bridegroom. To the ten virgins, that was the chief event of the night. If it had not been for his coming, they would not have gone forth with their lamps. It was because they knew he would surely come that they prepared themselves to join in the marriage procession and attend him with their songs to the place of his abode.

Yet, for a while, he did not come. The sun had gone down, and darkness had stolen over the whole landscape, but the bridegroom did not come. The dews of night were falling fast, yet still he did not come. The hours were long and slowly passed away one after the other, yet he did not come. It was waxing toward the middle of the night, and the eyes of the waiting virgins grew heavy with watching. Why was the bridegroom so long in coming? They had been bidden to look for him, they had fully expected him; yet he had not come.

But the bridegroom did come, as, in our case, the Heavenly Bridegroom will come. However long we may have waited for him, let us rest assured that he will come. As surely as he came once, so, "unto them that look for him shall he appear the second time without sin unto salvation" (Heb. 9: 28). It seems to me that it needs less faith to believe in the second Advent of Christ than in his first Advent. He has been here before, so he knows the way to come again. He has been here before, and wrought a wondrous work; surely, he will come back to receive the reward of his service. The Good Shepherd came to earth once to lay down his life for the sheep; he will surely come again as the Chief Shepherd to recompense the under-shepherds who have faithfully kept the night watches for him.

Yes, the bridegroom did come. Despite the waiting time, he did come; and then came the dreadful separation between those who had been waiting for his appearing. Scarcely by any act of his, the foolish and the wise were parted the one from the other. They were awakened by the sound of his approach; the herald that preceded him cried, "Behold, the bridegroom cometh," and the sleepers were all aroused. Then the true adherents of the bridegroom, the wise virgins, penitent for their guilty sleep, poured the oil into their lamps, which were burning low, and soon they were blazing up clear and bright. As the bridegroom's procession came near, "they that were ready went in with him to the marriage: and the door was shut." But the foolish virgins—those who had despised the secret stores of oil, those who had never gone to the Divine Spirit for his matchless grace—were separated from their wiser companions; not, indeed, by any special act of the bridegroom, but as the natural result of their own unprepared condition. They had to go away to buy oil of those that sold it, and when they came back, it was too late for them to go in to the marriage. They came up to the gate of the palace, and found the door fast closed against them, shut for ever, and learned that they must abide in the outer darkness, to weep and lament that they were not found worthy to behold the bridegroom's face.

First, then, let us think of THE READY AND THEIR ENTRANCE: "They that were ready went in with him to the marriage."

Let us meditate a little, first, about the entrance itself, and then talk together about the persons who enjoyed it.

Concerning their entrance, note that it was *immediate upon the coming of the bridegroom.* As soon as he appeared, there seems to have been no interval, but, at once, "they that were ready *went in* with him to the marriage." The manifestation of Christ shall be the glorification of his people. We shall want nothing else but to behold his face, and then our bliss shall be perfect and complete. Never entertain the slightest fear of any such purgatorial state as some have begun to dream of again. That lie, which the Reformers rightly called, "purgatory pick-purse," which filled the pope's treasury and was a curse to myriads of immortal souls, was exposed in all its naked ugliness by the light which God gave to Luther and Calvin; yet now, amid the abounding scepticism of these evil days, there is coming back this foul night-bird, or rather, this dragon of the dark ages; and sometimes even the children of God feel the influence of its pestilential presence. Dear Christian friends, be not afraid of any purgatory. If you die, you shall be absent from the body and present with the Lord at once, for this shall be your blessed portion in Christ. If you are alive and remain till Jesus comes again, your body shall be changed in a moment, in the twinkling of an eye, and you shall rise to meet your Lord in the air, and so shall be ever with him; but if you have fallen asleep in Jesus, those who are alive at his coming, shall have no preference over you, but you shall be raised incorruptible, and in the moment of that rising, when your spirit, by the divine fiat, shall have been reunited with your perfectly purified and glorified body, you shall go in with him to the marriage, and be for ever with him and like him. Do not trouble yourself, therefore, about what is to happen, or what is not to happen. Be you confident of this; if you sleep, you shall sleep in Jesus, and, when you wake up, you shall wake up in his likeness, and you shall never be parted from him whose company even now is your highest source of joy, and whose society shall be your delight for ever and ever.

Notice, next, that the entrance of the wise virgins into the marriage feast was not only immediate, it was also *intimate*. "They that were ready went in *with him* to the marriage." I like that expression "with him." I would go nowhere without him; and if I may go anywhere with him, wherever he shall lead me, it shall be a happy day to me; and so it shall be to all who love his appearing. You know that our Lord Jesus left it in his will that we are to be with him in his glory; listen to this clause out of his last will and testament: "Father, I will that they also, whom thou hast given me be with me where I am; that they may behold my glory." You who know what it is to be one with Jesus, crucified with him, risen with him, made to sit together with him in the heavenlies, you, I am sure, will find something more heavenly about heaven than otherwise had been there when that sweet sentence is true of you, "They that were ready went in *with him* to the marriage."

Our Lord Jesus himself shall escort us to our place in glory;

he shall conduct us to the sources of highest blessedness, for as the elder said to John in the Revelation, "The Lamb which is in the midst of the throne shall feed them, and shall lead them unto living fountains of waters" (Rev. 7: 17). This, it seems to me, is the very centre of the bliss of heaven. Heaven is like the Eshcol cluster of grapes; but the essence, the juice, the sweetness of the cluster, consists in this fact, that we shall be with Jesus, "for ever with the Lord." Ah, me! how else could we ever hope to go in to the marriage, if we did not go in with him, hidden behind him, covered with his righteousness, washed in his blood? John saw a great multitude, which no man could number, of all nations, and kindreds, and people, and tongues, standing before the throne, and before the Lamb, and it was of them that the elder also said, "These are they which came out of great tribulation, and have washed their robes, and made them white in the blood of the Lamb. Therefore are they before the throne of God, and serve him day and night in his temple: and he that sitteth on the throne shall dwell among them."

Then, next, notice how exceedingly *joyous* was the entrance: "They that were ready went in with him *to the marriage.*" It was not their portion to stand outside the door, to listen to the music and enjoy the light that might come streaming through when it was opened for a few seconds; but they "went in with him to the marriage." It was not the intention of our Lord to tell us in this parable in what capacity the saints shall enter heaven. The parable is meant to teach certain lessons, and it explains them very clearly. If it tried to teach us everything, we might miss the most important lesson of all; but from other passages of Scripture we know that we shall go in with Christ to the marriage, not as mere spectators of his joy, as friends of the Bridegroom who rejoice exceedingly in his gladness; but we shall go in with him to share his bliss.

Oh, matchless word! You, believer, shall go in with him to that heavenly marriage feast, as part of that wondrous bride, the Lamb's wife, who is then to find her bliss for ever consummated with her glorious Husband. We shall for ever be one with Christ by conjugal bands; nay, more than that, for even conjugal bands are only used as a humble metaphor of the eternal union between our souls and Christ. "This," said the apostle Paul, when referring to marriage, "is a great

mystery: but I speak concerning Christ and the church."
"They that were ready went in with him to the marriage,"
right up to the banqueting table, to partake of all the rare
dainties gathered from all the ages, brought from all the
dominions of the great King.

Even on earth, we always properly associate the highest
degree of joy with a marriage, when it is what it ought to be.
If ever there is any joy on earth that belongs naturally to us as
beings of flesh and blood, it is upon our marriage day. The
wedding of a loving couple is looked forward to with great
expectations, and often looked back upon with fond memories.
However much of blight and withering blast may in after life
fall upon that relationship which is commenced upon the
marriage day, yet the day itself is always the figure and emblem
of joy. See, then, what heaven is to be to the people of God;
it is a marriage, a perpetual festival, a banishment of everything
that is dolorous, a gathering together of all that is joyous. A
marriage on earth—well, we know what that is; but a marriage
in heaven—who can describe that? The marriage of men and
women—we are familiar enough with that; but this union of
which I am trying to speak is the marriage of the Christ of God
with his redeemed people.

"They that were ready went in with him to the marriage."
These words sound to my ear and heart like the pealing of
wedding bells. Listen. These people had been in the battle,
fighting as good soldiers of Jesus Christ; but, by-and-by, they
"went in with him to the marriage." They had been in their
Lord's vineyard, toiling amid the burden and heat of the day;
the sun had looked upon them, and they were bronzed and
browned with the burning heat; but in due time they "went
in with him to the marriage." They had sometimes seen their
Lord for a season, and then they had missed him for a while,
but they "went in with him to the marriage." They had even
wandered from him sometimes, and darkness had surrounded
them; ay! and they had wickedly fallen asleep when they ought
to have watched; but they "went in with him to the marriage."
Oh, the blessedness of being where all evil is for ever ended, and
all joy is begun, never to end; all sin and imperfection blotted
out by Christ's precious blood, and all holiness and perfection
put upon us for ever and ever!

Then comes this little sentence, which is so terrible to the ungodly, but, oh! so sweet to the gracious: "And the door was shut." These words show that the entrance of the righteous into heaven is *eternal*. The door was shut for two purposes, but chiefly, as I understand it, to shut in the godly; and before that door can be opened to let in the wicked, it will have to be opened to let out the righteous. These two declarations of our Lord stand side by side: "These shall go away into everlasting punishment: but the righteous into life eternal." If you deny the eternity of the one, you must deny the eternity of the other, for it is the same word in each case. You must break down the door which is the security of the saints within, ere there can be a change for the ungodly who are without; and that can never be.

I want you, next, to notice who these people were who went in with the Bridegroom. According to the text, they were *a prepared people*, a people that were ready: "They that were ready went in with him to the marriage." There are none among the sons of men who are naturally ready to go in to that marriage feast; before they can enter, they must undergo a wondrous change, they must, in fact, be born again. Think for a moment what creatures we are by nature, quite unfit to go in with Christ to the heavenly marriage. Then think of what Christ is, so bright, so pure, so holy; who is she who is fit to go into heaven, to be for ever with this glorious Bridegroom? Canst thou ever be "ready" to go in with him to the marriage? Not unless that same God, who became man that he might be a fit Husband for thee, shall make thee holy, that thou mayest be meet to be wedded to him for ever.

A great change has to be wrought in you, far beyond any power of yours to accomplish, ere you can go in with Christ to the marriage. You must, first of all, be renewed in your nature, or you will not be ready. You must be washed from your sins, or you will not be ready. You must be justified in Christ's righteousness, and you must put on his wedding dress, or else you will not be ready. You must be reconciled to God, you must be made like to God, or you will not be ready. Or, to come to the parable before us, you must have a lamp, and that lamp must be fed with heavenly oil, and it must continue to burn brightly, or else you will not be ready. No child of darkness can go into that place of light. You must be brought out of nature's darkness into God's marvellous light, or else you will never be ready to go in with Christ to the marriage and to be for ever with him.

I pray you often look to your readiness for going in to the marriage. Are you all ready now? If, at this moment, the archangel's trumpet voice should sound, or if now, as lately happened to certain dear friends of ours, you should be struck down with paralysis or apoplexy, and in a moment pass away, are you ready for the great change? Are you quite ready to go in with Christ to the marriage? I would advise you, not only to be ready in all the great things, but to be ready also in the little things, and in everything that concerns yourself in relation to your Lord. Perhaps you have not yet publicly put on Christ in baptism. Then, in that respect, you are not ready. Do not delay obedience to Christ's command, remembering his own words, "He that believeth and is baptized shall be saved." With your mouth confess the Lord Jesus, if with your heart you have believed on him. Disregard no commands of Christ. Perhaps you have never yet been to his table of communion. If that is the case, I do not think you can call yourself "ready" to go in with him to the marriage. Perhaps you call these things little matters, and they are small compared with that greater matter of which I have already spoken. But I would not wish you to die with a single command of Christ's neglected. You have not prayed with your boys and girls yet, have you? Well, then, you are not ready. You have not made your will, you have not set your house in order; I would have you get all such things quite ready, for a little unreadiness may greatly trouble you in your departing moments. You have not yet fulfilled what has been very nearly a vow toward God; you have not yet done what you ought to do of your work for the present generation; you have not yet been to that ungodly friend and warned him, as your heart a little while ago prompted you to do.

I have only a few minutes to spend upon the second part of my subject—THE UNREADY AND THEIR EXCLUSION. I will try to say much in a few words, and I beg you to let every word abide with you.

What, then, was this exclusion? "The door was shut." It

was not ajar, it was shut, and so tightly was it closed that *there was a complete severance* between the guests inside and the too-late foolish virgins outside.

Yet, *this severance was perfectly just.* The foolish virgins ought to have been there in time, they ought to have gone in with the bridegroom; was it not their very office to attend him and accompany him home? The time for entering in had fully come; it was the right and proper time. The bridegroom had given them all that night to get ready, and they had even complained of the length of the delay before he came; so, when the door was at last shut, it was very late. They had had all that time in which to get the oil and to trim their lamps. It was not as though the bridegroom had come in the first watch of the night, and they had said, "We had not time to trim our lamps." No, it was not so. So you have had all this life, all these years of your Lord's long-suffering and patient entreaty; and it will be just that the door should be shut when your last hour shall come. Oh, be wise ere it is too late!

When "the door was shut," *the exclusion was final.* In all my searchings of the Word, I have never found any kind of hope that the door, once shut, will ever be opened again. There may be a "larger hope" indulged in by some, but I implore you never to risk your souls upon that rotten plank, for there is no Scripture warrant for it whatsoever. Even if there were, what larger hope do you want than that which the Gospel itself affords? Why do you not get ready to enter in with Christ to the marriage? Why be left to tarry outside? Why should you throw away the certainty of a present salvation and immediate deliverance from the curse, which you may have at this moment—which you shall have at once if you believe in Jesus— under some foolish dream that perhaps the door of mercy may open after ages of weeping and wailing and gnashing of teeth? Nay, rather, be ready to enter in with Christ to the marriage, for, as the Lord liveth, I cannot clear my soul of all responsibility unless I tell you that, as I read the Bible more and more, I am more and more certain that, when that door has once been shut, it will never again be opened to any living soul. Where death meets you, judgment will find you, and there you will remain to all eternity. I pray you, risk not your eternal destiny, but "Seek ye the Lord while he may be found, call ye upon him while he is near: let the wicked forsake his way, and the unrighteous man his thoughts: and let him return unto the Lord, and he will have mercy upon him; and to our God, for he will abundantly pardon" (Isa. 55: 6, 7).

Who were these persons who were shut out when the door was closed? *They bore the name of virgins*, yet the door was shut against them. They were not rank outsiders, not mere tramps of the street; not infidels, not agnostics, but members of the church. They were called virgins, yet against them the door was shut; they also had lamps, and lamps that once burned as brightly as others. There was, for a while, no difference between the lustre of their lamps and the lustre of the wisest, yet they were shut out. They had at least some oil, they were for a time companions of the wise virgins, they went out with them to meet the bridegroom, and the wise virgins, probably, never suspected that these others were foolish till, in the middle of the night, they found too late that their lamps were going out. Shall we drink out of the same communion cup and eat of the same bread at the Lord's table, and be reminded of his broken body and his shed blood, and yet, shall some of us be shut in with God for ever, and shall some of you be shut out for ever because you have not received the Holy Ghost, because you have not the secret inward store of the oil of grace? May God prevent it by his grace!

Notice that *these people acted in much the same way as those acted who went in with the bridegroom.* They went forth to meet the bridegroom, they went on the same road and at the same rate as the others went; they went to sleep, alas! as the others went to sleep; they awoke as the others awoke; and they began to trim their lamps as the others were trimming theirs. Their spot seemed to be the spot of God's children, and they appeared to have many of the marks of the election of grace; yet they were not of it, nor in it, for they had no oil in their vessels with their lamps, no grace, no indwelling of the Holy Ghost, no supernatural operation of him who worketh in the saints to will and to do of his own good pleasure. They were so like the real bride of Christ that only the Bridegroom could tell the difference until the midnight came, and then the difference was apparent to all observers.

It seems to me also that these persons, who were shut out,

were *people who knew something about prayer*. They did not, that night, for the first time pick up the agonized cry, "Lord, Lord, open to us." They had probably been *habitués* of Prayer-Meetings, they had been where people called Christ "Lord," and they used that formula themselves. Perhaps they might have said, "Lord, Lord, have we not prophesied in thy name? and in thy name have cast out devils? and in thy name done many wonderful works?" Yet the door was shut against them, and they, outside, knew something of what was going on inside, and therefore would gnash their teeth all the more because they could not enter. The door was shut against those who had seen the light, but whose lamps had gone out. They had been carrying in their hand the very lamps which entitled them to claim a place in the procession, but those lamps had gone out; and therefore they were not entitled to any such place, and the door was shut against them. O you who are only professors of religion, will you shut yourselves outside the door of mercy? You will do so if you neglect to obtain that secret oil of grace which can only be supplied by the Holy Spirit.

Before another Sabbath comes round, your preacher may be suddenly struck down, as one of our brethren has been; I may never have another opportunity of speaking to you who are professors, and warning you to make sure that you are also possessors and that you really have the grace of God in your souls. Or, possibly, some of you may be taken away without a moment's warning, as one of our friends has been. Suppose that then you could turn round upon me, in another world, and say, "Preacher, we heard you again and again, we listened to all that came from your lips, yet you prophesied smooth things to us, and you said, 'Peace, peace, when there was no peace.'" I pray God that I may have no man's blood upon the skirts of my garments in that last tremendous day, and therefore I bid you now to escape from the wrath to come. Flee to Christ, flee to his dear Cross, and look up to his bleeding wounds, for "There is life for a look at the Crucified One." Flee from your sins, flee from yourselves. Flee from any worldly pursuits which entangle you, and put your trust in Jesus Christ and him crucified.

VIII

UNPROFITABLE SERVANTS

"And cast ye the unprofitable servant into outer darkness: there shall be weeping and gnashing of teeth."—Matt. 25 : 30.
"So likewise ye, when ye shall have done all those things which are commanded you, say, We are unprofitable servants: we have done that which was our duty to do."—Luke 17 : 10.
"His lord said unto him, Well done, thou good and faithful servant."—Matt. 25 : 21.

THERE is a narrow path between indifference and morbid sensibility. Some men seem to feel no holy anxiety: they place their Master's talent in the earth, leave it there, and take their pleasure and their ease without a moment's compunction. Others profess to be so anxious to be right that they come to the conclusion that they can never be so, and fall under a horror of God, viewing his service as a drudgery, and himself as a hard master—though probably they never say so. There are great perils in the consciousness that you have done well, and that you are serving God with all your might; for you may come to think that you are a deserving person, worthy to rank among the princes of Israel. The danger of being puffed up can hardly be overestimated: a dizzy head soon brings a fall.

But perhaps equally to be dreaded on the other side is that sense of unworthiness which paralyses all exertion, making you feel that you are incapable of anything that is great or good. Under this impulse have men fled from the service of God into a life of solitude; they felt that they could not behave valiantly in the battle of life, and therefore they fled from the field before the fight began, to become hermits or monks; as if it were possible to do the Lord's perfect will by doing nothing at all, and to discharge the duties to which they were born by an unnatural mode of existence. Blessed is that man who finds the strait and narrow way between high thoughts of self and hard thoughts of God, between self-esteem and a timid shrinking from all effort. May the Spirit of God bless our three texts and the three subjects suggested by them, so that we may be put right, and then by infinite mercy may be kept right until the great day of account.

Let us read Matthew 25: 30. "And cast ye the unprofitable servant into outer darkness: there shall be weeping and gnashing of teeth."

In this our first text we have THE VERDICT OF JUSTICE upon the man who did not use his talent. The man is here styled an "unprofitable servant" because he was slothful, useless, worthless. He did not bring his master interest for his money nor render him any sincere service. He did not faithfully discharge the trust reposed in him as his fellow servants did.

Notice, first, that *this unprofitable person was a servant*. He never denied that he was a servant; in fact, it was by his position as a servant that he became possessed of his one talent, and to that possession he never demurred. If he had been capable of receiving more, there is no reason why he should not have had two talents, or five; for the Scripture tells us that the master gave to every man according to his several ability. He owned the rule of his master even in the act of burying the talent, and in appearing before him to give an account. This makes the subject the more heart-searching for you and for me; for we, too, profess to be servants—servants of the Lord our God. Judgment must begin at the house of God; that is, with those who are in the house of the Lord as children and servants: let us, therefore, look well to our goings. If judgment first begin at us, "what shall be the end of them that obey not the Gospel of God?" "If the righteous scarcely be saved, where shall the ungodly and the sinner appear?" If this in our text be judgment upon servants, what will be the judgment upon enemies? This man acknowledged that he was a servant even to the last; and though he was impertinent and impudent enough to express a most wicked and slanderous opinion about his master, yet he neither denied his own position as a servant, nor the fact that his talent was his lord's, for he said, "Lo, there thou hast that is thine." In thus speaking he went rather further than some professing Christians do, for they live as if Christianity were all eating the fat and drinking the sweet and not serving at all; as if religion had many privileges but no precepts, and as if, when men were saved, they became licensed loiterers to whom it is a matter of honour to magnify free grace by standing all the day idle in the market-place. Alas, I know some who never do a hand's turn for Christ, and yet call him Master and Lord. Ill will it fare with them at his coming.

This man, though a servant, *thought ill of his master*, and disliked his service: he said, "I knew thee that thou art an hard man, reaping where thou hast not sown, and gathering where thou hast not strawed." Certain professors who have stolen into the Church are of the same mind: they dare not say that they regret their having joined the Church, and yet they so act that all may conclude that if it could be undone they would not do the like again. They do not find pleasure in the service of God, but continue to pursue its routine as a matter of habit or a hard obligation. They get into the spirit of the elder brother, and they say, "Lo, these many years do I serve thee, neither transgressed I at any time thy commandment: and yet thou never gavest me a kid, that I might make merry with my friends" (Luke 15: 29). They sit down on the shady side of godliness, and never bask in the sun which shines full upon it. They forget that the father said to the elder son, "Son, thou art ever with me, and all that I have is thine." He might have had as many feastings, as many lambs and kids as he desired, he would have been denied no good thing. The presence of his father ought to have been his joy and his delight; and better than all merry-makings with his friends; and it would have been so if he had been in a proper state of heart.

This unprofitable servant looked upon his master as one that reaped where he never sowed, and used the rake to gather together what he had never scattered: he meant that he was a hard, exacting, and unjust person, whom it was difficult to please. He judged his lord to be one who expected more of his servants than he had any right to look for, and he had such a hatred of his unjust conduct that he resolved to tell him to his face what he thought of him. This spirit may readily creep over the minds of professors; I fear it is brooding over many even now, for they are not content with Christ. If they want pleasure they go outside the church to get it: their joys are not within the circle of which Christ is the centre. Their religion is their labour, not their delight; their God is their dread, not their joy. They do not delight themselves in the Lord, and therefore he does not give them the desire of their hearts, and so they grow more and more discontented. It is no wonder when things come to this pass that a professor becomes an unprofitable servant; for who can do a work well which he hates to do? Forced service is not desirable. God wants not slaves to grace his throne.

Note next that, albeit this man was doing nothing for his master, *he did not think himself an unprofitable servant.* He exhibited no self-depreciation, no humbling, no contrition. He was as bold as brass, and said unblushingly, "Lo, there thou hast that is thine." He came before his master with no apologies or excuses. He did not join with those who have done all, and then say, "We are unprofitable servants"; for he felt that he had dealt with his Lord as the justice of the case deserved; indeed, instead of acknowledging any fault he turned to accusing his lord. It is even so with false professors. They have no idea that they are hypocrites, the thought does not cross their minds. They have no notion that they are unfaithful. Hint at it, and see how they will defend themselves. If they are not living as they ought to do, they claim to be pitied rather than blamed; the blame lies with Providence; it is the fault of circumstances: it is the fault of anybody but themselves. They have done nothing, and yet they feel more at ease than those who have done everything. They have taken the trouble to dig in the earth and hide their talent, and they as good as ask—what more do you want? Is God so exacting as to expect me to bring more to him than he gave me? I am as grateful and prayerful as God makes me—what more will he require?

Mark well that the verdict of justice at last may turn out to be the very opposite of that which we pronounce upon ourselves. He who proudly thinks himself profitable shall be found unprofitable, and he who modestly judges himself to be unprofitable may in the end come to hear his Master say, "Well done, good and faithful servant." So little are we able, through the defects of our conscience, to form a right estimate of ourselves, that we frequently reckon ourselves to be rich and increased in goods, and having need of nothing, when, indeed, we are naked, and poor, and miserable.

It should give rise to much searching of heart when we notice *what this unprofitable servant did, or, rather, what he did not do.*

He carefully deposited his capital where no one was able to find it and steal it; and there was an end of his service. We ought to observe that he did not spend that talent upon himself, or use it in business for his own benefit. He was not a thief, nor in any way a misappropriator of moneys placed under his charge. In this he excels many who profess to be the servants of God, and yet live to themselves only. What little talent they have is used in their own business, and never upon their Lord's concerns. They have the power of getting money, but their money is not made for Christ; such an idea never occurs to them. Their efforts are all for themselves, or—to use other words to express the same thing—*for* their families. Yonder is a man who has the gift of eloquent speech, and he uses it, not for Christ, but for himself, that he may win popularity, that he might arrive at a respectable position: the one end and object of his most earnest speech is to bring grist to his own mill, and gain to his own estate. Everywhere this is to be seen amongst professors, that they are living to themselves: they are not adulterers or drunkards, far from it; neither are they thieves or spendthrifts; they are decent, orderly, quiet sort of people; but still, they begin and end with self. What is this but to be an unprofitable servant? A professing Christian may toil till he becomes a rich man, an alderman in the City, a Lord Mayor, a member of Parliament, a millionaire; but what does that prove? Why, that he could work and did work well for himself; and, if all this while he has done little or nothing for Christ, he is all the more condemned by his own success: if he had worked for his Lord as he worked for himself, what might he not have accomplished?

Furthermore, the wicked servant did not go and mis-spend his talent: he did not waste it in self-indulgence and wickedness as the prodigal son did, who spent his substance in riotous living. Oh, no; he was a much better man than that. He never touched a penny of it for a feast or a revel, and therefore could not be accused of being a spendthrift with his lord's money; in all which he was superior to those who yield their strength to sin and use their abilities to gratify the guilty passions of themselves and others.

I grieve to add that some who call themselves servants of Christ lay out their strength to undermine the Gospel they profess to teach; they speak against the holy name by which they are named, and thus they use their talent against their Master. This man did not do so; he never employed learning in order to raise needless doubts, or to resist the plain doctrines of the Word of God.

His lord called this servant "wicked." Is it, then, a wicked thing to be unprofitable? Surely wickedness must mean some positive action. No. Not to do right is to be wicked; not to live for Christ is to be wicked; not to be of use in the world is to be wicked; not to bring glory to the name of the Lord is to be wicked; to be slothful is to be wicked. It is clear that there are many wicked people in the world who would not like to be called so. "Wicked and slothful"; these are the two words which are riveted together by the Lord Jesus, whose speech is always wise.

This man was condemned to outer darkness. Notice this: he was condemned to be *as he was*, for hell, in one light, may be described as the great Captain's saying, "As you were." "He that is unjust, let him be unjust still; and he that is filthy, let him be filthy still." In another world there is permanence of character: enduring holiness is heaven, continual evil is hell. This man was outside of the family of his lord. He thought his lord a hard master, and so proved that he had no love to him, and that he was not really one of his household. He was outside in heart, and so his lord said to him, "Remain outside." Besides that, he was in the dark: he had wrong notions of his master; for his lord was not an austere and hard man, he did not gather where he had not strawed, nor reap where he had not sown. Therefore his lord said, "You are wilfully in the dark: abide there in the darkness which is outside." This man was envious: he could not endure his master's prosperity; he gnashed his teeth at the thought of it. He was sentenced to continue in that mind, and so to gnash his teeth for ever.

This is a dreadful idea of eternal punishment, this permanence of character in an immortal spirit:— "He that is unjust, let him be unjust still." While the character of the ungodly will be permanent, it will also be more and more developed along its own lines: the bad points will become worse, and, with nothing to restrain it, evil will become viler still. What must it be to be for ever outside the family of God! Never to be God's child!

For ever in the dark! Never to see the light of holy knowledge, and purity, and hope! For ever to gnash one's teeth with painful contempt and abhorrence of God, whom to hate is hell! O for grace to be made to love him, whom to love is heaven. The unprofitable servant had the due reward of his deeds. O our God! grant that such may not be the lot of any one of us!

I must now call your attention to the second text:— "So likewise ye, when ye shall have done all those things which are commanded you, say, We are unprofitable servants: we have done that which was our duty to do."—Luke 17: 10.

This is THE VERDICT OF SELF-ABASEMENT, given forth from the heart of servants who had laboriously discharged the full work of the day. This is a part of a parable intended to rebuke all notions of self-importance and human merit. When a servant has been ploughing or feeding cattle, his master does not say to him, "Sit down, and I will wait upon you, for I am deeply in your debt." No, his master bids him prepare the evening meal and wait upon him. His services are due, and therefore his master does not praise him as if he were a wonder and a hero. He is only doing his duty if he perseveres from morning light to set of sun, and he by no means expects to have his work held up to admiration or rewarded with extra pay and humble thanks. Neither are we to boast of our services, but think little of them, confessing that "we are unprofitable servants."

Whatever of pain may have been caused by the first part of the discourse, I trust it will only prepare us the more deeply to enter into the spirit of our second text. Both these texts are graven on my heart as with an iron pen, by a merciless wound, inflicted when I was too feeble to bear it. When I was exceedingly ill in the South of France, and deeply depressed in spirit—so deeply depressed and so sick and ill that I scarce knew how to live—one of those malicious persons who commonly haunt all public men, and especially ministers, sent me anonymously a letter, openly directed to *"That unprofitable servant C. H. Spurgeon."* This letter contained tracts directed to the enemies of the Lord Jesus, with passages marked and underlined, with notes applying them to myself.

How many Rabshekahs have in their day written to me! Ordinarily I read them with the patience which comes of use, and they go to light the fire. I do not look for exemption from this annoyance, nor do I usually feel it hard to bear, but in the hour when my spirits were depressed, and I was in terrible pain, this reviling letter cut me to the quick. I turned upon my bed and asked—Am I, then, an unprofitable servant? I grieved exceedingly, and could not lift up my head, or find rest. I reviewed my life, and saw its infirmities and imperfections, but knew not how to put my case till this second text came to my relief, and answered as the verdict of my bruised heart. I said to myself, "I hope I am not an unprofitable servant in the sense in which this person intends to call me so; but I am assuredly so in the other sense." I cast myself upon my Lord and Master once again with a deeper sense of the meaning of the text than I had felt before: his atoning sacrifice revived me, and in humble faith I found rest.

This which is put into our mouths as a confession that "we are unprofitable servants" is meant to rebuke us when we think we are somebody, and have done somewhat worthy of praise. Our text is meant to rebuke us if we think that we have done enough, that we have borne the burden and heat of the day a long time, and have been kept at our post beyond our own watch. If we conclude that we have achieved a fine day's work of harvesting, and ought to be invited home to rest, the text upbraids us. If we feel an inordinate covetousness after comfort, and wish the Lord would give us some present and striking reward for what we have done, the text shames us. This is a proud, unchildlike, unservantlike spirit, and it must be put down with a firm hand.

In the first place, *in what way can we have profited God?* Eliphaz has well said, "Can a man be profitable unto God, as he that is wise may be profitable unto himself? Is it any pleasure to the Almighty, that thou art righteous? or is it gain to him, that thou makest thy ways perfect?" (Job 22: 2,3). If we have given to God of our substance, is he our debtor? In what way have we enriched him to whom all the silver and gold belongs? If we have laid our lives out with the devotion of martyrs and missionaries for his sake, what is that to him, whose glory fills the heavens and the earth? How can we dream of putting the Eternal in debt to us? The right spirit is to say with David, "O my soul, thou hast said unto the Lord, Thou art my Lord: my goodness extendeth not to thee; but to the saints that are in the earth, and to the excellent, in whom is all my delight." How can a man place his Maker under an obligation to him? Let us not dote so blasphemously.

We ought to recollect that *whatever service we have been able to render has been a matter of debt.* I hope our morality is not fallen so low that we take credit to ourselves for paying our debts. I do not find men in business priding themselves and saying, "I paid a thousand pounds this morning to such an one." "Well, did you give it to him?" "Oh no; it was all owing to him." Is that any great thing? Have we come to such a low state of spiritual morals that we think we have done a great deal when we give to God his due? "It is he that made us, and not we ourselves" (Ps. 100: 3). Jesus Christ has bought us: "we are not our own," for we are "bought with a price." We have also entered into covenant with him, and given ourselves over to him voluntarily. Were we not baptized into his name and into his death? Whatever we may do is only what he has a right to claim at our hands from our creation, redemption, and professed surrender to him. Why boast we, then, or cry for a discharge, or look for thanks?

Over and above this there is the sad reflection that, alas, *in all we have done we have been unprofitable through being imperfect.* In the ploughing there have been baulks, in the feeding of the cattle there have been harshness and forgetfulness, in the spreading of the table the viands have been unworthy of such a Lord as we serve. How must our service appear to him of whom we read, "Behold, he put no trust in his servants, and his angels he charged with folly." Can any of you look back upon your service of your Lord with satisfaction? If you can, I cannot say I envy you, for I do not sympathise with you in the least degree, but tremble for your safety. As for myself, I am compelled to say with solemn truthfulness that I am not content with anything I have ever done. Whatever grace has done for me I acknowledge with deep gratitude; but so far as I have done anything myself I beg pardon for it. I pray God to forgive my prayers, for they have been full of fault; I beseech him to forgive even this confession, for it is not as humble as it ought to be; I beseech him to wash my tears and purge my devotions, and to baptize me into a true burial with my Saviour, that I may be quite forgotten in myself, and only remembered in him.

Once more, we cannot congratulate ourselves at all, even if we have had success in our Lord's work, since *for all that we have done we are indebted to our Lord's abundant grace.* If we had done all our duty, we should not have done anything if his grace had not enabled us to do it. If our "zeal no respite knows," it is he that keeps the fire burning. If our tears of repentance flow, it is he that strikes the rock and fetches the waters from it. If there be any virtue, if there be any praise, if there be any faith, if there be any ardour, if there be any likeness to Christ, we are his workmanship, created by him, and therefore to ourselves we dare not take a particle of the praise. Of thine own have we given unto thee, great God!

Try to be more profitable, and ask for more grace. The servant's business is not to hide himself in a corner of the field and cry, but to go on ploughing; not to bleat with sheep, but feed them, and so prove your love to Jesus. You are not to stand at the head of the table and say, "I have not spread the table for my Master so well as I could have desired." No, go and spread it better. Have courage; you are not serving a hard Master after all; and, though you very properly call yourself an unprofitable servant, be of good cheer, for a gentler verdict shall be pronounced upon you ere long. You are not your own judge either for good or ill; another judge is at the door, and when he cometh he will think better of you than your self-abasement permits you to think of yourself: he will judge you by the rule of grace and not by law, and he will end all that dread which comes of a legal spirit and hovers over you with vampire wings.

Thus I have brought you to the third text, "His lord said unto him, Well done, thou good and faithful servant" (Matt. 25: 21).

I shall not try to preach upon that cheering word, but shall only say a word or two upon it. It is much too grand a text to be treated upon at the end of a sermon. We find the Lord saying to those who had used their talents industriously, "Well done, good and faithful servant." This is THE VERDICT OF GRACE. Blessed is the man who shall own himself to be an unfaithful servant; and blessed is the man to whom his Lord shall say, "Thou good and faithful servant."

Observe here that the "Well done" of the Master is *given to faithfulness*. It is not "Well done, thou good and brilliant servant;" for perhaps the man never shone at all in the eyes of those who appreciate glare and glitter. It is not, "Well done, thou great and distinguished servant;" for it is possible that he was never known beyond his native village. He conscientiously did his best with his "few things," and never wasted an opportunity for doing good, and thus he proved himself faithful.

The same praise was given to the man with two talents as to his fellow-servant with five. Their stations were very different; but their reward was the same. "Well done, good and faithful servant," was won and enjoyed by each of them. Is it not very sweet to think that though I may have only one talent I shall not thereby be debarred from my Lord's praise? It is my faithfulness on which he will fix his eye, and not upon the number of my talents. I may have made many mistakes and have confessed my faults with great grief; but he will commend me as he did the woman of whom he said, "She hath done what she could." It is better to be faithful in the infant school than to be unfaithful in a noble class of young men. Better to be faithful in a hamlet over two or three score of people, than to be unfaithful in a great city parish, with thousands perishing in consequence. Better to be faithful in a cottage meeting, speaking of Christ crucified to half-a-hundred villagers, than to be unfaithful in a great building where thousands congregate.

This verdict was *given of sovereign grace*. The reward was not according to the work, for the servant had been "faithful in a few things," but he was made "ruler over many things." The verdict itself is not after the rule of works, but according to the law of grace. Our good works are evidences of grace within us; our faithfulness, therefore, as servants, will be the evidence of our having a loving spirit towards our Master, evidence, therefore, that our heart is changed, and that we have been made to love him for whom once we had no affection. Our works are the proof of our love, and hence they stand as evidence of the grace of God. God first gives us grace, and then rewards us for it. He works in us, and then counts the fruit as our work. We work out our own salvation, because "he worketh in us to will and to do of his own good pleasure." If he shall ever say, "Well done" to you and to me it will be because of his own rich grace, and not because of our merits.

Lastly, with what infinite delight will Jesus fill our hearts if, through divine grace, we are happy enough to hear him say, "Well done, good and faithful servant." Oh, if we shall hold on to the end despite the temptations of Satan, and the weakness of our nature, and all the entanglements of the world, and keep our garments unspotted from the world, preaching Christ according to our measure of ability, and winning souls for him, what an honour it will be! What bliss for him to say, "Well done." The music of these two words will have heaven in them to us. How different it will be from the verdict of our fellow-men, who are often finding fault with this and that, though we do our best. We never could please them, but we have pleased our Lord. Men were always misinterpreting our words and misjudging our motives, but he sets all right by saying, "Well done!" Little will it matter then what all the rest have said: neither the flattering words of friends nor the harsh condemnaticns of enemies will have any weight with us when he says, "Well done!" Not with pride shall we receive that eulogium; for we shall reckon ourselves even then to have been unprofitable servants; but oh how we shall love him for setting such an estimate upon the cups of cold water we gave to his disciples, and the poor broken service we tried to render him. What condescension to call that "well done" which we feel was so ill done!

I pray God's servants, who first began with searching themselves, and then went on to confess their imperfections, now to close by rejoicing in the fact that, if we are believing in Christ Jesus, and are really consecrated to him, we shall conclude this life and begin the next with that blessed verdict of "Well done!" Go on, and think not of resting till your day's work is done. Serve God with all your might. Do more than the Pharisees, who hope to be saved by their zeal. Do more than your brethren expect of you, and then, when you have done all, lay it at your Redeemer's feet with this confession, "I am an unprofitable servant." It is to those who blend faithfulness with humility and ardour with self-abasement that Jesus will say, "Well done, good and faithful servant: enter thou into the joy of thy Lord."

IX

WHAT FARM LABOURERS CAN DO

"And he said, So is the kingdom of God, as if a man should cast seed into the ground; and should sleep, and rise night and day, and the seed should spring and grow up, he knoweth not how. For the earth bringeth forth fruit of herself; first the blade, then the ear, after that the full corn in the ear. But when the fruit is brought forth, immediately he putteth in the sickle, because the harvest is come."—Mark 4 : 26–29.

OUR subject on this occasion will mainly be the measure and limit of human instrumentality in the Kingdom of Grace. If we shall be taught of the Spirit of God we shall find this Scripture to be full of instruction upon the matter.

It is remarkable that the parable before us is peculiar to Mark. No other evangelist has recorded it, but we do not think any the less of it on that account; as it is told us but once, we will give the more earnest heed to a voice which speaketh once for all. We are glad that the Holy Spirit led Mark to reserve this pearl out of the many excellent things which our Lord said which have been lost. Many of the things that Jesus said floated about, no doubt, for a time, and were gradually forgotten, and we have to be thankful to the Spirit of God for perpetuating this choice similitude by the hand of his servant Mark. Preserved in the amber of inspiration, this choice instruction is of priceless value.

Here is a lesson for sowers, for the labourers upon the farm of God. It is a parable for all who are concerned in the Kingdom of God. It will be of little value to those who are in the kingdom of darkness, for they are not bidden to sow the good seed: "Unto the wicked God saith, what hast thou to do to declare my statutes?" But all who are loyal subjects to King Jesus, all who are commissioned to scatter seed for the Royal Husbandman, will be glad to know how the kingdom advances, glad to know how the harvest is preparing for him whom they serve. Listen, then, ye that sow beside all waters; ye that with holy diligence seek to fill the garners of your God; listen, and may the Spirit of God speak into your ears as you are able to bear it.

We shall, first, learn from our text WHAT WE CAN DO AND WHAT WE CANNOT DO. Let this stand as our first head.

"So is the Kingdom of God, as if a man should cast seed into the ground": this the gracious worker can do. "And the seed should spring and grow up, he knoweth not how": this is what he cannot do, it belongs to a higher power. Man can neither make the seed spring nor grow up, he is out of the field in that respect, and may go home "to sleep, and rise night and day." Seed once sown is beyond human jurisdiction and is under divine care. Yet ere long the worker comes in again: "When the fruit is brought forth, immediately he putteth in the sickle." We can reap in due season, and it is both our duty and our privilege so to do. You see, then, that there is a place for the worker at the beginning, and though there is no room for him in the middle passage, yet another opportunity is given him further on when that which he sowed has actually yielded fruit.

Notice, then, that *we can sow*. Any man who has received the knowledge of the grace of God in his heart can teach others. I include under the term "man" all who know the Lord, be they male or female. We cannot all teach alike, for all have not the same gifts; to one is given one talent, and to another ten. Neither have we all the same opportunities, for one lives in obscurity and another has far-reaching influence. Yet there is not within the family of God an infant hand which may not drop its own tiny seed into the ground. There is not a man among us who needs to stand idle in the market-place, for work suitable to his strength is waiting for him. There is not a saved woman who is left without a holy task; let her do it and win the approving word. "She hath done what she could." Something of sacred service is within the reach of everyone's capacity, whether it be the mother in the family, the nurse-girl with the infant, the boy in the school, the workman at the bench, or the nurse at the bedside. Those with the smallest range of opportunities can, nevertheless, do something for Christ and his cause.

Having selected the seed, we shall have plenty of work if we go forth and sow it broadcast everywhere, for every day brings its opportunity, and every company furnishes its occasion. "In the morning sow thy seed, and in the evening withhold not thy hand." "Sow beside all waters." Imitate the sower in the parable, who was not so penny-wise that he would only cast the seed where, according to his judgment, all was good soil, but who, feeling that he had other work for his judgment besides the selecting of the soil, threw the seed right and left as he went on his way, and denied not a handful even to thorny and rocky soils. You, dear fellow-workers, will have enough to do if at all times and in all places, as prudence and zeal suggest, you spread abroad the living word of the living Lord.

Still, wise sowers discover favourable opportunities for sowing, and gladly seize upon them. There are times when it would clearly be a waste to sow; for the soil could not receive it, it is not in a fit condition. After a shower, or before a shower, or at some such time as he that hath studied husbandry knows, then is the time to be up and doing. So while we are to work for God always, yet there are seasons when it were casting pearls before swine to talk of holy things; and there are other times when if we were slothful it would be a shameful waste of propitious seasons. Sluggards in the time for ploughing and sowing are sluggards indeed, for they not only waste the day, but throw away the year. If you watch for souls, and use hours of happy vantage, and moments of sacred softening, you will not complain of the scanty space allowed for agency. Even should you never be called to water, or to reap, your office is wide enough if you fulfil the work of the sower.

For little though it seem to teach the simple truth of the Gospel, yet it is essential. How shall men hear without a teacher? The farm never brings forth a harvest without sowing. Weeds will grow without our help, but not so wheat and barley. The human heart is so depraved that it will naturally bring forth evil in abundance, and Satan is quite sure not to let it lie without a sowing of evil seed; but if ever a man's soul is to yield fruit unto God the seed of truth must be cast into it from without. Servants of God, the seed of the Word is not like thistledown, which is borne by every wind, nor like certain seeds wafted by their own parachutes here, there, and everywhere, but the wheat of the kingdom needs a human hand to sow it, and without such agency it will not enter into men's hearts, neither can it bring forth fruit to the glory of God. The preaching of the Gospel is the necessity of every age; God grant that our country may never be deprived of it. Even if the Lord should send us a famine of bread and a famine of water, may he never send us a famine of the Word of God. Faith cometh by hearing, and how can there be hearing if there is no teaching? Scatter ye, scatter ye, then, the seed of the kingdom, for this is essential to the harvest. The spreading of the Gospel is not a thing that ye may do or may not do, according to your pleasure, but it is a duty urgently needful, to be neglected at your peril.

This seed should be sown often, for the times are such that one sowing may not suffice. Sow again and again, for many are the foes of the wheat, and if ye repeat not your sowing ye may never see a harvest. The seed must be sown everywhere, too, for there are no choice corners of the world that you can afford to let alone, in the hope that they will be self-productive. Ye may not leave the rich and intelligent under the notion that surely the Gospel will be found among them, for it is not so: the pride of life leads them away from God. You may not leave the poor and illiterate, and say, "Surely they will of themselves feel their need of Christ." Not so: they will sink from degradation to degradation unless you uplift them with the Gospel. No tribe of man, no peculiar constitution of the human mind, may be neglected by us, but everywhere we must preach the word, in season and out of season.

I have heard that Captain Cook, the celebrated circumnavigator, was in one respect an admirable example to us. Wherever he landed, in whatever part of the earth it might be, he took with him a little packet of divers English seeds, and he was often observed to scatter them in suitable places. He would leave the boat and wander up from the shore. He said nothing to anybody, but quietly scattered English seeds wherever he went, so that he belted the world with the flowers and herbs of his native land. Imitate him wherever you go; sow spiritual seed in every place that your foot shall tread upon.

Let us now think of what you cannot do. *You cannot, after the seed has left your hand, cause it to put forth life.* I am sure you cannot make it grow, for you do not know how it grows. The text saith, "And the seed should spring and grow up, he knoweth not how." That which is beyond the range of our knowledge is certainly beyond the reach of our power. Can you make a seed germinate? You may place it under circumstances of damp and heat which will cause it to swell and break forth with a shoot, but the germination itself is beyond you. How is it done? We know not. After the germ has been put forth, can you make it further grow and develop its life into leaf and stem? No; that, too, is out of your power. And when the green, grassy blade has been succeeded by the ear, can you ripen it? It will be ripened; but can *you* do it? You know you cannot; you can have no finger in the actual process, though you may promote the conditions under which it is produced. Life is a mystery; growth is a mystery; ripening is a mystery: and these three mysteries are as fountains sealed against all intrusion.

The philosopher may say that he can explain life and growth, and straightway he will, according to the ordinary process of philosophy, bamboozle you with terms which are less understandable than the ordinary talk of infants; and then he will say, "There is the whole matter! It is as clear as possible." He cloaks his ignorance with learned jargon, and then calls it wisdom. To this day it still remaineth true of the growth of the commonest seeds, "He knoweth not how." The scientific man may talk about chemical combinations and physical permutations, and he may proceed to quote analogies from this and that; but still the growth of the seed remains a secret, it springs, "He knoweth not how."

Certainly this is true of the rise and progress of the Word of God in the heart. It enters the soul and roots itself ye know not how. Naturally men hate the Word, but it enters and it changes the heart, so that they come to love it, but we know not how. Their whole nature is renewed, so that instead of producing sin it yields repentance, faith and love, but we know not how. How it is that the Spirit of God deals with the mind of man, how he creates the new heart and the right spirit, how we are begotten again unto a lively hope, how we are born of the Spirit, we cannot tell. The Holy Ghost enters into us; we hear not his voice, we see not his light, we feel not his touch; yet he worketh an effectual work upon us, which we are not long in perceiving. We know that the work of the Spirit is a new creation, a resurrection, a quickening from the dead; but all these words are only covers to our utter ignorance of the mode of his working, with which it is not in our power to meddle. We do not know how he performs his miracles of love, and, not knowing how he works, we may be quite sure that we cannot take the work out of his hands.

This work of God having proceeded in the growth of the seed, what next? *We can reap the ripe ears.* After a season God the Holy Spirit uses his servants again. As soon as the living seed has produced first of all the blade of thought, and afterwards the green ear of conviction, and then faith, which is as full corn in the ear, then the Christian worker comes in for further service, for *he can reap.* "When the fruit is brought forth, immediately he putteth in the sickle." This is not the reaping of the last great day, for that does not come within the scope of the parable, which evidently relates to a human sower and reaper. The kind of reaping which the Saviour here intends is that which he referred to when he said to his disciples, "Lift up your eyes, and look on the fields; for they are white already to the harvest" (John 4: 35). After he had been sowing the seed in the hearts of the Samaritans, and it had sprung up, so that they began to evince faith in him, the Lord Jesus cried, "The fields are white unto the harvest." The apostle saith, "One soweth, and another reapeth." Our Lord said to the disciples, "I sent you to reap that whereon ye bestowed no labour." Is there not a promise, "in due season ye shall reap if ye faint not"?

Christian workers begin their harvest work by watching carefully to see when men evince signs of faith in Christ. They are eager to see the blade and delighted to mark the ripening ear. They often hope that men are believers, but they long to be sure of it: and when they judge that at last the fruit of faith is put forth, they begin to encourage, to congratulate, and to comfort. They know that the young believer needs to be housed in the barn of Christian fellowship, that he may be saved from a thousand perils. No wise farmer leaves the fruit of the field long exposed to the hail which might beat it out, or the mildew which might destroy it, or the birds which might despoil it. Evidently no believing man should be left outside of the garner of holy fellowship; he should be carried into the midst of the church with all the joy which attends the home-bringing of sheaves.

The worker for Christ watches carefully, and when he discerns that his time is come he begins at once to fetch in the converts that they may be cared for by the brotherhood, separated from the world, screened from temptation, and laid up for the Lord. He is diligent to do it at once, because the text saith, "immediately he putteth in the sickle." He does not wait for months in cold suspicion; he is not afraid that he shall encourage too soon when faith is really present. He comes with the word of promise and the smile of brotherly love at once, and he says to the new believer, "Have you confessed your faith? Is not the time come for an open confession? Hath not Jesus bidden the believer to be baptized? If you love him, keep his commandments." He does not rest till he has introduced the convert to the communion of the faithful. For our work is but half done when men are made disciples and baptized. We have then to encourage, to instruct, to strengthen, to console, and succour in all times of difficulty and danger.

The reaper is the man who gathers in the converts, and he fulfils an honourable and useful office. Observe the sphere of agency. We can introduce the truth to men, but that truth the Lord himself must bless; the living and growing of the Word within the soul is the operation of God alone. When the mystic work of growth is done we are able to introduce the saved ones into the church. To bring them into the fellowship of the faithful is our work, and we must not fail to do it. For Christ to be formed in men the hope of glory is not of our working, that remains with God; but when Jesus Christ is formed in them, to discern the image of the Saviour and to say, "Come in, thou blessed of the Lord, wherefore standest thou without?" this is our duty and delight. To create the divine life is God's, to cherish it is ours. To cause the hidden life to grow in secret is the work of the Lord; to see the uprising and perfecting of that life, and to rejoice in it is the work of the faithful, even as it is written, "when the fruit is brought forth, immediately he putteth in the sickle, because the harvest is come."

Our second head is like unto the first, and consists of WHAT WE CAN KNOW AND WHAT WE CANNOT KNOW.

First, *what we can know*. We can know when we have sown

the good seed of the Word that it will grow; for God has promised that it shall do so. Not every grain in every place; for some will go to the bird, and some to the worm, and some to be scorched by the sun; but as a general rule God's Word shall not return unto him void, it shall prosper in the thing whereto he hath sent it. This we can know. And we can know that the seed when once it takes root will continue to grow; that it is not a dream or a picture that will disappear, but a thing of force and energy, which will advance from a grassy blade to corn in the ear, and under God's blessing will develop to actual salvation, and be as the "full corn in the ear." God helping and blessing it, our work of teaching will not only lead men to thought and conviction, but to conversion and eternal life.

We also can know, because we are told so, that the reason for this is mainly because there is life in the Word. In the Word of God itself there is life, for it is written—"The word of God is quick and powerful,"—that is, "living and powerful." It is "the incorruptible seed which liveth and abideth for ever." It is the nature of living seeds to grow, and the reason why the Word of God grows in men's hearts is because it is the living Word of the living God. We know this, because the Scriptures teach us so. Is it not written, "Of his own will begat he us by the word of truth"?

Moreover, the earth, which is here the type of the man, "bringeth forth fruit of herself." We must mind what we are at in expounding this, for human hearts do not produce faith of themselves; they are as hard rock on which the seed perishes. But it means this—that as the earth under the blessing of the dew and the rain is, by God's secret working upon it, made to take up and embrace the seed, so the heart of man is made ready to receive and enfold the Gospel of Jesus Christ within itself. There is a something congruous in the earth to the seed which is sown in it, so that the seed is adopted and nourished by the soil. Just so is it by the heart of man when God makes it honest and good ground. Man's awakened heart wants exactly what the Word of God supplies. Moved by a divine influence the soul embraces the truth, and is embraced by it, and so the truth lives in the heart, and is quickened by it. The man's love accepts the love of God; man's faith wrought in him by the

Spirit of God believes the truth of God; man's hope wrought in him by the Spirit of God lays hold upon the things revealed, and so the heavenly seed grows in the soil of the soul.

Still, there is *a something which we cannot know:* a secret into which we cannot pry. I repeat what I have said before, you cannot look into men's inward parts and see exactly how the truth takes hold upon the heart, or the heart takes hold upon the truth. Many have watched their own feelings till they have become blind with despondency, and others have watched the feelings of the young till they have done them rather harm than good by their rigorous supervision. In God's work there is more room for faith than for sight. The heavenly seed grows secretly. You must bury it out of sight, or there will be no harvest. Even if you keep the seed above ground, and it does sprout, you cannot discover *how* it grows; even though you microscopically watched its swelling and bursting, you could not see the inward vital force which moves the seed. Behind the veil which conceals the secret working of God in the mysteries of natural life and growth you cannot pry; and as for the divine life in man, it must for ever be hidden from all mortal eyes. The result of it you shall be able to see, and something about the way of its development you shall be able to know; but the actual *modus operandi* (the mark of operation), the secret and innermost mystery of the new birth, it shall not be given to you to perceive. Thou knowest not the way of the Spirit. His work is wrought in secret, and thou canst not tell whence he cometh or whither he goeth. "Explain the new birth," says somebody. My answer is, "Experience the new birth, and you shall know what it is." So far shall thy knowledge go, but no further; and thou mayest thank God it is so, for thus he leaves room for faith, and gives cause for prayer.

Thirdly, our text tells us WHAT WE MAY EXPECT IF WE WORK FOR GOD, AND WHAT WE MAY NOT EXPECT. According to this parable we may expect to see fruit. The husbandman casts his seed into the ground, and the seed springs and grows, and he may expect a harvest. I wish I could say a word to stir up the expectations of Christian workers; for I fear that many work without faith. If you have a garden or a field, and you sow seed in it, you would be very greatly surprised and grieved if it did not come up at all; but many Christian people seem quite content to work on, and they never reckon upon result so much as to look for it expectantly. This is a pitiful kind of working—pulling up empty buckets by the year together. Surely I must either see a result for my labour and be glad, or else, failing to see it, I must be ready to break my heart if I be a true servant of the great Master. We ought to expect results: if we had expected more we should have seen more, but a lack of expectation has been a great cause of failure in God's workers.

But we may not expect to see all the seed which we sow spring up the moment we sow it. Sometimes, glory be to God, we have but to deliver the Word, and straightway men are converted: the reaper overtakes the sower, in such instances, but it is not always so. Some sowers have been diligent for years upon certain plots of ground, and apparently all has been in vain, till at the last the harvest has come, a harvest which, speaking after the manner of men, had never been reaped if they had not persevered to the end.

This world, as I believe, is to be converted to Christ; but not to-day, nor to-morrow, peradventure not for many an age; but the sowing of the centuries is not being lost, it is all working on towards the grand ultimatum. A crop of mushrooms may soon be produced, but a forest of oaks will not reward the planter till generations of his children have mouldered into the dust. We are to expect results, but not to be dispirited if we see them not to-day or on the morrow.

We are also to expect to see the good seed grow, but not always after our fashion. We are nearly all of us like children, for still there are not many fathers, and like children we are apt to be impatient. Your little boy sowed mustard and cress yesterday in his little garden. This afternoon Master Johnny will be turning over the ground to see if the seed is growing. There is no probability that his mustard and cress will come to anything, for he will not let it alone long enough for it to grow. So is it with hasty workers; they must see the result of the Gospel directly, or else they will leave off, and distrust the blessed Word. Although the people may have taken the Word into their minds and may be considering it, certain preachers are in such a hurry that they will allow no time for thought, no space for counting the cost, no opportunity for men to consider their ways and turn to the Lord with full purpose of heart. All other seeds take time to grow but the seed of the Word must grow before the speaker's eyes like magic, or he thinks nothing has been done. Such good brethren are so eager to produce blade and ear there and then, that they make men think that they are converted, and thus effectually hinder them from coming to a saving knowledge of the truth. I am solemnly convinced that some men are prevented from being saved by being told that they are saved already, and by being puffed up with a notion of perfection when they are not even broken in heart. Perhaps if such people had been taught to look for something deeper they might not have been satisfied with receiving seed on stony ground; but now they are content with that which comes of seed sown on unbroken rocks, they exhibit a rapid development, and an equally rapid decline and fall.

You are in a hurry, but it were better to exhibit the patience of principle than the heat of passion. Let all men be in a hurry to be saved, but let those who are preaching the truth be content to see men convinced of sin, delivered from self-confidence, enlightened as to the grace of God, and thus led by sure steps to faith. Some of the best of Christians do not know the exact point at which they were converted; it was a gradual process, from green blade to ripe ear, and they cannot tell exactly when the actual fruit of faith was formed in them. Some of the most thoughtful minds are not jerked on a sudden into religion, but are brought gradually into light, even as the noon of day draweth on by degrees. With many there is at first nothing but a little blade, you cannot tell whether it is not grass and grass only; their feeling looks like a natural emotion caused by the fear of hell, and this might lead to nothing effectual. Then follows a little belief, so formed as to be like the wheat-ear of faith, and yet it may be only a notion: it takes time with such persons before they show the full corn of assured faith in Jesus.

We may expect also to see the seed ripen. Our work will lead up by God's grace to real faith in those he hath wrought upon by his Word and Spirit, but we must not expect to see it perfect at the first. How many mistakes have been made here. Here is a young person under impression, and some good sound brother talks with that young person and asks profound questions. He shakes his experienced head and knits his furrowed brows. He goes into the corn-field to see how the crops are prospering, and though it is early in the year, he laments that he cannot see an ear of corn; indeed, he perceives nothing but mere grass. "I cannot see a trace of corn," says he. No, of course you cannot; for you will not be satisfied with the blade as an evidence of life, but must insist upon seeing everything at full growth at once. If you had looked for the blade you would have found it; and it would have encouraged you. For my own part, I am glad even to perceive a faint desire, a feeble longing, a degree of uneasiness, or a measure of weariness of sin, or a craving after mercy. Will it not be wise for you, also, to allow things to begin at the beginning, and to be satisfied with their being small at the first? See the blade of desire, and then watch for more. Soon you shall see a little more than desire; for there shall be conviction and resolve, and after that a feeble faith, small as a mustard seed, but bound to grow. Speak to him about his being a sinner, and Christ a Saviour, and you will in this way water him, so that his grace in the ear will become the full corn. It may be that there is not much that looks like wheat about him yet, but by-and-by you shall say, "Wheat! ah, that it is, if I know wheat. This man is a true ear of corn, and gladly will I place him among my Master's sheaves." Expect grace in your converts, but do not look to see glory in them just yet. It is enough if you see heaven begun: do not look to see it complete in them here below.

Expect, then—for you may expect it—to see a harvest, but do not expect to find every seed springing up. "There," says one, "that is a discouraging word." It may be so, but it is a true word. If you young people who begin to work for God expect that every word you speak will be useful to all who hear it, it will not happen, and you will grow discouraged; therefore I would raise your expectation as high as truth permits, and no higher. I never like to see a man expecting what he will not obtain. Now, I know that some of our seed will fall among thorns, and some in stony places, and I do not despair when it happens to be so. I do not expect when I preach the Gospel that everybody who hears it will receive it, because I know it will be a savour of life unto life to some, and of death unto death to others. I pull the net in, hauling away with all my might; but I know that when it comes to shore it will contain some queer things that are not fish, which will have to be thrown away, and I am heartily glad that there will also be in it a cheering number of good fishes. The results of our ministry in these days will be mixed, even as they were when Paul preached, and some believed and some believed not; we must be prepared for that, and yet I bid you let your expectations be very large, for you may have sixty or a hundred-fold of fruit from the seed if God be with you, and that will abundantly repay you, even if the crows and the worms should eat their share of the grain.

The last head is this, WHAT SLEEP WORKERS MAY TAKE, AND WHAT THEY MAY NOT TAKE; for it is said of this sowing man, that he sleeps and rises night and day, and the seed springs and grows up he knoweth not how. They say a farmer's trade is a good one because it is going on while he is abed and asleep; and surely ours is a good trade, too, when we serve our Master by sowing good seed, for it is growing even while we are asleep.

But how may a good workman for Christ lawfully go to sleep? I answer, first, he may sleep the sleep of restfulness born of confidence. You are afraid the Kingdom of Christ will not come, are you? Who asked you to tremble for the ark of the Lord? Afraid for the infinite Jehovah that his purposes will fail? Shame on you! Your anxiety dishonours your God. You degrade him by a suspicion of his failing. Shall Omnipotence be defeated? You had better sleep than wake to play the part of Uzzah. Rest patiently, God's will be done, and his kingdom will come, and his chosen will be saved, and Christ shall see of the travail of his soul. Take the sweet sleep which God gives to his beloved, the sleep of perfect confidence, such as Jesus slept in the hinder part of the ship when it was tossed with tempest. The cause of God never was in jeopardy, and never will be; the seed sown is insured by omnipotence, and must produce its harvest. In patience possess your soul, and wait till the harvest comes, for the pleasure of the Lord must prosper in the hands of Jesus.

Also take that sleep which leads to a happy waking of joyful expectancy. Get up in the morning and feel that the Lord is ruling all things for the accomplishment of his own purpose.

Look for it. If you do not sleep you certainly will not wake up in the morning refreshed and ready for more work. If it were possible for you to sit up all night and eat the bread of carefulness you would be unfit to attend to the service which your Master appoints for the morning; therefore take your rest and be at peace, and work with calm dignity; for the matter is safe in the Lord's hands.

Take your rest because you have consciously resigned the work into God's hands. After you have spoken the word resort to God in prayer, and commit it into God's hand, and then do not fret about it. It cannot be in better keeping—leave it there.

But do not sleep the sleep of unwatchfulness. The farmer sows his seed, but he does not therefore forget it. He has to mend his fences to keep the cattle out; it may be he has to drive away birds, to remove weeds, or to prevent floods. While he is not sitting down to watch the growth, he has plenty else to do. He never sleeps the sleep of indifference or even of inaction; for each season has its demand upon him. His sleep is but an interlude that gives him strength to continue in his occupations.

I want you to come to that point to-day. "Lord, this is thy work. Lord, thou canst do thine own work. Lord, do thine own work—we entreat and beseech thee to do it. Lord, help us to do *our* work, both at the beginning of the chapter and at the end of the chapter, confident that thou wilt not fail in the middle of the chapter; but that thou wilt do thy work. Help us to exercise faith in thee, and to go about our labour in the confidence that thou art with us, and we are workers together with thee."

X

BANKRUPT DEBTORS DISCHARGED

"And when they had nothing to pay, he frankly forgave them both."—Luke 7 : 42.

THE two debtors differed very considerably in the amounts which they owed: the one was in arrears five hundred pence, and the other fifty. There are differences in the guilt of sins, and in the degrees of men's criminality. It would be a very unfair and unrighteous thing to say that all men are exactly alike in the extent of their transgression. Some are honest and upright, kind and generous, even though they be but natural men: while others appear to be of a malicious, envious, selfish disposition, and rush into evil, sinning, as it were, with both hands greedily. The man who is moral, sober, and industrious is only a fifty pence debtor as compared with the vicious, drunken blasphemer whose debt is written at five hundred pence. Our Saviour recognizes the distinction, because it exists and cannot justly be overlooked. There are distinctions among unconverted men, very great distinctions. One of them, a young man, came to Jesus, and he had so many fine traits in his character that the Lord looking upon him loved him; whereas when the Pharisees gathered about him our Lord looked round upon them with indignation. The soil, which was none of it yet sown with the good seed, yet varied greatly, and some of it was honest and good ground before the sower came to it.

But I call your particular notice to this fact—that though there was one point of difference in the two debtors, there were three points of similarity; for they were both debtors: and so all men have sinned, be it little or be it much: and, secondly, they were both alike bankrupt, neither of them could meet his debt; the man who owed fifty pence could no more pay than he who owed five hundred pence, so that they were both insolvent debtors. But what a mercy it is that they were alike in a third point! for "when they had nothing to pay," their creditor "frankly forgave them both."

Oh, we are all alike in the first two things! Oh that we might be all of us alike in this last point, that the Lord our God may grant to every one of us the free remission of sins according to the riches of his grace through Christ Jesus! Why should it not be so, since Jesus is exalted on high to give repentance and remission of sins? There is forgiveness with God. He delighteth in mercy. He can cast all our sins into the depths of the sea, that they may not be mentioned against us any more for ever.

First, let us think of THEIR BANKRUPTCY. This was their condition. They were unquestionably in debt. If they could have disputed the creditor's claim, no doubt they would have done so. If they could have pleaded that they were never indebted, or that they had already paid, no doubt they would have been glad to have done so; but they could not raise a question; their debt would not be denied. Another fact was also clear to them, namely, that they had nothing to pay with. No doubt they had made diligent search; they had turned out their pockets, their cash-boxes, and their lockers, and they had found nothing; they had looked for their household goods, but these had vanished piece by piece. They had nothing at home or abroad that they could dispose of. Things had come to such a pass with them that they had neither stock nor money, nor anything in prospect which they could draw upon: they were brought to the last extremity, reduced to absolute beggary. Meanwhile, their great creditor was pressing them for settlement. That idea lies in the heart of the text. The creditor had evidently brought his over-due accounts and had said to them, "These claims must be met. There must be an end to this state of affairs; your accounts must be discharged." They were just brought to this condition—they must confess the debt, and they must also humbly acknowledge that they had nothing to meet it with: the time for payment had come, and it found them without a penny. No condition could be much more wretched.

So far I have stated the parable, and it most truly sets forth *the condition* of every man who has not come to Jesus Christ and so received the frank forgiveness of his sins. Upon this we will enlarge. We are all by nature and by practice plunged in debt, and this is the way in which we came to be so. Hear it and mark it well. As God's creatures we from the very first owed to him the debt of obedience. We were bound to obey our Maker. It is he that made us, and not we ourselves; and we were, therefore, bound reverently to recognize our Creator, affectionately to worship him, and dutifully to serve him. This is an obligation so natural and reasonable that nobody can dispute it. If you are the creatures of God, it is nothing more than right that you should honour him. If you receive daily the breath in your nostrils and the food that you eat from him, then you are bound to him by the ties of gratitude, and should do his will.

But we have not done his will. We have left undone the things we ought to have done, and we have done the things we ought not to have done, and so we have come in a second sense into his debt. We now stand liable to penalty, yea, we are condemned already. There is due from us to God, in vindication of his broken law, both suffering and death; and in the Word of God we find that the righteous penalty for sin is something utterly overwhelming. "Fear him," saith Christ, "which is able to destroy both soul and body in hell." Yea, I say unto you, fear him! Very terrible are the metaphors and symbols by which the Holy Spirit sets forth the misery of a soul upon which the Lord pours forth his fiery indignation. The pain of loss and pain of woe which sin at last brings upon guilty men are inconceivable: they are called "the terrors of the Lord." There is not one among us, apart from the Lord Jesus Christ, but what owes to God's law a debt which eternity cannot fully meet, even though it be crowded with agonizing regrets. A life of forgetfulness of God and breaking of his law must be recompensed by a future life of punishment. That is where we stand: can any man be at rest while this is his condition before God?

And we are utterly unable to make any amends for this. If he should meet with us and call us to account we cannot answer him one of a thousand. We cannot excuse ourselves, and we cannot by any possibility render to him his righteous due. If any think they can, let me remind them of this, that to cancel the debt which we owe to God we must pay it all. God demands, righteously demands, from us the keeping of his entire law. He tells us that he that is guilty in one point is guilty of all: for

God's law is like a fair vase of alabaster, lovely in its entireness; but, if it be chipped in any part, it may not be presented in his court; the least flaw in it mars its perfection and destroys its value. A perfect obedience to a perfect law is that which is required by the justice of the Most High; and is there any one of us who can render it, or who can attempt to pay the penalty due for not rendering it? Our inability to obey comes of our own fault and is part of our crime. Ah me! may none of us ever have to bear the penalty! To be banished from his presence, and from the glory of his power; to be cast away from all hope and light and joy for ever!

Remember, too, that if there is anything that we can do for God in the way of obedience it is already due to him. All that I can do if I love God with all my heart and soul and strength, and my neighbour as myself, throughout the rest of my life, is already due to God: I shall but be discharging new duties as they occur—how will this affect old disobediences?

> *Could my tears for ever flow,*
> *Could my zeal no respite know,*
> *All for sin could not atone;*
> *Christ must save, and Christ alone.*

Moreover, the debt is immense and incalculable! Fifty pence is but a poor representation of what the most righteous person owes; five hundred pence is but an insignificant sum compared with the transgressions of the greater offenders. Oh, when I think of my life it seems to be like the sea, made up of innumerable waves of sin; or like the sea-shore, constituted of sands, that cannot be weighed nor counted. My faults are utterly innumerable, and each one deserving death eternal. Our sins, our heavy sins, sins against light and knowledge, our foul sins, our repeated sins, our aggravated sins, our sins against our parents, our sins against all our relationships, our sins against our God, our sins with the body, our sins with the mind, our sins of forgetfulness, our sins of thought, our sins of imagination—who can reckon them up in order unto God? Who knoweth the number of his trespasses? Now, to think that we can ever meet such a debt is indeed to bolster up ourselves with a notion utterly absurd: we have nothing to pay.

This being the case, I want to spend a minute in noticing *certain temptations* to which all bankrupt sinners are much subject. One of these is to try and forget their spiritual estate altogether. Some of you to-day have never given serious thought to your souls and to your condition before God. It is an unpleasant subject. You suspect that it would be still more unpleasant if you looked into it. You want amusement, something to while away the time, because you do not care to examine into the state of your heart before God. Solomon exhorts the diligent man to know the state of his flocks, and look well to his herds; but he that is careless and idle would rather leave such enquiries, and let things go as they please. The man who is going backward in business has no pleasure in stock-taking. "Oh," says he, "don't bring me my books; I shall not sleep at nights if I look into *them*." He knows that he is sinking lower and lower and will soon be a ruined man; and the only way in which he can endure his life is to drive dull care away by drink, or by going into company, or idle amusement. He labours to beguile the hours that he may conceal from himself his true condition. But what a fool he is! Would it not be infinitely wiser if he would look the thing in the face and have it out, and know his actual state? Such ignorance as he chooses is not bliss to a right-hearted man, but suspense and misery. I have often prayed this prayer, "Lord, let me know the very worst of my case," for I do not wish to entertain a hope that will at last deceive me. This is the temptation of the bankrupt soul, to shut its eyes to unwelcome truth. However forgetful you may be, God does not forget your sins.

Another temptation to a man in this condition is to make as good a show as he can. A man who is very near bankruptcy is often noticed for the dash he cuts. What fashionable parties he gives! Just so, he desires to keep up his credit as long as ever he can. He is going to make a smash of it by-and-by, but for a season he assumes the airs of my lord, and everybody near him imagines that he has money enough and to spare. The governor of a besieged city threw loaves of bread over the wall to the besiegers, to make them believe that the citizens had such large supplies that they could afford to throw them away; yet they were starving all the while. There are some men of like manners; they have nothing that they can offer unto God, but yet they exhibit a glittering self-righteousness. Oh, they have been so good, such superior people, so praiseworthy from their youth up; they never did anything much amiss. They make a fair show in the flesh with morality and formality, and a smattering of generosity. Besides, they profess to be religious: they attend divine service, and pay their quota of the expenses. Who could find any fault with such good people? There is nothing at all in you, and there never was, if you are as nature has made you; wherefore then do you try to brazen it out, and make yourself to seem somewhat when you are nothing? You may by this means deceive yourself, but certainly you will not deceive God.

Another temptation which lurks in the way of a bankrupt sinner is that of making promises of what he will do. Men in debt are generally very promising men; they will pay next week for certain; but when that next week comes, they meant the next week further on, and then payment shall be doubly certain; yet they put in no appearance even then, or, if they do, they give a bill. Is not that a precious document? Is it not as good as the money itself? They evidently think so, for they feel quite as easy as if they had really paid that debt. But when the bill falls due, what then? It falls, never to rise again. A bill is often just a lie with a stamp on it. So will debtors go on as long as they can. This is what every sinner does before he becomes cleared by the sovereign grace of God. He cries, "I mean to do better." Never mind; tell us no more what you mean to do, but do it. To promise and vow so falsely is only adding to your sins! "Oh! but you know I do not intend to go on in this way always. It is a long lane that has no turning. I shall pull up short one of these days, and then you will see." What shall we see? What we shall see; and that will not be much. Yes. We shall see the dew of promise disappear, and the morning cloud of resolution pass away. Neither God nor man will trust you; you have promised these twenty years, and in no one year have you made a real move in the right direction. You have not lied unto men only, but unto God, and how will you answer for it? Know you not that every promise that you make to God which you do not keep is a great addition to your transgressions and helps to fill up the measure of your iniquities?

Another temptation is, always to ask for more time, as if this was all that was needed. When the debtor, in another parable, was arrested, he said to his creditor, "Have patience with me, and I will pay thee all." We cannot pay any of our debt to-day, and yet dote upon to-morrow. Yes, it does seem such a relief to get a little longer time; somehow a vague shadowy hope seems to pervade the months to come. The sinner cries, "Go thy way for this time; when I have a convenient season, I will call for thee." It is not convenient just now, but do wait a little bit, a suitable hour will come. What are the fabled virtues of to-morrow? Why do men dote upon the unknown future? To immediate decision I would press you at this moment; and may God by his divine Spirit deliver you as a bird from the hand of the fowler, that you may no longer procrastinate and waste your life in disobedient delay.

This being the temptation, let me hint to those of you who are bankrupt what *your wisdom* is. It is your wisdom to face the business of your soul. Your soul-matters are the most important things you will ever have on hand, for when your wealth must be left, and your estate shall see you no more, and when your body is dead, your soul will still be living in eternal happiness or endless woe; therefore, do not let your state in reference to God have the go-by. Give it the first place.

Take care that you face it, like an honest man, and not as one who makes the best of a bad story. When you face the matter, be very true and sincere with yourself and with God; because you are not now dealing with creditors who may be cheated, but you are dealing with One who knows the secret thoughts and intents of your heart. Before God nothing but truth can stand; the painted hypocrite is spied out immediately.

One thing more: it will be your wisdom to give up all attempts to pay, because you have nothing to pay with. Do not delude yourself into the idea that you will pay one day, for you never will; but take quite another course, plead absolute poverty, and appeal to mercy. Say, "Lord, I have nothing, I am nothing, I can do nothing. I must throw myself upon thy grace." Of this grace I am now going to speak.

Our second head is, THEIR FREE DISCHARGE. "He frankly forgave them both." What a blessing they obtained by facing the matter! These two poor debtors, when they went into the office, were trembling from head to foot, for they had nothing to pay, and were deeply involved; but see! they come out with light hearts, for the debt is all disposed of, the bills are receipted, the records are destroyed. Even thus the Lord has blotted out the handwriting that was against us, and has taken it out of the way, nailing it to his Cross.

In this free discharge I admire, first of all, *the goodness* of the great creditor. What a gracious heart he had! He said, "Poor souls, you can never pay me, but you need not be cast down because of it, for I freely cancel your debts." Oh, the goodness of it! Oh, the largeness of the heart of God! I was reading of Cæsar the other day. He had been at fierce war with Pompey, and at last he conquered him, and when he conquered him he found among the spoil Pompey's private cabinet, in which were contained letters from the various noblemen and senators of Rome who had sided with him. In many a letter there was fatal evidence against the most eminent Romans, but what did Cæsar do? He destroyed every document. He would have no knowledge of his enemies, for he freely forgave them and wished to know no more. In this Cæsar proved that he was fit to govern the nation. But look at the splendour of God when he puts all our sins into one cabinet, and then destroys the whole. If the sins of his people be sought for they cannot now be found. He will never mention them against us any more for ever. Oh, the goodness of the infinite God, whose mercy endureth for ever!

But, then, observe *the freeness* of it—"He frankly forgave them both." They did not stand there and say, "Oh, good sir, we cannot pay," and plead and beg, as for their lives; but he freely said to them, "You cannot pay, but I can forgive. You ought never to have got into my debt, and you ought not to have broken your promises to me; but behold, I make an end of all this weary business: I freely blot out all your obligations!" Did not this open a fountain in their eyes? Did they not hasten home to their wives and children, and tell them that they were out of debt, for the beloved creditor had forgiven it all most freely? This is a fair picture of the grace of God. When a poor sinner comes to him bankrupt, he says, "I forgive you freely: your offence is all gone. I do not want you to earn a pardon by your tears, and prayers, and anguish of soul. You have not to make me merciful, for I am merciful already; and my dear

Son Jesus Christ has made such a propitiation that I can be just and yet can forgive you all this debt. Therefore, go in peace."

Furthermore, this debt was *fully* discharged. The creditor did not say, "Come, my good fellow, I will take fifty per cent off the account if you find the remainder." As they had nothing wherewith to pay, they would not have been a bit the better if he had reduced them ninety per cent; but still their case would have been hopeless, since they had not a farthing of their own. Now the Lord, when he blots out his people's sin, leaves no trace of it remaining. My own persuasion is that when our Lord Jesus died upon the Cross he made an end of all the sins of all his people and made full and effectual atonement for the whole of those who ever shall believe in him.

Does not the Spirit of God himself ask the question, "Who shall lay anything to the charge of God's elect?" (Rom. 8: 33.) The Lord has frankly forgiven their debt, and he has not done so in part, but as a whole. Hallelujah!

Observe that it was a very *effectual* forgiveness too. The only person that can forgive a debt is he to whom the debt is due. God only can forgive sin, seeing it is a debt to him. Suppose I were to forgive you for injuries done by you to the Queen, of what value would my forgiveness be? He against whom I have transgressed is the only one that can pronounce my pardon; but if he absolves me, how effectual is the sentence! When the creditor said, "I freely forgive you both," why, the deed was done: his lips had power, he had finished the debt by his word. What an effectual pardon it is!

And I believe that when this is done, I may add another adjective—it is an *eternal* discharge. That creditor could never summon those debtors again for debts which he had remitted. He could never think of such a thing with any show of justice. He had frankly forgiven them, and they were forgiven. God does not play fast and loose with his creatures, and forgive them and then punish them. I never shall believe in God's loving a man to-day, and casting him away to-morrow. The gifts and calling of God are without repentance on his part. Justification is not an act which can be reversed, and followed with damnation. No, no; "whom he justified, them he also glorified."

Only one more remark on this point: this frank forgiveness *applied to both the debtors*—"he frankly forgave them both." The man that owed only fifty pence needed a free discharge as truly as the debtor who owed five hundred; for though he was not so deep in the mire, yet he was as truly in the slough. Take note that you cannot be saved except by the free forgiveness of God through the precious blood of Christ. The fifty pence debtor must obtain his discharge by grace alone. It is also a most blessed thing to perceive that he forgave the five hundred pence debtor with equal freeness.

Perhaps I have some who have never made any pretence of being good, who from their childhood have gone from bad to worse. There is a possibility of free and instantaneous forgiveness for you at this moment. You that are over head and ears in debt to God can be freely forgiven by the same Lord who forgives the smaller debtors. When a man has his pen in his hand and is writing receipts, it takes him no more trouble to write a receipt for five hundred pounds than it does for a bill of fifty—the same signature will suffice: and when the Lord has the pen of his Spirit in his hand, and he is about to write upon a conscience the peace which comes of reconciliation, he can write upon one as well as upon another. Ho, you with a little bill, bring it here that infinite grace may write upon it "CANCELLED!" Ho, you with a more weighty account, come and place it near that gracious right hand, for though your bill be never so long and heavy, the hand of Infinite Love can write "CANCELLED" in a moment! My joy overflows at having such a Gospel to preach to you: whatever your guilt, my gracious God is ready to forgive you for Jesus' sake, because he delighteth in mercy.

I now beg your very special attention to the last point, and that is THE CONNECTION BETWEEN THIS BANKRUPTCY AND THIS FREE DISCHARGE. It is said "*When* they had nothing to pay, he frankly forgave them both." There is a time when pardon comes, and that time is when self-sufficiency goes. If any person in this place has in his own conscience come to this point, that he feels he has nothing to pay, he has come to the point at which God is ready to forgive him. He that will own his debt and confess his own incapacity to meet it, shall find that God frankly blots it out. The Lord will never forgive us until we are brought to the starvation of pride and the death of boasting. A sense of spiritual bankruptcy shows that a man has become *thoughtful;* and this is essential to salvation. Must there not be serious thought before we can hope for mercy? Would you have God save us while we are asleep, while we are giddy, frivolous, trifling, and without concern about our sin? Surely that would be giving a premium to folly! God acts not so. He will have us know the seriousness of our danger, for else we shall treat the whole matter with lightness; and *we* shall miss the moral effect of pardon, while *he* will be robbed of his glory.

Next, when we come to feel our bankruptcy we then *make an honest confession,* and to that confession a promise is given— "he that confesseth his sin shall find mercy." They humbled themselves before their creditor, and then he said, "I frankly forgive you." As for you, poor trembler, here is comfort for you: when you go unto God in your chamber and cry, "Lord, have mercy upon me, for I am guilty, and I cannot justify myself before thee, nor offer any excuse to thee": then it is that he will say, "Be of good cheer; I have put away thy sin; thou shalt not die." When you are brought to your worst, you shall see the Lord at his best.

It is in their utter destitution that *men value a discharge.* If God were to give his mercy to every man at once, without his ever having had any sense of sin at all, why men would count it cheap and think nothing of it. "God is merciful," is a common saying everywhere; and it is such a bit of valueless talk with them, that they let it roll glibly out as if it were no matter. They do not worship him for his mercy or serve him for his grace. They say, "Oh, God is merciful," and then they go on to sin worse than ever; the idea has no effect upon their hearts or lives; they have no esteem for that mercy of which they speak so freely. So the Lord takes care that the sinner shall know his need of mercy by feeling the pinch of conscience and the terror of the law. If I may so speak, he puts in the sheriff's officer, and makes a distraint upon the soul by convincing the man of sin, of righteousness, and of judgment. The Lord puts an execution into the heart, and then it is, when the poor creature cries, "I have nothing to pay with," that free discharge is given by the Lord, and heartily prized by him to whom it comes. Christ is precious when sin is bitter.

Under conviction a poor soul *sees the reality of sin and of pardon*. You will never believe in the reality of forgiveness till you have felt the reality of sin. I remember when I felt the burden of sin, and though but a child, my heart failed me for anguish, and I was brought very low. Sin was no bugbear to scare me; it was a grim reality; as a lion it tore me in pieces. And now, to-day, I know the reality of pardon: it is no fancy, no dream, for my inmost soul feels its power. I know that my sins are forgiven, and I rejoice therein; but I should never have known the real truth of this happy condition if I had not felt the oppressive load of sin upon the conscience.

I do believe that the Lord will give us our quittance when we have got to our last farthing, and not till then, because *only then do we look to the Lord Jesus Christ*. As long as we have anything else to look to, we never will look to Christ. As long as a man has one rusty counterfeit farthing hidden away in the corner of his till, he will never accept the riches of redeeming love; but when it is all up with him, when he has neither stick nor stock left, then he prizes Jesus and his salvation. When we cannot give, God can forgive. If any of you have any goodness of your own you will perish for ever. If you have anything you can trust to of your own you will be lost as sure as you are living men and women; but if you are reduced to sore extremity, and God's fierce wrath seems to burn against you, then not only may you have mercy, but mercy is yours already.

Blessed are ye poor, for ye shall be rich! Blessed are ye hungry, for ye shall be fed! Blessed are ye that are empty, for ye shall be filled! But woe unto you that are rich and are increased in goods, and have need of nothing, and boast of your own goodness! Are you a sinner? Then Christ is the Saviour of sinners. Join hands with him by faith, and the work is done: you are saved for ever!

XI

THE GOOD SAMARITAN

"Which now of these three, thinkest thou, was neighbour unto him that fell among the thieves? And he said, He that showed mercy on him. Then said Jesus unto him, Go, and do thou likewise."—Luke 10: 36, 37.

OUR text is the whole story of the Samaritan; but as that is very long, suppose, for our memories' sake, we consider the exhortation in the thirty-seventh verse to be our text. *"Go, and do thou likewise."*

Our Lord was a great practical preacher. He frequently delivered addresses in which he made answer to questioners, or gave direction to seekers, or upbraided offenders, and he gave a prominence to practical truth such as some of his ministers dare not imitate. Jesus tells us over and over again the manner in which we are to live towards our fellow-men, and he lays great stress upon the love which should shine throughout the Christian character.

The story of the good Samaritan, which is now before us, is a case in point, for our Lord is there explaining a point which arose out of the question, "What shall I do to inherit eternal life?" The question is legal, and the answer is to the point. But let it never be forgotten that what the law demands of us the Gospel really produces in us. The law tells us what we ought to be, and it is one object of the Gospel to raise us to that condition. Hence our Saviour's teaching, though it be eminently practical, is always Evangelical: even in expounding the law he has always a Gospel design. Two ends are served by his setting up a high standard of duty: on the one he slays the self-righteousness which claims to have kept the law by making men feel the impossibility of salvation by their own works; and, on the other hand, he calls believers away from all content with the mere decencies of life and the routine of outward religion, and stimulates them to seek after the highest degree of holiness —indeed, after that excellence of character which only his grace can give. I shall not speak of obedience to the law as the road to heaven, but I shall show you the pathway which is to be followed by the faith which works by love.

Our first observation will be that THE WORLD IS VERY FULL OF AFFLICTION. This story is but one among a thousand based upon an unhappy occurrence. "A certain man went down from Jerusalem to Jericho, and fell among thieves." He went upon a short journey, and almost lost his life on the road. We are never secure from trouble; it meets us around the family hearth and causes us to suffer in our own persons or in those of the dearest relatives; it walks into our shops and counting-houses, and tries us; and when we leave home it becomes our fellow-traveller and communes with us on the road. "Although affliction cometh not forth of the dust, neither doth trouble spring out of the ground; yet man is born unto trouble, as the sparks fly upward."

Frequently the greater afflictions *are not occasioned by the fault of the sufferer.* Nobody could blame the poor Jew that when he was going down to Jericho about his business the thieves beset him and demanded his money, and that when he made some little resistance they wounded him, stripped him, and left him half dead. How could he be blamed? It was to him a pure misfortune. Believe me, there is a great deal of sorrow in the world which does not arise out of the vice or folly of the persons enduring it: it comes from the hand of God upon the sufferer, not because he is a sinner above others, but for wise ends unknown to us. Now, this is the kind of distress which above all others demands Christian sympathy, and the very kind which abounds in our hospitals. The man is not to blame for lying there beaten and bruised: those gaping wounds from which his life is oozing are not of his own inflicting, nor received in a drunken brawl or through attempting a foolhardy feat; he suffers from no fault of his own, and therefore he has a pressing claim upon the benevolence of his fellow-men.

Still, *very much distress is caused by the wickedness of others.* The poor Jew on the road to Jericho was the victim of the thieves who wounded him and left him half dead. Man is man's worst enemy. If man were but tamed to peace the wildest beast in the world would be subdued; and if evil were purged from men's hearts, the major part of the ills of life would cease at once. The drunkard's wastefulness and brutality, the proud man's scorn, the oppressor's cruelty, the slanderer's lie, the trickster's cheat, the heartless man's grinding of the faces of the poor,—these put together are the roots of almost all the poisonous weeds which multiply upon the face of the earth to our shame and sorrow. When we see innocent persons suffering as the result of the sin of others our pity should be excited. How many there are of little children starving, and pining into chronic disease through a father's drunkenness, which keeps the table bare! Wives, too, who work hard themselves are brought down to pining sickness and painful disease by the laziness and cruelty of those who should have cherished them. Work-people, too, are often sorely oppressed in their wages, and have to work themselves to death's door to earn a pittance. Those are the people who ought to have our sympathy when accident or disease bring them to the hospital gates "wounded and half dead."

The man in the parable was quite helpless, he could do nothing for himself; there he must lie and die, those huge wounds must bleed his very soul away unless a generous hand shall interfere. It is as much as he can do to groan; he cannot even dress his wounds, much less arise and seek a shelter. He is bleeding to death among the pitiless rocks of the descent to Jericho, and he must leave his body to be fed upon by kites and crows unless some friend shall come to his help. Now, when a man can help himself, and does not, he deserves to suffer; when a man flings away opportunities by his idleness or self-indulgence a measure of suffering ought to be permitted to him as a cure for his vices; but when persons are sick or injured, and are unable to pay for the aid of the nurse and the physician, then is the time when true-hearted philanthropy should promptly step in and do its best. So our Saviour teaches us here.

Certain paths of life are peculiarly subject to affliction. The way which led from Jerusalem to Jericho was always infested by robbers. Jerome tells us that it was called the "bloody way," on account of the frequent highway robberies and murders which were there committed; and it is not so long ago as to be beyond the memory of man that an English traveller met his death on that road, while even very recent travellers tell us that they have been either threatened or actually attacked in that particularly gloomy region, the desert which goes down to the city of palm trees. So also in the world around us there are paths of life which are highly dangerous and fearfully haunted by disease and accident. Years ago there were many trades in which from want of precaution death slew its thousands. I thank God that sanitary and precautionary laws are better regarded, and men's lives are thought to be somewhat more precious.

Yet still there are ways of life which may each be called "the bloody way": pursuits which are necessary to the community, but highly dangerous to those who follow them. Our mines, our railways, and our seas show a terrible roll of suffering and death. When I think of the multitudes of our working people in this city who have to live in close, unhealthy rooms, crowded together in lanes and courts where the air is stagnant, I do not hesitate to say that much of the road which has to be trodden by the poor of London is as much deserving of the name of the way of blood as the road from Jerusalem to Jericho. If they do not lose their money it is because they never have it: if they do not fall among thieves, they fall among diseases which practically wound them and leave them half dead. Now, if you have not to engage in such avocations, if your pathway does not lead you from Jerusalem to Jericho, but takes you, perhaps, full often from Jerusalem to Bethany, where you can enjoy the sweetnesses of domestic love and the delights of Christian fellowship, you ought to be very thankful, and be all the more ready to assist those who for your sakes, or for the benefit of society at large, have to follow the more dangerous roads of life. Do you not agree with me that such persons ought to be among the first to receive of our Christian kindness?

Secondly, THERE ARE MANY WHO NEVER RELIEVE AFFLICTION. Our Saviour tells us of two at least who "passed by on the other side," and I suppose he might have prolonged the parable so as to have mentioned two dozen if he had chosen to do so, and even then he might have been content to mention but one good Samaritan, for I hardly think that there is one good Samaritan to two heartless persons. I wish there were, but I fear the good

Samaritans are very few in proportion to the number who act the part of the priest and the Levite.

Now, notice who the persons were that refused to render aid to the man in distress.

First, they were *brought to the spot by God's providence on purpose to do so.* What better thing could the Lord himself do for the poor man half dead than to bring some man to help him? An angel could not well have met the case. How should an angel, never wounded, understand binding up wounds and pouring in wine and oil? No, a man was wanted who would know what was necessary, who would with brotherly sympathy cheer the mind while doctoring the body. In our English version we read, "*By chance* there came down a certain priest that way;" but learned Greek scholars read it, "*By a coincidence.*" It was in the order of divine providence that a priest should come first to this afflicted person, that so he might go and examine the case as a man of education and skill, and then when the Levite came afterwards he would be able to carry on what the priest began; and if one could not carry the poor man, the two might between them be able to bear him to the inn, or one might remain to guard him while the other ran for help. God brought them to this position, but they wilfully refused the sacred duty which providence and humanity demanded of them. Now, you that are wealthy are sent into our city on purpose that you may have compassion upon the sick, the wounded, the poor, and the needy. God's intent in endowing any person with more substance than he needs is that he may have the pleasurable office, or rather let me say, the delightful privilege, of relieving want and woe.

Alas, how many there are who consider that store which God has put into their hands on purpose for the poor and needy to be only so much provision for their excessive luxury, a luxury which pampers them but yields them neither benefit nor pleasure. Others dream that wealth is given them that they may keep it under lock and key, cankering and corroding, breeding covetousness and care. Who dares roll a stone over the well's mouth when thirst is raging all around? Who dares keep the bread from the women and the children who are ready to gnaw their own arms for hunger? Above all, who dares allow the sufferer to writhe in agony uncared for, and the sick to pine into their graves unnursed? This is no small sin: it is a crime to be answered for to the Judge when he shall come to judge the quick and dead.

They were both of them persons, too, who ought to have relieved him, because *they were very familiar with things which should have softened their hearts.* If I understand the passage, the priest was coming down from Jerusalem. I conclude that he was going from Jerusalem to Jericho, because it says, "By chance there came *down* a certain priest that way." It was quite literally going down, for Jericho lies very low. I conclude that he was going home to Jericho, after having fulfilled his month's engagements in the temple, where he had been familiar with the worship of the Most High, as near to God as man could be, serving amidst sacrifices and holy psalms and solemn prayers, and yet he had not learned how to make a sacrifice himself. He had heard those prophetic words which say, "I will have mercy, and not sacrifice," but he was entirely forgetful of such teaching: he had often read that law, "Thou shalt love thy neighbour as thyself," but he regarded it not.

The Levite had not been quite so closely engaged in the sanctuary as the priest, but he had taken his share in holy work, and yet he came away from it with a hard heart. This is a sad fact. They had been near to God, but were not like him. You may spend Sabbath after Sabbath in the worship of God, or what you think to be so, and you may behold Christ Jesus set forth visibly crucified among you, and themes which ought to turn a heart of stone to flesh may pass before your minds, and nevertheless you may return into the world to be as miserly as ever, and to have as little feeling towards your fellow-men as before. It ought not to be so. I beseech you suffer it not to be so in any case again.

These two persons, moreover, were *bound by their profession to have helped this man,* for though it was originally said of the high priest yet I think it could be said of any priest that he was taken from among men, that he might have compassion. If anywhere there should be compassion towards men, it should be in the heart of the priest who is chosen to speak for God to men and for men to God. And oh, you Christian ministers, and all of you who teach in schools, or who undertake any service of Christian ministry—and you ought all to do so, for

the Lord hath made all his people to be priests unto him—
there ought to be in you from your very profession a readiness
of heart towards the kindliest actions for those who need
them.

And there is one thing to be mentioned also against this priest
and Levite, that *they were very well aware of the man's condition.*
They came close to him and saw his state. It is a narrow track-
way down to Jericho, and they were obliged to go almost over
his wounded body: the first comer looked at him, but he hurried
on; the second appears to have made a further investigation,
to have had sufficient curiosity, at any rate, to begin to examine
the state of the case; but his curiosity being satisfied his compassion was not aroused, and he hurried away. Half the neglect
of the sick poor arises from not knowing that there are such
cases, but many remain wilfully in ignorance, and such ignorance is no available excuse. In the case of the hospitals, you
do know that there are persons in them at this moment suffering, persons suffering grievously, for no fault of their own, and
you know that these need your aid.

Yet the pair had capital excuses: both the priest and the
Levite had excellent reasons for neglecting the bleeding man.
I never knew a man refuse to help the poor who failed to give
at least one admirable excuse. I believe that there is no man
on earth who wickedly rejects the plea of need who is not
furnished with arguments that he is right: arguments eminently
satisfactory to himself, and such as he thinks should silence
those who press the case. For instance, the priest and Levite
were both in a hurry. The priest had been a month away at
Jerusalem from his wife and dear children, and he naturally
wanted to get home; if he lingered the sun might be down; it
was an awkward place to be in after sundown, and you could
not expect him to be so imprudent as to stay in a lone place
with darkness coming on. A very excellent excuse was this:
but he also felt that he really could not do much good. He did
not understand surgery, and could not bind up a wound to save
his life; he shrank from it; the very sight of blood turned his
stomach, he could not bring himself to go near a person who
was so frightfully mangled. If he did try to bind up a wound
he felt he should be sure to make a muddle of it. The poor man,
moreover, was evidently half dead, and would be quite dead

in an hour or two, and therefore it was a pity to waste tim e on a hopeless case. Then the priest was only one person, and could not be expected to carry a bleeding man, and yet it would be idle to begin with the case and leave him there all night.

True, he could almost hear the sound of the Levite's feet, indeed he hoped he was coming up behind, for he felt very nervous at being alone with such a case; but then that was all the more reason for leaving the matter, since the Levite would be sure to attend to it. Better still was the following line of excuse—you would not have a person stop in a place where another man had been half killed by thieves. The thieves might be back again, they were scarcely yet out of hearing even then, and a priest after a month's scrvice ought to have some fees in his purse, and it was important not to run the risk of losing the support of his family by stopping in a place which was evidently swarming with highwaymen. He might be wounded too, and then there would be two people half dead, and one of them a valuable clergyman. Really, philanthropy would suggest that you take care of yourself, as you could not possibly do any good to the poor man. Did not all the principles of prudence suggest that the very best thing that he could do was to get out of the way as quickly as possible?

Moreover, he could pray for the man, you know, and he was glad to find that he had a tract with him which he would leave near him, and what with the tract and the prayer what more could a good man be expected to do? With this pious reflection he hastened on his way. It is just possible also that he did not wish to be defiled. A priest was too holy a person to meddle with wounds and bruises. Who would propose such a thing? He had come from Jerusalem in all the odour of sanctity; he felt himself to be as holy as he could conveniently be, and therefore he would not expose such rare excellence to worldly influences by touching a sinner. All these powerful reasons put together made him content to save trouble, and leave the doing of kindness to others.

You have smiled over what the priest might have said, but if you make any excuses for yourselves whenever real need comes before you, and you are able to relieve it, you need not smile over your excuses, the devil will do that; you had better cry over them, for there is the gravest reason for lamenting that your heart is hard toward your fellow-creatures when they are sick, and perhaps sick unto death.

In the third place THE SAMARITAN IS A MODEL FOR THOSE WHO DO HELP THE AFFLICTED. He is a model, first, if we notice *who the person was that he helped.* The parable does not *say* so, but it implies that the wounded man was a Jew, and, therefore, the Samaritan was not of the same faith and order. The apostle says, "As we have opportunity, let us do good unto all men, especially unto them who are of the household of faith." This man was not of the household of faith, as far as the Samaritan's judgment went, but he was one of the "all men." The Jew and he were as much apart in religious sympathy as they well could be. Ay, but he was a man: whether he was a Jew or not, he was a man, a wounded, bleeding, dying man, and the Samaritan was another man, and so one man felt for another man and came to his aid. Do not ask whether a sick man believes in the Thirty-nine Articles, or the Westminster Assembly's catechism. Let us hope that he is sound in the faith, but if he is not his wounds need staunching just as much as if he held a perfect creed. You need not enquire whether he is a sound Calvinist, for an Arminian smarts when he is wounded; a Churchman feels as much pain as a Dissenter when his leg is broken, and an infidel needs nursing when he is crushed in an accident. It is as bad for a man to die with a heterodox creed as with the orthodox faith; indeed, in some respects it is far worse, and therefore we should be doubly anxious for his cure. We are to relieve real distress irrespective of creed, as the Samaritan did.

Moreover, the Jews were great haters of the Samaritans, and no doubt this Samaritan might have thought, "If I were in that man's case he would not help me. He would pass me by and say, 'It is a Samaritan dog, let him be accursed.'" The Jews were accustomed to curse the Samaritans, but it did not occur to the good man to remember what the Jew would have said: he saw him bleeding and he bound up his wounds. Our Saviour has not given us for a golden rule, "Do ye to others as others would do to you," but "as ye would they should do to you." The Samaritan went by that rule, and though he knew of the enmity in the Jewish mind he felt that he must heap coals of fire upon the wounded man by loving help; therefore he went straight away to his relief. Perhaps at another time the Jew would have put off the Samaritan and refused even to be touched by him; but the tender-hearted sympathizer does not think of that: the poor man is too sick to hold any crotchets or prejudices, and when the Samaritan bends over him and pours in the oil and wine he wins a grateful glance from the son of Abraham.

That poor, wounded man was one who *could not repay him.* He had been stripped of all that he had, even his garments were taken from him; but charity does not look for payment, else were it no charity at all. The man was *a total stranger* too. The Samaritan had not even seen him before. What did that matter? He was a man, and all men are akin. "God hath made of one blood all nations that dwell upon the face of the earth": the Samaritan felt that touch of nature which makes all men kin, and he bent over the stranger and relieved his pains.

He might have said, "Why should *I* help? He has been *rejected by his own people;* the priest and the Levite have left him; his first claim is upon his own countrymen." So have I known some say, "These persons have no claim; they ought to go to their own people." Well, suppose they have gone and failed, now comes your turn; and what the Jew would not do for the Jew let the Samaritan do, and he shall be blessed in the deed.

He is a model to us next in *the spirit in which he did his work.* He did it without asking questions. The man was in need, he was sure of that, and he helped him at once; doing so without hesitation, and making no compact nor agreement with him, but at once proceeding to pour in the oil and wine. He did it without attempting to shift the labour from himself to others.

He did it without any selfish fear: the thieves might have been upon him, but he cared nothing for thieves when a life was in danger. Here is a man in want, and the man must be relieved, thieves or no thieves, and he does it. He does it with self-denial, for he finds oil and wine, and money at the inn, and everything, though he was by no means a rich man, for he gave two pence, a larger sum than it looks, but still a small sum. It was a poor Samaritan who did this rich and noble act: the poorest can help the poor; even those who feel distress themselves may manifest a generous Christian spirit, and give their services. Let them do so as they have opportunity.

This man helped his poor neighbour with great tenderness and care. He was like a mother to him. Everything was done with loving thought and with whatever of skill he possessed. He did the best he could. Let what we do for others always be done in the noblest style. Let us not treat the poor like dogs to whom we fling a bone, nor visit the sick like superior beings who feel that they are stooping down to inferiors when they enter their rooms; but in the sweet tenderness of real love, learned at Jesus' feet, let us imitate this good Samaritan.

But *what did he do?* Well, first he came to where the sufferer was, and put himself into his position. Then he put forth all his skill for him, and bound up his wounds, no doubt rending his own garment to get the bands with which to bind up the wound. He poured in oil and wine, the best healing mixture that he knew of, and one which he happened to have by him. He then set the sick man on his mule, and of course he had to walk himself, but this he did right cheerfully, supporting his poor patient as the mule proceeded. He took him to an inn, but he did not leave him at the caravanserai and say, "Anybody will take care of him now," but he went to the manager of the establishment and gave him money, and he said, "Take care of him." I admire that little sentence, because it is first written, "he took care of him," and next he said, "Take care of him." What you do yourself you may exhort other people to do.

The Samaritan did not cease till he had gone through with his kindness. He said, "This money may not be sufficient, for it may be a long time before he is able to move. That leg may not soon heal, that broken rib may need long rest. Do not hurry him away, let him stop here, and if he incurs additional expense, I will be sure to pay it when I come back from Jerusalem again." There is nothing like the charity which endures even to the end.

But now, fourthly, WE HAVE A HIGHER MODEL than even the Samaritan—our Lord Jesus Christ. I do not think that our divine Lord intended to teach anything about himself in this parable, except so far as he is himself the great exemplar of all goodness. He was answering the question, "Who is my neighbour?" and he was not preaching about himself at all. There has been a great deal of straining of this parable to bring the Lord Jesus and everything about him into it, but this I dare not imitate. Yet by analogy we may illustrate our Lord's goodness by it. This is a picture of a generous-hearted man who cares for the needy: but the most generous-hearted man that ever lived was the Man of Nazareth, and none ever cared for sick and suffering souls as he has done. Therefore, if we praise the good Samaritan, we should much more extol the blessed Saviour whom his enemies called a Samaritan, and who never denied the charge, for what cared he if all the prejudice and scorn of men should vent itself on him?

Now our Lord Jesus Christ has done better than the good Samaritan, because our case was worse. As I have already said, the wounded man could not blame himself for his sad estate; it was his misfortune, not his fault; but you and I are not only half dead, but altogether dead in trespasses and sins, and we have brought many of our ills upon ourselves. The thieves that have stripped us are our own iniquities, the wounds which we bear have been inflicted by our own suicidal hand. We are not in opposition to Jesus Christ as the poor Jew was to the Samaritan from the mere force of prejudice, but we have been opposed to the blessed Redeemer by nature; we have from the first turned away from him. Alas, we have resisted and rejected him. The poor man did not put his Samaritan friend away, but we have done so to our Lord. How many times have we refused Almighty love! How often by unbelief have we pulled open the wounds which Christ has bound up! We have rejected the oil and wine which in the Gospel he presents to us. We have spoken evil of him to his face, and have lived even for years in utter rejection of him, and yet in his infinite love he has not given us up, but he has brought some of us into his church, where we rest as in an inn, feeding on what his bounty has provided. It was wondrous love which moved the Saviour's heart when he found us in all our misery, and bent over us to lift us out of it, though he knew that we were his enemies.

The Samaritan was akin to the Jew because he was a man, but our Lord Jesus was not originally akin to us by nature: he is God, infinitely above us, and if he was "found in fashion as a man" it was because he chose to be so. If he journeyed this way, *via* Bethlehem's manger, down to the place of our sin and misery, it was because his infinite compassion brought him there. The Samaritan came to the wounded one because in the course of business he was led there, and, being there, he helped the man; but Jesus came to earth on no business but that of saving us, and he was found in our flesh that he might have sympathy with us. In the very existence of the man Christ Jesus you see the noblest form of pity manifested.

And being here, where we had fallen among robbers, he did not merely run risks of being attacked by thieves himself, but he was attacked by them: he was wounded, he was stripped, and not half dead was he, but altogether dead, for he was laid in the grave. He was slain for our sakes, for it was not possible for him to deliver us from the mischief which the thieves of sin had wrought upon us excepting by suffering that mischief in his own person; and he did suffer it that he might deliver us.

What the Samaritan gave to the poor man was generous, but it is not comparable to what the Lord Jesus has given to us. He gave him wine and oil, but Jesus has given his heart's blood to heal our wounds: "he loved us and gave himself for us." The Samaritan *lent* himself with all his care and thoughtfulness, but Christ *gave* himself even to the death for us. The Samaritan gave two pence, a large amount out of his slender store, and I do not depreciate the gift, but "he that was rich for our sakes became poor that we through his poverty might be rich." Oh, the marvellous gifts which Christ has bestowed upon us! Who is he that can reckon them? Heaven is among those blessings, but his own self is the chief boon.

The Samaritan's compassion did but show itself for a short time. If he had to walk by the side of his mule it would not be for many miles, but Christ walked by the side of us, dismounted from his glory, all through his life. The Samaritan did not stop long at the inn, for he had his business to attend to, and he very rightly went about it; but our Lord remained with us for a lifetime, even till he rose to heaven: yea, he is with us even now, always blessing the sons of men.

When the Samaritan went away he said, "Whatsoever thou spendest more I will repay thee." Jesus has gone up to heaven, and he has left behind him blessed promises of something to be done when he shall come again. He never forgets us.

The good Samaritan, I dare say, thought very little of the Jew in after years; indeed, it is the mark of a generous spirit not to think much of what it has done. He went back to

Samaria and minded his business, and never told anybody "I helped a poor Jew on the road." Not he. But of necessity our Lord Jesus acts differently, for because we have a constant need he continues to care for us, and his deed of love is being done, and done, and done again upon multitudes of cases, and will always be repeated so long as there are men to be saved, a hell from which to escape, and a heaven to win.

Jesus has redeemed you, brought you into his church, put you under the care of his ministers, bidden us take care of you, and promised to reward us if we do so in the day when he comes. *Seek, then, to be true followers of your Lord* by practical deeds of kindness, and if you have been backward in your gifts to help either the temporal or the spiritual needs of men, begin from to-day with generous hearts, and God will bless you. O divine Spirit, help us all to be like Jesus.

XII

JUDGMENT THREATENING
BUT MERCY SPARING

"Cut it down; why cumbereth it the ground? And he
answering said unto him, Lord, let it alone this year also."—
Luke 13: 7, 8.

THE comparison of a man to a tree, and of human works to
fruit, is exceedingly common in Scripture, because it is
most suggestive, natural, and appropriate. As fruit is the
production of the tree's life, and the end for which the tree
exists, so obedience to the divine will, and holiness unto the
Lord, should be the product of man's life, and for it he was at
first created. When men plant trees in a vineyard, they very
naturally expect to find fruit thereon; and, if at the age and
season of fruitbearing they find no produce, their natural and
justifiable expectation is disappointed. Even thus, speaking
after the manner of men, it is natural that the great Maker of all
should look for the good fruit of obedience and love from the
men who are the objects of his providential care, and be grieved
when he meets with no return. Man is very much more God's
property than a tree can ever be the property of the man who
plants a vineyard; and as God has spent so much more skill and
wisdom in the creation of a man than a husbandman can have
spent in the mere planting of trees, it becomes the more natural
that God should look for fruit from his creature, man; and the
more reasonable that his most righteous requirements should
not be refused.

Trees that bring not forth fruit must be cut down; and sinners
who bring not forth repentance, faith, and holiness, must die.
It is only a matter of time as to whether or not the vineyard
shall be cleared of the incumbrance of its barren trees; it is
but a matter of time as to when the world shall be delivered
from the burdensome presence of barren souls. There is a time

143

for felling fruitless trees, and there is an appointed season for hewing down and casting into the fire the useless sinner.

We shall not linger on the threshold of our solemn work now, for our burden is very heavy, and we would fain be rid of it speedily. We shall address ourselves at once to those persons who are living without God and without Christ, among whom many of you must be numbered. We shall speak to those who are not saved: there are such in the professing Church everywhere. O may the Holy Spirit find them out by our word, and bring them in real earnest to consider their ways. To all unprofitable, unfruitful sinners, we utter this hard, but needful sentence: TO CUT YOU DOWN WOULD BE MOST REASONABLE. It is right and reasonable to fell barren trees, and it is just as right and reasonable that *you* should be cut down.

This will appear in the first place, if we reflect that *this is the shortest and the surest way to deal with you;* it will cost the least trouble, and be most certainly effectual in removing you from the place to which you are an injury rather than a benefit. When the owner of the vineyard says to the gardener concerning the tree, "Cut it down," the remedy is very sharp, but it is very simple; the felling is soon done, the clearance is thorough, and when another tree is planted the benefit is evident. To spare is difficult and involves trouble; to cut down is easy and effectual. Unconverted hearer, to preach the Gospel to you, to call you to repentance, to entreat, exhort, and warn you, is a laborious process, and will probably be unsuccessful after all. The work will require much thought; providential agencies must be directed with wisdom, saints must pray with earnestness, ministers must plead with tears, the Scriptures must be written, and those Scriptures must be expounded and explained; all this is more than thou hast any natural right to expect that God should do with thee, when he has in his hands a far simpler remedy by which he may at once ease himself of his adversary, and prevent thy being any further offence: he has but to take away thy breath and permit thy body to descend into the grave and thy soul into hell, and the vineyard is clear, and there is room for another tree.

This sharp, short, simple process, is one which commends itself to men in the case of trees, and it is one which it is a thousand wonders that the Lord has not used with thee.

There will be no more blaspheming God, sinner, when the axe has laid thee low! There will be no more rejecting the promise of his mercy, no more violating of Sabbath days, no more despising Scripture, when the day of doom arrives! Death shall end all these abominations for ever. We shall no more have to agonize for you in vain, no more shall we weep bitterly because of your hardness of heart, no longer study to meet your objections, and sigh at your constant oppositions. Sinner, I ask you, is not the readiest plan to be rid of you suggested by the text, "Cut it down"? You yourself would do thus with a tree; what reason is there why the Lord should not deal thus with you?

Do you argue that you are of far greater importance than a tree? How do you make this appear? A tree is far more valuable to you than you can be supposed to be to the infinite God. The gardener would lose something possibly by cutting down his tree, but how canst thou suppose that thy ruin would be any damage to the great God? You yourself could not well complain of being cut down, for you do not think much of your own soul; you are not concerned about its salvation; you trifle with its best interests. Why should you expect another to value you at a higher rate than you have set upon yourself? You fling away your soul for passing joys; you neglect the great salvation; you live in daily disobedience against God, who alone can do you good; even the preaching of the Gospel, that all-powerful engine, seems to have no effect upon you, because you despise your own self. You have wantonly used the axe to yourself on many occasions, why should not the proper executioner use it in earnest? Some men ruin their health by their sins; they wildly dash the axe against their own root and wound themselves terribly. On your soul you are using that axe continually, for you damage it by sin, and seek out folly, and choose the way to damnation, and labour to be lost. You cannot, therefore, complain. Beware, O rebellious, unrepentant sinner! My love yearns for your salvation, but my reason approves of your ruin, foresees it, and expects it speedily except you turn unto the Lord and live.

Another reason makes the argument for judgment very powerful, namely, *that sufficient space for repentance has already been given.* I do not know what can be done for some of you more than has been done. You have been digged about—the digging, I suppose, is to loosen the roots of their hold upon the earth—and you have had affliction, trial, and trouble, like the gardener's great spade, to wean you from earth, and loosen your hold of carnal things; you have had sickness—you have tossed to and fro upon the bed of pain; you have been in the jaws of death and the horrid teeth seemed above and beneath you, as though they would enclose you for ever; but all this has been of no avail. Why should you be stricken any more? You will revolt more and more. Those great and grievous afflictions have not been sanctified to you, but rather you have gone on offending against God and provoking the Most High.

The gardener spoke of dunging as well as of digging, and some of you have had plentiful helps towards repentance. The Gospel has been put close by your roots, hundreds of times; you have a Bible in every house; you have, some of you, had the advantage of godly training from your youth up. You have been warned again, and again, and again, sometimes sternly, sometimes affectionately; you have heard the wooing voice of mercy, and the thundering notes of judgment; but yet, though Jesus Christ's own Gospel has been laid close to your root, O barren tree, you are barren still. What is the use then of sparing you? Sparing has been tried, and it has had no effect: the other remedy is certain—"*Cut it down.*" O sinner, you may well say—

I have long withstood his grace,
Long provoked him to his face;
Would not hearken to his calls;
Grieved him by a thousand falls.

Depths of mercy! can there be
Mercy still reserved for me?
Can my God his wrath forbear?
Me, the chief of sinners spare?

Sinner, I argue thy case somewhat harshly, thou thinkest. Ah! would God I could make thee think *me* harsh, if thou wouldst but have pity on thine own soul, for my harshness is only apparent, not real, and thy carelessness for thy soul is real harshness, for thou carest not for thine own soul, but treatest it as a thing to be cast away, and its ruin to be laughed at, as though it were contemptible. *All this while there has been no sign of improvement whatever in thee.* If there had been some little fruit, if some tears of repentance had been flowing from thine eyes, if there had been some seeking after Christ, if thine heart had been a little softened, if thou hadst but a little faith in Jesus, though it were but as a grain of mustard seed, then there were indeed reasons for sparing thee; but, sorrowful to add, *thy sparing has had an ill effect upon thee.* Because God hath not punished thee, therefore thou hast waxed wanton and bold; thou hast said, "Doth God know? Is there knowledge in the Most High?"

Strange madness of evil, that thou shouldst pervert the long-suffering which calls thee to repentance into a reason for running to greater lengths of sin! What, when Jehovah spares thee that thou mayst turn to him, shall that very sparing make thee lift up the foot of thy rebellion and spurn him? It has done so. Up to this time thou hast grown hardened instead of softened. Thou hast grown older, but thou art no wiser, except it be with Satan's subtlety to be more wise in sin. The Gospel has not now the effect it had once on thee. This voice could make thy soul shiver and thy very blood chill in its veins, but it cannot do so now. These eyes have sometimes looked on thee and seemed as though they flashed with fire, but now they are dull as lead to thee. Once, when we spoke to thee of the wrath to come, the tears would flow: there were some tears of gentle pity for thine own soul; but ah! it is not so with thee now. You will go your way, and our most earnest tones will seem but as the whistling wind, and our most importunate entreaties as a child's playful song. O God, it is reasonable indeed that thou shouldst uplift that sharp axe of thine and say, "Cut it down." I think I could abundantly justify the severity of God, if now he were to use it, when I thus perceive that all his sparing has had no effect but to make you worse, when I perceive that, notwithstanding these years of waiting, there are no tokens of improvement. If he saith, "Cut it down," justice and reason say, "Ay, Lord, it is well it should be so."

But there are other reasons why "Cut it down" is most reasonable, *when we consider the owner and the other trees.* First of all, *here is a tree which brings forth no fruit whatever, and therefore is of no service.* It is like money badly invested, bringing in no interest; it is a dead loss to the owner. What is the use of keeping it? And even so with thee, sinner; what is the use of thee? Thou art of use to thy children, to thy family; in business thou mayst be of some service to the world; but then the world did not make thee; and thy children, and thy family, they did not create thee. God has made thee, God has planted thee, God is thy proprietor—thou hast done nothing for God. Even in coming up to his house to-day, you did not come with any desire to honour God; and to-morrow, if you should chance to give something to the poor, it will not be because they are God's, nor out of love to *him.* You neither pray to God, nor praise God, nor live for God; you live for anything, for everything, for nothing, sooner than live for the God that made you.

Then what is the good of you to God? All his other creatures praise him. "The ox knoweth his owner, and the ass his master's crib" (Isa. 1: 3); but thou dost not know. Wouldst thou keep a horse that never did thee service? Thou wouldst say, "What is the good of this? A servant in my house to feed upon my bread, to be clothed with my bounty, and yet never to obey me, but to live in constant reckless disregard of my most reasonable commands!" You would say to such a servant, "Get thee gone; thou art no servant of mine." Well might the Lord say this of thee. All these years preserving goodness has winked at the past; longsuffering has borne with thy follies and thy faults, but it cannot be so for ever, for reason demands that a useless thing should not always stand, and "Cut it down" is the natural inference from the uselessness of thy life.

Thou costest God much; much patience, much bounty, much skill, much power. Wherefore should he spare thee? What is there in thee, that he should go on with thee in this manner? Sinner, if you were in God's place and were as ill-treated by your creature, as the Lord is by you, would you lavish love and goodness upon him, to receive hardness of heart and rebellion in return? Assuredly not. Judge then whether it be not right that the Lord should say, "Cut it down."

But there is a worse consideration, namely, that *all this while you have been filling up a space which somebody might have been filling to the glory of God.* Where that barren tree stands there might have been a tree loaded with fruit. You are cumbering the ground, as the text says, that is, doing nothing but just being a cumbersome nuisance. If another mother had those children, she would pray for them and weep over them, and teach them of Christ, but you do no such thing. If another man had that money it would be laid out for God's glory, and you lay it out for your own pleasure and forget the God who gave it to you. If another had sat in that seat which you occupy, it may be that he had long ago repented in sackcloth and ashes; but you, like the men of Capernaum, have been hardened instead of being softened under the Gospel.

It may be, man of influence, if another had stood where you have stood in the world's judgment, he would have led hundreds in the path of right, but you, standing there, have done no such thing. Oh! if another had your gifts, young man, he would not be making a company laugh at the tavern, but pleading with all his might for Jesus. If another had but your gifts of utterance, he would be spending in prayer and teaching what you now spend in fun and frolic to make amusement for fools. Oh! if another had that time to live in, he would live in earnest for his Master. If that young saint, just going through the flood, had your health and vigour, how would he spend and be spent!

Moreover, and to make bad worse even to the worst degree, *all this while ungodly men are spreading an evil influence.* Well may the question arise: "Whence to me this waste of love?"

It is so apparently a waste of longsuffering and mercy that some transgressors should be spared at all, that they may well marvel. Look at it, and I think you will see it very clearly so, *the very fact that God does not punish sin on the spot is mischievously interpreted.* Men in all ages have drawn a wicked inference from the patience of the great Judge. The Preacher, in Ecclesiastes, says, "Because sentence against an evil work is not executed speedily, therefore the heart of the sons of men is fully set in them to do evil" (Eccles. 8:11). "Why," you say, "So-and-so drinks and swears, and he has lived to be a hale, hearty old man. Such an one has plunged into all sorts of folly and wickedness; he was a thief, and everything bad besides, and yet he prospers in the world and grows rich. Instead of God sinking him down at once to hell, he has favoured him, and fattened him as a bullock in rich pasture." "Oh," the worldling says, "there is no justice in God. He does not punish sin." The very fact that you are spared, O sinner, is doing mischief in the world. Do you see that? Your mere existence in this world is to others an inducement to continue in sin; for while you are spared, others look at you and say, "God has not punished him." Therefore they infer that he will not punish sin at all.

Moreover, how many there are of you *whose example is fearfully contagious;* whose lips and lives combine to lead your associates astray from God. In a dreadful murrain which ravaged our fields and destroyed the cattle, farmers were advised, as soon as ever the cow was attacked with the disease, to kill it on the spot and bury it five feet deep out of the way. Let us reflect that the murrain of sin is much more pestilential and more certain to kill than this murrain among the cattle, and therefore stern justice cries, "Let the sinner be at once sent where he cannot increase the plague of iniquity: it is of no use sparing him; he grows no better; all the means used only make him worse, and meanwhile we must look to the welfare of others, lest he perish not alone in his iniquity. He teaches his children to swear; he makes others worldly; the whole current of his life is to incite men to rebel against God: let his desperate course be stopped at once. The leprosy is upon him, and all that he touches he pollutes: for high sanitary reasons, therefore, he must be removed." It is better that one die than that many should be smitten, and, therefore, the highest consideration for the good of mankind in general renders it necessary that the mandate should go forth, "Cut it down."

Our second most solemn work is to remind thee, O impenitent sinner, that FOR GOD TO HAVE SPARED YOU SO LONG IS A VERY WONDERFUL THING. That the infinitely just and holy God should have spared you, up till now, is no small thing, but a matter for adoring wonder.

Consider, *negatively, God is not sparing you because he is insensible towards your sins:* he is angry with the wicked every day. If the Lord could be indifferent towards sin, and could bring his holy mind to treat it as a mere trifle, then it would be no wonder that he should let the transgressor live; but he cannot endure iniquity—all the day long his anger smokes and burns towards evil, and yet he holds back the thunderbolt and does not smite the guilty. If *you* had been angry half-an-hour, you would have come to hard words or blows; but here is the Judge of all the earth angry every day for twenty, thirty, forty, fifty, sixty, seventy, or eighty years with some of you, and yet he has not smitten. *It is not because the offence is at a distance*, and therefore far from his observant eye; no—your sins are like smoke in his nose; your iniquities provoke him to his face; you touch the apple of his eye, and yet, for all that, though this accursed thing called sin intrudes into his presence every instant, yet still he has spared you until now.

He said to the foolish rich man, "This night thy soul shall be required of thee," and he never saw the morning; and he might as easily have sent the same sad message to you, *and what then?* As I have said before, this great patience is not manifested towards your sinful soul because the Lord is at all dependent upon you; your living will not increase, and your dying will not diminish his glory. Admire and wonder at this longsuffering.

Remember that this wonder is increased, when you *think of the fruit he deserved to have had of you.* A God so good and so gracious ought to have been loved by you. He has treated you so well, and given you such capacities for pleasure that he ought to have had some service of you. God gives to you not only your daily food, but your very life—you are wholly dependent upon him. You ought to have served him, to have delighted in that service, to spend and to have been spent for your Lord. He asks no more of you than he ought to have had, and yet he asks you to love the Lord your God with all your heart, your soul, your strength—this was his first and great commandment—but this you have constantly, persistently broken.

I have to touch upon a very solemn part of the business now, when I notice again that some, perhaps, *have been guilty of very God-provoking sins.* Some offences provoke God much more than others—I believe that *cursing* does, for it is wanton insolence, by which nothing can be gained. It is altogether a gratuitous piece of insult. To swear, to imprecate the curse of God upon one's limbs and souls is an unnecessary, supernumerary sin. There cannot be any pleasure in pronouncing oaths, any more than in uttering any other form of words. It is just because man *will* hate his Maker, and will provoke him, that he does this. O sinner, did you ever ask God to damn you and are you not astonished that he has not done it? Did you ever desire that the blast should come upon you, and do you not marvel that he has not long ago swept you where his wrath would wither you for ever? Swearing is a sin that provokes the Most High. O sinner, abhor this most detestable of vices.

How many are guilty of *infidelity*? How provoking to God for a man to deny his very existence; standing up and breathing God's air and living upon God's life, and yet saying that there is no God. An insignificant worm dares challenge the Almighty to prove his Godhead and existence by a tremendous act of justice. This is a God-provoking sin.

So again is *persecution*. There may be some who have persecuted wife and child because of their following Christ. "He that toucheth you toucheth the apple of mine eye," saith God. Beware, sinner, you will not touch the Lord's eye long without feeling his heavy hand. If any man injures your children the blood is in your cheek at once, if you are a father, and you feel that you will show yourself strong in their defence, even so the heavenly Father will avenge his own elect. Therefore, take heed lest thou persevere in *this* heaven-provoking sin.

And *slander*, too, lying against God's servants, inventing and spreading wicked tales against those who walk in God's fear,— this is another evil which awakes the anger of God, and stirs up righteous fury against the man who is guilty of it. Beware! beware!

Filthiness, filthiness of body and of life, will also provoke the Most Holy One. This once brought hell out of heaven upon Sodom; God sent down fire and brimstone because of the lusts of the flesh that made Sodom to stink in his nostrils; the harlot and the adulterer, and the fornicator, shall know that they sin not without provoking God very terribly.

And, among these God-provoking sins, there is that *quenching of conscience* of which some of you have been guilty. Ah, there are not many of you to whom I spoke under these first heads, for I know that very few of you would indulge in these grosser sins; but there are some of you quite as bad in another sense, for you know the right and choose the wrong; you hear of Christ and do not give your hearts to him. We had hoped of some of you that long ere this we should have seen you walking in the Lord's fear, but you are still strangers to Christ. You must have had hard work to do this. You must have had a terrible tug with conscience, some of you; I know you have been stifling many a holy desire, and when the Spirit of God has been striving with you, you have been so desperately set on mischief, that still you have gone on in the error of your ways. Shall God be always provoked? Shall mercy be preached to you for ever in vain? Shall Christ be presented and always rejected, and will you continue to be his enemies, and shall he never proclaim war against your souls? It is a marvel, it is a wonder that these God-provoking sins have so long been borne with, and that you are not yet cut down.

And now, WHAT IS THE REASON FOR ALL THIS LONGSUFFERING? Why is it that this cumber-ground tree has not been cut down? The answer is, because *there is One who pleads for sinners.* I have shown you, and some of you will think I have shown you with very great severity too, how reasonable it is that you should be cut down. I wish you felt it, for, if you felt how reasonable it was that God should send you to hell, then you would begin to tremble, and there would be some hope of you. But what has been the secret cause that you have been kept alive? The answer is, *Jesus Christ has pleaded for you, the crucified Saviour has interfered for you.* And you ask me "Why?" I answer, because *Jesus Christ has an interest in you all.* We read of some who denied the Lord that bought them. No one who is bought with blood for eternal salvation ever tramples on that blood; but Jesus Christ has shed his blood for the reprieve of men that they may be spared, and those who turn God's sparing mercy into an occasion for fresh sin, do trample on the blood of Jesus Christ.

Thou hadst not been on praying ground and pleading terms with God if it had not been for that dear Suffering One. Our text represents the gardener as only *asking* to have it spared; but Jesus Christ did something more than ask; he pleaded, not with his mouth only, but with pierced hands, and pierced feet, and pierced side; and those prevailing pleas have moved the heart of God, and you are yet spared.

May I speak to thee then? If thy life had been spared, when thou wast condemned to die, by my intervention—suppose such a case—would you despise *me?* If I had power at the Court, and when you were condemned to die, had gone in and pleaded for you, and you had been reprieved, year after year would you hate me? Would you speak against me? Would you rail at my character? Would you find fault with my friends? I know you better: you would love me; you would be grateful for the sparing of your life. O sinner, I would you would treat the Lord Jesus as you would treat man. I would you would think of the Lord Jesus Christ as you would think of your fellow-man who had delivered you from death. You are not in hell, where you would have been if he had not come in and pleaded for you. I do beseech you, think of the misery of lost souls, and recollect that *you* would have been in such a woeful case yourself now, if he had not lifted up that hand once pierced for human sin.

Where are your companions, your old companions? You sat in the pothouse with them; they are in hell, but you are not. When you were younger you sinned with them, and they are lost, but you are not. Why is this difference made? Why are they cast away and you spared? I can only ascribe it to the gracious longsuffering of Jehovah. O, I pray you look at him who spared you, and weep and mourn for your sin. May the Spirit of God come down on you to-day and draw you to the foot of his dear Cross, and as you see the blood which has spared your blood, and the death which has made you live until now, I do trust that the divine Spirit may make you fall down and say, "O Jesus, how can I offend thee? How can I stand out against thee? Accept me and save me for thy mercy's sake."

I tell you that God will forgive you, but you will never forgive yourselves for having stood out and resisted so long. Oh, may eternal mercy, which has not yet said, "Cut it down," now dig about you that you may bring forth fruit, and then it shall be all to the praise of him whose precious blood has saved us from eternal wrath.

XIII

A STRAIGHT TALK

"I cannot come."—Luke 14: 20.

THERE are different ways of replying to the invitation of the Gospel when you mean to refuse it. They are all, at bottom, bad, and they may all be classed under one head; for "they all with one consent began to make excuse"; but yet some are more decently worded than others and have a greater show of reason about them. The first two sets of people, who were invited to the supper, said to the servant, apologetically, with some appearance of courtesy, "I pray thee have me excused." But the third man did not beat about the bush at all, or pray to be excused; but he said tersely, bluntly, sharply, "*I cannot come.*" This was a final reply; he did not intend, nor wish, to come to the supper. "*I cannot come,*" was a snappish word; but as he had married a wife, he thought the idea of his coming was utterly unreasonable, and he needed no sort of excuse.

Now, what did that mean? Well, it meant that he thought very lightly of the giver of the feast. He had no respect for this "certain man," who had made a great supper. He had an opportunity of slighting him by refusing his invitation, and he did so outspokenly, saying, "*I cannot come.*"

It also showed that he had a very low opinion of the supper itself. It might be a respectable meal, but he did not want it: he could have quite as good a supper at home. He was better off than those people in the streets. Those hedge-birds might be glad enough of a supper for nothing; but he was not dependent upon anybody, and he could do very well for himself. Do you not know many in this world who have no opinion of Christ, no love to God? Religion is to them mere nonsense—an unpractical, dreamy matter, about which they have no time to concern themselves. It is a pitiful thing that the God, whom angels worship, they will not even think of; and the Christ who is the loveliest of the lovely—in him they see no beauty; and the priceless provisions of mercy, the pardon of sin, the salvation of the soul, the heaven of God—they neglect these things, as if they did not need them, or could get them whenever they please. Thousands are proudly independent of the free grace of God; they are good enough, and virtuous enough; and need not cry for mercy, like the wicked and profane. In their own judgment, they are quite able to fight their own way to heaven. They want not the charities of the Gospel. Contempt of the great Feast-maker, and contempt of the feast itself—these two pieces of proud disdain induce a man to say, "*I cannot come.*"

But there was more than common pride in this brief, brusque speech, for this man had, at the first, made a promise to come. He had been bidden, and it is implied in the parable that he had at that time accepted the invitation. He had accepted the cards of invitation to the supper; and, though he had done so, he now flies in the face of his own self, and says, "I cannot come." I think that I am addressing some who have pledged themselves many a time to come to Christ. If I remember rightly, you asked the prayers of friends, and promised that you would be in real earnest. You looked your wife in the face, and said, "I hope that it will not be long before I am with you in the church of God, and shall no longer have to go away and leave you alone at the Lord's table." You asked some of your Christian friends to make a point of praying for you; but you have never carried out your intention of becoming a true Christian. Your resolutions may be still read in God's eternal book of record; but they are there as witnesses to your falseness and changeableness. You accepted the invitation on the spur of the moment; but when worldliness had got the upper hand with you, you went back to your own obstinacy, and said, "I cannot come." It matters little whether you say it angrily or quietly; for, if you do not come, the practical result is the same.

In saying, "I cannot come," the man intended, as it were, to dismiss the matter. He wished to be understood as having made up his mind, and he was no longer open to argument. He did not parley; he did not talk; but he just said, off-hand, "I want no more persuading; I cannot come, and that settles it." Certain of you have come to such a condition of heart that they would gladly silence our gospel expostulations: with a kindly but determined tone they would say, "*I cannot come. Do not trouble me any more.*"

I suppose that this man, after he had made that positive declaration, felt that there was truth in what he had stated. He said, "*Therefore* I cannot come." He had reason to support him in what he said, and he went home, sat down, and enjoyed himself, and felt that he was a righteous man, quite as good as those who had gone to the supper, and perhaps rather better. He could not blame himself, for when a man cannot do it, why, of course, he cannot do it; and why should he be censured for an impossibility? "I cannot come": how can I help that? So he sat down with a cool indifference to eat his own supper. It was nothing to him whether the great giver of the feast was grieved or not; whether his oxen and fatlings were wasted or not. He had said it to his conscience very often, till he half believed it—"I cannot come, and there is no disputing it."

I have no doubt that many, who have never come to Christ, have made themselves content to be without him by the belief that they cannot come. Although the impossibility, if it did exist, would involve the greatest of all calamities, yet they speak of it with very little concern. Practically, they say, "I cannot be saved. I must remain an unbeliever." What an awful thing for any mortal to say! Yet you have said it till you almost believe it; and you wish us now to leave you quite alone for this dreadful reason. You do not want to be troubled to-day. The text already begins to startle you a little, and you do not like it. If the Lord helps me, I will trouble you far more before long: I have heavy tidings from the Lord for you. With kindly importunity I would plead with you and try to show you that this little speech of yours, "*I cannot come,*" is a wretched speech. You must throw it to the winds, and prove that you can come by coming at once, and receiving of the great feast of love, and honouring him that spreads it for hungry souls.

Two or three things I would like to say about this case, for *it is very serious*. It was bad enough for this man to say, "I cannot come," but it is far worse for you to say, "I cannot come to Christ." Remember, if the invited guests did not come, and come at once, they could never come, for there was only that one supper, and not a series of banquets. The great man who made the feast did not intend to prepare another. A very grave offence would be committed by their not coming to the one supper. There is only one time of grace for you, and, if that be ended, you will not have a second opportunity. There is only one Christ Jesus; there is no more sacrifice for sin. There is only one way of eternal love and mercy; do not forsake it. I pray you, do not turn away from the one door of life, the one way of salvation. If it is slighted now, and the feast is over, as it will be when you die, then you have lost the great privilege, and you have been guilty of a gross neglect, from the consequences of which you never will be able to escape. Note this, and beware.

Besides, it is not merely a supper that you will lose when you say, "I cannot come." To lose a supper would be little and might soon be set right when breakfast-time came round. But you lose eternal life, and that loss in time can never be found in eternity. You lose the pardon of sin, reconciliation to God, adoption into the family of love—these are heavy losses. You lose the joy of faith for life, and you lose comfort in death— who can estimate this damage? Lose not your immortal soul! Oh, lose not *that!* For, if you gain the whole world, it will not recompense you for such a loss. Lose what you will, but lose not your soul, I pray you!

Besides, once more, if you do not come to Christ, it will imply the greatest insult that you can put upon your Maker. You have already grieved him by breaking his laws; but what will be his indignation when you refuse his mercy? When you turn your back on his Son, when you refuse not only your God, but your crucified Saviour, hanging there with outstretched arms, bleeding his life away, that he may save you? Trample not upon the blood of Christ; but you will do so if you refuse his great salvation. If you will not come to him to be saved, you have as good as said that you will be damned rather than be loved by God—that you will be damned rather than be saved through Jesus Christ his Son.

Having said so much by way of preface, I am now going to take these words, "*I cannot come*," and handle them a little with the hope that you may grow ashamed of them.

First, this man declared, "I cannot come," because he said, "I HAVE MARRIED A WIFE." He had promised to come to the supper, and he was bound to fulfil his promise. Why did he want to get married just then? Surely, he had not been compelled to marry all in a hurry, so that he could not keep engagements already made. He was bound to keep his promise to the maker of the feast; and that promise was claimed of him by the messenger. He could not say that his wife would not let him come. Such a declaration might be true in England; but in the East the men are always masters of the situation, and women seldom bear rule in the family. No Oriental would say that his wife would not let him come. Nor in these Western regions, where the woman more nearly gains her rights, can any man truthfully say that his wife will not allow him to be a Christian. I do not believe that any of you will be able to say, when you come to die, that your wife was responsible for your not being a Christian. Most men would be angry if we told them that they were hen-pecked, and could not call their souls their own. He must be a fool, indeed, who would let a woman lead him down to hell against his will. The fact is, a man is a mean creature when he tries to throw the blame of his sin upon his wife.

I know that Father Adam set us a bad example in that respect; but the fact that this was a part of the sin which caused the ruin of our race should act as a beacon to us. You certainly, as a man, ought not to demean yourself so much as to say, "I cannot come, for my wife will not let me." If one of you, however, continues to whine "My wife is my ruin. I am unable to be a Christian because of my wife," I must ask you a question or two before I believe your pitiable story. Do you let her rule you in everything else? Does she keep you at home of an evening? Does she pick all your companions for you? Why, my dear man, if I am not much mistaken, you are a self-willed, cross-grained, pig-headed animal about everything else; and then, when it comes to the matter of religion, you turn round, and whine about being governed by your wife! I have no patience with you. You know that the blame lies with yourself alone; if you wished to seek the best things, the little woman at home would be no hindrance to you.

This man said, "*I cannot come.*" Why? Because he had a

wife! Strange plea! For surely that was a reason why he should come, and bring her with him. If any man, unhappily, has a wife opposed to the things of God, instead of saying, "I cannot be a Christian, for I have an unconverted wife," he should seek for double grace that he may win his wife to Christ. If a woman laments that she has an unconverted husband, let her live the nearer to God that she may save her husband.

I remember hearing Mr. Jay tell a story about a Nonconformist servant-girl, who went to live in a family of worldly people who attended the Church of England, although they were not real believers. They were outside buttresses of the church, and they had very little to do with the inside of it; and outsiders are generally the most bigoted. They were very angry with their servant for going to the little meeting-house and threatened to discharge her if she went again. But she went all the same, and very kindly but firmly assured them that she must continue to do so. At last she received notice to go: they could not, as good Church-people, have a Dissenter living with them. She took their rough dismission very patiently; and it came to pass that, the day before she was to leave her situation, a conversation took place somewhat of this sort. The master said, "It is a pity, after all, that Jane should go. We never had such a good girl. She is very industrious, truthful, and attentive." The wife said, "Well, I have thought that it is hardly the thing to send her away for going to her chapel. You always speak up for religious liberty, and it does not look quite like religious liberty to turn our girl away for worshipping God according to her conscience. I am sure she is a deal more careful about her religion than we are about ours." So they talked it over, and they said, "She has never answered us pertly, nor found fault with us about our going to church. Her religion is a greater comfort to her than ours is to us. We had better let her stay with us, and go where she likes." "Yes," said the husband, "and I think we had better go and hear the minister that she goes to hear. Evidently she has got something that we have not got. Instead of sending her away for going to chapel, we will go with her next Sunday, and judge the matter for ourselves." And they did, and the master and mistress were not long before they were members of that same church. Do not say, therefore, "I cannot come, because my master and mistress object to it." Do not make idle excuses out of painful facts which are reasons why you should be more determined than ever, even if you have to go to heaven alone, that you will be a follower of Christ. Keep to your resolve, and you may entertain the hope and belief that you will lead others to the Saviour's feet.

A second reason is even more common. It is not everybody who can say, "I have married a wife"; but everywhere you can meet with a person who pleads, "I HAVE NO TIME." You say, "Sir, I cannot attend to religion, for I have no time." I remember hearing an old lady say to a man who said that he had no time, "Well, you have got all the time there is." I thought that it was a very conclusive answer. You have had the time, and you still have all the time there is—why do you not use it? Nobody has more than twenty-four hours in a day, and you have no less. You have no time? That is very singular! What have you done with it? You certainly have had it! Time flies with you, I know, but so it does with me, and with everybody. What do you do with it? You have robbed God of that part of time which was due to him, and you have given up to some inferior thing what your great Lord and Master could rightly claim for the highest purposes.

You have time enough for common things. You have time to dress your bodies, and no time to dress your souls with the robe of Christ's righteousness? Do not tell me that! I do not meet any one of our friends saying, towards evening, "I am ready to faint, for I have had nothing to eat since I got up. I have had no time to get a morsel of meat." No, no, they have had their breakfast, and they have had their dinner, and so on. "Oh, yes, we have time to eat," says one. Do you tell me that you have time to feed your bodies, and that God has not given you time in which to feed your souls? People find time to look in the glass, and wash their faces, and brush their hair. Have you no time whatever to look at yourself, to see your spiritual spots, and to wash in the fountain that is open for sin and for uncleanness?

You have no time? How much do many of us spend in silly talk? How much time do certain persons spend in frivolous amusements? I have heard people say that they have no time, when I am sure I do not know what they can have to occupy them. They are living without an object—purposeless, aimless lives; and yet they talk about not having time! Such pretences will not do.

You have no time, and yet you undertake more secular work. You keep a shop, do you not? "Yes, I have a large shop." You are going to enlarge it, are you not? Will you have time, do you think, to attend to it when the business grows? "Oh, yes, I dare say that I shall find time: at any rate, I must make time, somehow or other." You are going to take a second shop, are you not? How will you manage it? "Oh, I shall find time." Yes, you can find time for all those enlargements, and speculations, and engagements; let me be plain with you and say that you could find time for thought about your soul if you had a mind to do so. To plead that you have no time for religion is a fraud. It is lying unto God to say that you have no time. When a man wants to do a thing, if he has no time, he makes time. "Where there's a will there's a way." Where there is a heart to religion there is plenty of time for it.

Besides, time is not the great matter. Did the Lord demand of you a month's retirement from business? Did we command you to spend two days in a week in prayer? Did we tell you that you could not be saved unless you shut yourself up an hour every morning for meditation? I would to God you could have an hour for meditation! But, if you cannot, who has demanded it of you? The command is that you believe on the Lord Jesus Christ, and forsake your sin; and this is a matter which will not interfere with your daily work.

A man can turn the potter's wheel, and pray. A man can lay bricks, and pray. A man can drive the plane, and pray. A man can walk behind a plough, and yet he can be walking with God. A woman can scrub a floor, and commune with God. A man can be riding on horseback, and yet he can still be in communion with the Most High. A woman can be making the beds, and growing in grace. It is not a matter in which time comes in so much as to interfere with any of the ordinary duties of life. Therefore throw away that excuse, and do not say any longer, "I cannot come because I have no time." At once repent of sin, and believe in the Lord Jesus; and then all your time will be free for the service of the Lord, and yet you will have not a moment the less for the needful duties of your calling.

There is a third form of this excuse, and a very common one: "I HAVE MORE IMPORTANT THINGS TO DO." Now, come! I shall contradict you flatly. *You have nothing more important to do.* That would be utterly impossible. Nothing under heaven can be of one-hundredth part of the importance of your being reconciled to God, and saved through Jesus Christ. What is that more important business? To make money? Where is the importance of that? You may get a pile of it, and the net result will be greater care, and the more to leave when you die. But you tell me you must have an opportunity for study. Well, that is better; but what are you going to study? Science? Art? Politics? Are these important as compared with the saving of your soul? Why, if you have an educated mind, and it is lost, it will be as bad to lose it in culture and learning as to lose it in ignorance. Your first duty is to be right with your God, who made you. Has Christ redeemed you? Rest not till you know the truth of that redemption by being reconciled to God through the death of his Son. Nothing can be so important to a man as to be pardoned through the Saviour, and changed by the power of the Holy Spirit from an enemy of God into a friend of God.

"Oh!" say you, "but my business occupies so much of my time." Yes; but do you not know that very likely your business would go on better if you were right with God? In a little church on the Italian mountains I saw, amongst many absurd daubings, one picture which struck me. There was a ploughman who had turned aside at a certain hour to pray. The rustic artist drew him upon his knees before the opened heavens; and, lest there should be any waste of time occasioned by his devotion, an angel was going on with the ploughing for him. I like the idea. I do not think an angel ever did go on with a man's ploughing while he was praying, but I think that the same result often comes to pass, and that when we give our hearts to God, and seek first the Kingdom of God and his righteousness, all these things are added unto us.

I have heard some use the excuse "I CANNOT AFFORD TO BE A CHRISTIAN." Well, let us have a talk about *that.* Cost you more than you can afford? What do you mean? What cost? Cost you money? It need not. It will cost you no more than you like to spend upon it with a glad heart. God will give you a generous spirit, which will make you love to support his cause, and to help the poor, and contribute your share to all Christian mission work. But in the Kingdom of Christ there is no taxation. Giving becomes a gratification, liberality a luxury. Nothing will be dragged from you by force. Surely, our God abhors money that comes into his exchequer by anything but the freewill offerings of loving hearts. It will not cost you much in that way, I am sure, for you are only to give as God has prospered you.

Will you pay as much in a year to hear the Gospel as many pay for one night at the play? Ay, and do not many at a horse-race spend a hundred times more than they ever gave throughout their whole existence either to the poor or to the Church of God? What you will save by holy, gracious, thrifty habits, will render this no loss to you, but a gain.

"Oh, but I meant that I could not afford it, for I should have to lose several friends." Is that friend worth keeping who is an enemy to God? The woman who would lead you away from God, or the man who would keep you out of heaven—are friends of that sort worth having?

"Oh," says one, "but I mean that I should lose so much in trade." Ah, well! I will not ask you to explain what you mean by that; for there is an ugly look about that statement. You know more about your trade than I do. No doubt there are trades which pander to the vices of men, and become all the more profitable in proportion to the growth of drunkenness and impurity. These must be given up. Moreover, there are traders who live by puffery, and lying, and cheating; and I do not recommend you to profess to be a Christian if that is your line of things. It is better to give up all profession of religion when you go in for unrighteous gain. What? Did I hear a hint about adulteration? Did I also hear that you do not give full weight and true measure? Ah, give up that game at once, whether you become a Christian or not; but certainly, if that is what you mean, the loss of dishonest profits will be a great gain to you, both for this life and the next.

"Well," says one, "I should have to give up a good many pleasures." Pleasures which block the road to heaven ought to be given up at once. You may think me a very melancholy sort of person; but I fancy that I am about as happy as any man in

England. I appreciate a merry thought and a cheerful speech as much as anybody. I can laugh, and I can enjoy good, clean, humorous remarks as well as most people; and I bear my witness that I have never had to relinquish a single pleasure for which I have felt a deliberate desire. As soon as you are renewed in heart, you are changed in your pleasures; and that which might have been a pleasure once to you would then be a misery. If I had to sit in some people's company, and hear what some people talk about, it would be hell to me. You will lose no pleasure if you come to Christ.

I hear one other person say, "I cannot come." Why not? "Well, sir, I do not mean that I shall not come one of these days; but IT WOULD NOT BE CONVENIENT JUST NOW. I could not yield my heart to the Lord just now." No; I know. You have an engagement to-morrow which must be attended to, but it would not be quite the thing for a Christian. Just so. It would not be convenient just now, nor on Monday, nor will it be on Tuesday, depend upon it. Your anxious thoughts will have gone by then. It will not be convenient to be saved! You want to see a little "life," do you not? "Life" in London means death. "Oh, but just now I am only an apprentice!" Then at once be bound apprentice to Christ. "But I am a journeyman. When I get a little business of my own, then will be the time." Will it? Oh, that you would become a journeyman to Christ! "But I have associations just now that render it difficult." That is to say, God must wait your convenience. Is that the way the poor treat the doctors who receive patients gratis? Do they say, "Doctor, it is not convenient for me to call upon you before ten or eleven o'clock in the morning. It is not convenient for me to come to your house. I shall be glad to see you if you come to my house about half-past eleven in the evening." Would you send a message to a physician in the West End, that you will be pleased for him to attend to you for nothing if he will come at your time? "Oh," say you, "I should not think of insulting a doctor like that, if he is kind enough to attend to me for nothing." And yet you will insult your God! You mean that God is not worthy of your strength and health; but, when you are old and worn out, then you mean to sneak into heaven, and cheat the devil. It is dirt mean of you! I can say no better. Though the Lord is exceedingly gracious and merciful, yet, when men make up their minds to it that they will only give him the fag-end of life, it is small wonder that they die in their sins. What must God think of such treatment?

I have heard people say, "I cannot come, sir, for I CANNOT UNDERSTAND IT. I am a poor man, I never had any education." What is it that you cannot understand? Can you not understand that you have broken God's law, and that the just God must punish you for it? You can understand that. Can you not understand that, if you trust the Lord Jesus Christ, then it is certain that he took your sin, and bore it in his own body on the tree, and put your sin away, for his name is the "Lamb of God, which taketh away the sin of the world"? Can you not understand that, if you trust in him, you have him to stand in your room, and place, and stead; for the Scripture says, "He hath made him to be sin for us, who knew no sin; that we might be made the righteousness of God in him." You *can* understand it, if you wish to do so. There is nothing in the Gospel which the poorest and the least educated cannot understand if their minds be made willing to know and receive the truth. If the Spirit of God will come upon them, they cannot only understand the Gospel, but grasp it, and enjoy it, and begin to teach it to others, too; for the Lord makes the babes to have knowledge and discretion in his ways, while the wise and learned in scientific matters often miss the way to the eternal kingdom.

May I ask you to do another thing? If you still intend to say, "I cannot come," will you speak the truth now? Will you alter a word, and get nearer the truth? Say, "I will not come." "I cannot come," is Greek, or double Dutch; but the plain English is, "I WILL NOT COME." I wish you would say *that* rather than the other, because the recoil of saying, "I will not come: I will not believe in Jesus: I will not repent of sin: I will not turn from my wicked ways"—the recoil, I say, from that might be blessed by God to you to make you see your desperate state. I wish you would then cry, "I cannot sit down, and make my own damnation sure by saying that I will not come to Christ."

Will you now, instead of refusing to come, resolve to come at once? Say, "I will come to Jesus. Tell me how." You can only come to Christ by trusting him. Trust yourself with him, and he will save you. Never did anyone trust Jesus in vain.

XIV

ONE LOST SHEEP

"How think ye? if a man have an hundred sheep, and one
of them be gone astray, doth he not leave the ninety and nine,
and goeth into the mountains, and seeketh that which is gone
astray? And if so be that he find it, verily I say unto you, he
rejoiceth more of that sheep, than of the ninety and nine
which went not astray."—Matt. 18 : 12, 13.

THIS passage occurs in a discourse of our Saviour against
despising one of those little ones that believe in him. He fore -
tells a dreadful doom for those who, in their contempt for the
little ones, cause them to stumble ; and he forbids that contempt
by a variety of forcible arguments, upon which we cannot now
dwell. There is a tendency, apparent at this present time, to
think little of the conversion of individuals, and to look upon
the work of the Holy Spirit upon each separate person as much
too slow a business for this progressive age.

We hear grand theories of a theocracy of a kind unknown to
Holy Scripture: a semi-political dominion of the Lord over
masses wherein the individuals are unregenerate. We listen
to great swelling words about the uplifting of nations and the
advancement of the race ; but these lofty ideas do not produce
facts, nor have they any moral power. Our "cultured"
teachers, weary of the humdrum work of bringing individual
souls into light, pine to do it wholesale, by a far more rapid
process than that of personal salvation. They are tired of the
units, their great minds dwell upon "the solidarity of the race."
I am bold to assert that, if ever we despise the method of
individual conversion, we shall get into an unsound order of
business altogether, and find ourselves wrecked upon the rocks
of hypocrisy. Even in those right glorious times when the
Gospel shall have the freest course, and shall run the most
quickly, and be the most extensively glorified, its progress will
still be after the former manner of the conviction, conversion,

and sanctification of individuals, who shall each one believe and be baptized, according to the Word of the Lord.

I fear lest in any of you there should be even the least measure of despising the one lost sheep, because of the large and philosophical methods which are now so loudly cried up. If the wanderers are to be brought in in vast numbers, as I pray they may be, yet must it be accomplished by the bringing of them in one by one. To attempt national regeneration without personal regeneration is to dream of erecting a house without separate bricks. Let us settle it in our minds that we cannot do better than obey the example of our Lord Jesus, given us in the text, and go after the one sheep which has gone astray.

Our text warns us that *we are not to despise one person, even on account of evil character.* The first temptation is to despise *one*, because only one; the next is to despise one, because that one is so little; the next, and perhaps the most dangerous, form of the temptation, is to despise one, because that one has gone astray. The individual is not in the right path, not obeying law, nor reflecting credit on the church, but doing much that vexes the spiritual and grieves the holy; yet we are not, therefore, to despise him. Read the eleventh verse: "The Son of man is come to save that which was lost." In the Greek, the word "lost" is a very strong word: we may read it, "that which is destroyed." It does not mean "that which is non-existent," as you will clearly see; but that which is destroyed as to usefulness to the shepherd, as to happiness to itself, and as to working out the intent for which it was created. If any are so effectually destroyed by sin that their existence is a greater calamity than their non-existence would have been; if they are now dead in trespasses and sins, and even offensive in character; yet must we not despise them. The Son of man did not despise such, since "He has come to seek and to save that which was lost." Many a soul that has been so destroyed as to be lost to itself, lost to God, lost to his people, lost to anything like hope and holiness, the Lord Jesus Christ has saved by his gracious power. *He values each one;* this is the lesson which I would teach to the utmost of my power. May the Holy Spirit teach it also.

First, then, in the words before us, OUR SAVIOUR SHOWS PECULIAR INTEREST IN ONE LOST SOUL.

Note, in the commencement, that for the sake of those lost ones *our Lord assumes a special character*. The eleventh verse puts it, "The Son of man is come to save that which was lost." He was not originally known as "the Son of man," but as "the Son of God." Before all worlds, he dwelt in the bosom of the Father, and "thought it not robbery to be equal with God." But in order to redeem men, the Son of the Highest became "the Son of man." He was born of the Virgin, and by birth inherited the innocent infirmities of our nature, and bore the sufferings incident to those infirmities. Then did he also take upon himself our sin and its penalty, and therefore died upon the Cross. He was in all points made like unto his brethren. He could not be the Shepherd of men without becoming like to them, and therefore the Word condescended to be made flesh. Behold the stupendous miracle of Incarnation! Nothing can excel this marvel—Immanuel, God with us! "Being found in fashion as a man, he became obedient unto death, even the death of the cross" (Phil. 2: 8). O lost one, conscious of your loss, take heart to-day when the name of Jesus is named in your hearing; he is God, but he is man, and as God-and-man he saves his people from their sins.

Next, to show how Jesus values one lost soul, he *makes a very wonderful descent*. "The Son of man is come." He was always known as "The Coming One"; but as to the salvation of the lost he has actually come. For judgment he is "The Coming One" still; but for salvation we rejoice that our Saviour has already come. Quitting the assemblies of the perfect, he has been here as the Friend of publicans and sinners. From being the Lord of angels, he has stooped to be "a Man of Sorrows, and acquainted with grief." Yes, he has come; and not in vain. Those who preached the coming Saviour had such a joyous message to deliver that their feet were beautiful upon the mountains, and their voices were as heavenly music; but as for us who preach that he has come, and, coming, has finished the work which he undertook to perform—surely ours is the choicest of messages. Our Lord Jesus has completed the atoning sacrifice, and the justifying righteousness, by which lost men are saved: happy is the preacher of such tidings, and blessed are your ears that hear them! The good Shepherd has performed all that is necessary for the salvation of the flock which his

Father has given into his hands. Beloved, let us take heart. Lost as we are, Christ has come to save us. He has come to the place of our ruin and woe. His coming and seeking will not be in vain. How greatly ought we to value the souls of men when Jesus for their sake becomes a man, and comes into this sinful world among our guilty race that he may work the salvation of the lost!

Note, here, that *he does this for those that are still straying.* I have marked, in looking at the Greek text, that it is written, "He seeketh that which goeth astray." The Shepherd seeks while the sheep strays: seeks it because it strays and needs seeking. Full many of the Lord's redeemed are even now going astray, and even now is the Shepherd going after them. The Saviour seeks those who are even now sinning. That he should have a love to those who are repenting I can well understand; but that he should care for those who are wilfully going astray is far more gracious. Jesus seeks those whose backs are towards him, who are going further and further away from the fold; herein is grace most free, most full, most sovereign. Indeed it is so. Though thou dost harden thyself against the Lord, though thou dost refuse to turn at his rebuke, yet if thou be his redeemed, his eye of love marks thee; in all thy wilful wanderings he follows thee. He sees thee, he seeks thee; oh that thou mayest yield, and find that he saves thee! O ye that are now in the flock, think of the love of Christ to you when you were outside the fold; when you had no wish to return; when, seeing him pursuing you, you only ran the faster to escape his almighty love! Let us sing together,

> *Determined to save, he watched o'er my path,*
> *When, Satan's blind slave, I sported with death.*

Notwithstanding all my rebellion, and all my wilful transgression, he still loved me with his heart, and pursued me with his Word. Oh, how we ought to love sinners, since Jesus loved us, and died for us while we were yet sinners! We must care for drunkards while they still pass round the cup; swearers even while we hear them swear; and profligates while we mourn to see them polluting our midnight streets. We must not wait till we see some better thing in them, but feel an intense interest for them for what they are—straying and lost.

The shepherd takes a peculiar interest in the lost, not only as now straying, but as *having already gone very far away.* Carefully consider these words—"If so be that he find it." That "if" tells its own tale. The sheep had become so terribly lost that it was not likely to be found again: it had wandered into so dense a thicket, or strayed into so wild a region, that it seemed scarcely within the bounds of hope that it would ever be discovered and brought back. We do not often meet with an "if" in reference to the work of Christ; but here is one— "If so be that he find it." This does not show weakness in the Shepherd, but the desperate danger of the sheep. I have often heard it said, by those who come to confess Christ and to acknowledge his love to them, that they are struck with wonder that they, above all others, should be doing any such thing. When we sit at the Lord's table, the feast is very wonderful; but the greatest wonder is the Guest, when I am there. But it is so. The good Shepherd is to-day seeking many whose salvation seems highly improbable, if not utterly impossible. Herein is love that he should go after those whose finding is by no means a certainty, nor even a probability!

Moreover, those toward whom our Lord has these thoughts of love have often sinned so as to have *brought themselves into the deadliest danger.* "For the Son of man is come *to save* that which was lost." Saving implies ruin, peril, jeopardy—yea, destruction already in a measure present. Are not many now playing with the fire of hell? For what is that unquenchable fire but sin, in its nature and results? Playing with edged tools is nothing in danger compared with sporting with your lusts; and many are doing so. Yet, despite their danger, Jesus seeks them. If you be but one inch this side of hell, love will pursue you, and mercy will follow you.

If we rightly consider the parable before us, we shall see that *he takes a special interest in these stray sheep because they are his own.* This man did not go after wild beasts, nor after other men's sheep; but he had a hundred sheep of his own, and when he had counted them, he missed one. The hireling, whose own the sheep are not, would have said, "We have nearly the hundred: we need not be particular about an odd one." But these hundred sheep belonged to the Shepherd himself; they were his own by choice, by inheritance, by divine gift, by glorious capture, and by costly purchase, and he could not accept ninety and nine for a hundred. "None of them is lost," saith he. "Those that thou gavest me I have kept, and none of them is lost, but the son of perdition; that the Scripture might be fulfilled" (John 17: 12). Ninety-nine is not a hundred, and the Saviour will not consider it such; for well he knows that "it is not the will of your Father which is in heaven, that one of these little ones should perish" (Matt. 18: 14). Since Jesus takes such an interest even in one stray soul, you must not think it little that you should be called to care for a single soul. Value one soul more than a world's purchase.

Secondly, may the Spirit of God help me while I remind you that OUR LORD PUT FORTH SPECIAL EXERTION TO SAVE ONE SOLITARY INDIVIDUAL.

Observe in the parable—for it is a parable, though briefly told—that we see the Shepherd *leaving happier cares.* He felt himself at home with his attached and faithful flock; they had not gone astray, and they gathered about him, and he fed them, and took pleasure in them. There is always a great deal to do with sheep: they have many diseases, many weaknesses, many needs; but when you have an attached, affectionate flock about you, you feel at home with them. So the great Shepherd describes himself as leaving the ninety and nine, his choice flock, the sheep that had fellowship with him, and he with them. Yes, he leaves those in whom he could take pleasure, to seek one that gave him pain. I will not dwell upon how he left the paradise above, and all the joy of his Father's house, and came to this bleak world; but I pray you remember that he did so. It was a wonderful descent when he came from beyond the stars to dwell on this beclouded globe, to redeem the sons of men. But, remember, he still continually comes by his Spirit. His errands of mercy are perpetual. The Spirit of God moves his ministers, who are Christ's representatives, to forego the feeding of the gathered flock, and to seek, in their discourses, the salvation of the wandering ones, in whose character and behaviour there is nothing to cheer us. He would not have his Church expend all her care on the flock which he has led into her green pastures, but he would have her go afield after those who are not yet in her blest society.

According to the text, the Shepherd goes into the mountains:

among difficulties and dangers. He will do and dare for the saving of the lost: no hardships can daunt his mighty love. A sheep in the East is more light of foot than our sheep; it will leap like a gazelle, and climb the mountains like a chamois; and so are sinners very swift in transgression, and very daring in presumption. They leap in their iniquities where the children of God would shudder to follow them even in thought. They make nothing of leaps of profanity which would curdle the blood of him that has been taught the fear of God at the feet of Jesus Christ. Yet the Lord Jesus went after these desperadoes. What difficulties he conquered, what sufferings he endured, what mountains he overleaped, that he might seek and save! The same heart is in him still: he goes forth continually in the preaching of the Word. With many a sigh and many a groan on the part of his chosen ministers, he goes among the mountains to seek that which has gone astray.

To show his exertion for the lost, our Lord describes himself as *seeking with persevering diligence.* Possibly the lost sheep is in yonder gully! It is a long way to go, but he is so intent on his purpose that he is soon there; but the sheep is not to be seen. Where can it be? He travels on with swift foot, for he does not know what may become of his sheep while he delays. Every now and then he stops: he thinks he hears a bleating. Surely it is the voice of his sheep! He is mistaken. His love makes his ear the father of sounds which are not sounds at all. He has neither seen nor heard it these long hours; but he will continue seeking till he finds it. The concentrated omniscience of Christ is set upon a soul that goes astray, looking after it in all its evil desires and evil emotions; watching the growth of anything that looks like repentance; and observing with sorrow the hardening of its heart.

At the last he saves—completely saves. He has not come to make the salvation of his people possible, but to save them. He has not come to put them in the way of saving themselves, but to save them. He has not come to half save them, but to save them altogether. When my Lord comes forth in the majesty of his sovereign grace to save a soul, he achieves his purpose, despite sin, and death, and hell. The wolf may grind his teeth, but the Shepherd is the wolf's master. The sheep itself may for a long time have wandered, and at the last may struggle against him; but he grips its feet, and throws the creature on his shoulders, and bears it home; for he is resolved to save it. The sheep is glad to be so borne, for with a touch the Shepherd moulds its will to his more perfect will. His grace is the triumphant energy by which the lost one is restored.

Notice, in the third place, that our Lord FEELS A SPECIAL REJOICING AT THE RECOVERY OF A WANDERING SHEEP. Do not make a mistake here. Do not suppose that our Lord loves more the one soul that has wandered than the ninety and nine who have been preserved by his grace from going astray. Oh, no! he thinks ninety-nine times more of ninety-nine than of one; for his sheep are each one equally precious to him. We must not suppose that he looks upon any one soul of his redeemed with a tenderness ninety-nine times greater than he gives to another. But you will see the meaning of the passage by an illustration from your own experience. You have a family, and you love all your children alike. But little Johnny is very ill; he has a fever, and is like to die: now you think more of him than of all the rest. He recovers, and you bring him downstairs in your arms, and just then he is the dearest child of the whole company. Not that he is really more valued than his brothers and sisters, but the fact that he has been so ill and was likely to die, has brought him more before your mind and caused you more anxiety, and therefore you have more joy in him because of his recovery. The great deeps of Christ's love are the same to all his flock, but on the surface there is sometimes a holy storm of joy when any one of them has been newly restored after wandering.

Learn the occasion of this demonstrative joy. The wandering one has caused great sorrow. Our Lord is still more grieved than we are. In proportion to the sorrow felt over the wanderer, is the joy manifested when he is restored. Moreover, great apprehensions were aroused; we feared that he was not the Lord's, and that he would go back into perdition. We trembled for him. That black dread is all over now: the sheep is safe, the doubtful one is saved and restored to the fold.

Besides, the Shepherd rejoices when he brings back the lost sheep because *he makes that rescue an occasion and opportunity for having a special gala day.* He wishes all his sheep to learn his delight in them all by seeing his delight in one. I know it is so in the Church. I bless the Lord when he keeps the feet of his saints: I bless him every day for preserving grace; but, when some grievous wanderer is restored, then we bless him more emphatically. Then we have music and dancing. The elder brother wonders what these overflowing joys can mean: but everybody else can see good reason for special mirth when the lost one is found. Shepherds and their flocks cannot have holiday every day; but, when a lost one has been recovered, they feel such mutual delight in each other, and such a common delight in the saving of the lost, that they seize upon the occasion for rejoicing. I want you all to recognize that, if you love the Church of Christ, you are bound to keep a feast-day when fallen ones are raised up; and, that you may hold that festival, you are bound to put out all your strength to bring in the lost one.

Now we come to the tug-of-war, that is, to look upon our divine Shepherd as HE SETS US A STRIKING EXAMPLE.

We may view this text as *our personal missionary warrant.* We arc all of us to be missionaries for Christ, and the text presents a warrant for each one to work earnestly as a soul-winner.

What shall we do, then, to imitate our Lord? The answer is— Let us *go after one* soul. I cannot make a selection for you now, but I do entreat all who are workers together with God to go after the ones. There is a kind of knack in speaking to individuals; everybody does not possess it, but every believer should labour to acquire it. Seek the souls of men one by one. It is far easier work to me to speak to you all than it would be to take each one apart and speak to him personally of his soul; and yet such speaking to you one by one might be more successful than this sermon to you in the mass. I entreat you, as the great Shepherd goes after one, do not think you will demean yourself by going after one poor man, or woman, or child; but do it now.

Listen again: *let that one be somebody that is quite out of the way.* Try and think of one who has grievously gone astray; it may be there is one such in your family, or you meet with one such in the course of trade. Think carefully of that one soul, and reflect upon its sin and danger. You would like to pick out a hopeful case, in order that you might feel sure of success.

Take another course this time: seek the one which is going astray, and seems hopeless. Follow your Lord's example, and go after one who is the least likely to be found. Will you try this plan?

"I have a class and a work," says one. Yes, I want you, for a little, to *leave the ninety and nine.* I pray that you may feel called to look after some one greatly depraved person, or some utterly neglected child. Keep up your ninety-and-nine class, if you possibly can, but, at all hazards, go after the one. Make an unusual effort; go out of your way; let ordinary service be placed second for the time being. It will be a healthy change for you, and, perhaps, a great relief. You are getting a little mouldy; and you are just a wee tired of the monotony of your work. Every Sunday the same girls, or the same boys, and the same form of lesson. Well, cut the whole concern for a little, and go after the one sheep that has gone astray.

When you go after that one, *have all your wits about you.* Go and *seek*; and that you cannot do, unless you are on the alert. Follow up the straying one. Did you say that you would wait till he called at your house? Is that your notion of seeking lost sheep?

> *O come, let us go and find them,*
> *In the paths of death they roam.*

Go after them, for so the Shepherd did. He braved the mountain's slippery side. I do not suppose the Shepherd had any greater love for mountain tracks than you have; but up the rough tracks he climbed, for the sheep's sake. Go after sinners into their poverty and wretchedness, until you find them.

Here is one thing to cheer you. If you should win such a soul as that, *you will have more joy, a great deal, than in saving those for whom you regularly labour*—more joy over that lost one than over the ninety and nine hopeful ones. It will be such a support to your faith, such a fillip for your joy, such a bright light to your labour, to have won such a specially guilty one. Such converts are our crown of rejoicing. May I specially recommend that you make a trial of this extra sheep-seeking? If you do not succeed, you will have done no harm; for you will have copied your Lord and Master. But you will succeed, for he is with you, and his Spirit works by you.

When you know that people are very wicked, the usual plan is to wish them well, but keep out of their way. Prudence makes you hide yourself from them. The whole street may swarm with harlots, but then you have gone to bed, and the door is shut. What has their sin to do with you? There are many drunken men about; but you do not drink to excess, what has their drinking to do with you? That is what is meant by hiding ourselves from them. How easily that can be done!

Take an illustration which is worth the telling. A vessel was crossing the Atlantic, and it fell in with that disabled emigrant ship, *The Danmark*. Suppose the captain had kept on his course. He might have looked another way, and resolved not to be detained. He might have argued, "I am bound to do the best for my owners. It will hinder me greatly if I go pottering about after this vessel. I had better go by, and not see it; or make haste to port and send out help." It could have been done, and nobody would have been the wiser; for the ship would have gone down soon. The captain of that vessel was a man of a nobler breed. He did not hide himself, nor turn the blind eye towards the vessel in distress. But what did the captain do? All honour to him, he came near, and took the ship in tow. This was not all: he found that she could not keep afloat, and he resolved to take those hundreds of emigrants on board his own ship. But he could not carry them and his cargo too. What then? The decision was greatly to his honour. Overboard goes the cargo! God's blessing rest on the man! Into the sea went the freight, and the passengers were taken on board, and carried to the nearest port.

He could have easily hidden himself, could he not? So can you, you Christian people, as you call yourselves. Can you go through this world and always have a blind eye to the case of lost sinners? Will you let them go to hell unwarned and uninstructed? Can you hide yourselves from them! How dare you call yourselves Christians? How will you answer for it at last? Brothers, sisters, let us shake off this inhuman indifference, and deny ourselves rest, ease, credit, that we may save poor sinking souls. Overboard with cargo cheerfully, that you may, in the power of the Holy Ghost, save souls from death.

Once more, this text is *the great missionary warrant for all the Church of God*. We are to go, as the Saviour did, to seek and to save that which was lost; and we are to do this, not on account of the numbers of the heathen, but for one of them. I grant you there is a great power in the argument of numbers—so many hundreds of millions in China, so many hundreds of millions in India; but, if there were only one person left un-saved in any part of the world, it would be worth while for the entire Christian Church to go after that one person; for he who is greater than the Church, as the Bridegroom is greater than the bride, quitted heaven, ay, and quitted the sweet society of his own beloved, that he might go after the one that has gone astray. Do not care, therefore, about numbers: save the smallest tribes. Have an eye to the hamlets in England. I believe that the scattered cottages of our land are in a worse condition than the villages. Care for the ones. Your Lord did so, and here is your warrant for doing the like.

Next, notice, that we ought never to be moved by the sup-posed superiority of a race. I have heard it said that it would be far better to try and convert the superior races than to consider the more degraded. Is it not better to bring in the educated Brahmins than the wild hill-tribes? "What a fine sort of people these are, these philosophical Hindoos! If we could win them they would be worth converting!" That is not at all according to the mind of Christ. Let us feel that the degraded Africans, the dwarfs of the woods, the cannibals of New Guinea, and all such, are to be sought quite as much as more advanced races. They are men; that is enough.

The motive for missionary enterprise must never be the excellence of the character of the individuals. The Shepherd did not go after the sheep, because it never went astray, nor because it was docile, but because it did go astray, and was not docile. The sin of men is their claim upon the Church of God. The more sin, the more reason for abounding grace. Oh that the Church would feel it to be her duty, if not to go to the most degraded first, yet not to leave them to the last! Where you seem least likely to succeed there go at once, for there you will find room for faith; and where there is room for faith, and faith fills the room, God will send a blessing.

XV

THE PRODIGAL'S CLIMAX

"When he came to himself."—Luke 15: 17.

THERE are different stages in the sinner's history, and they are worth marking in the prodigal's experience. There is, first, the stage in which the young man sought independence of his father. The younger son said, "Father, give me the portion of goods that falleth to me." We know something of that state of mind; and, alas! it is a very common one. As yet there is no open profligacy, no distinct rebellion against God. Religious services are attended, the father's God is held in reverence; but in his heart the young man desires a supposed liberty, he wishes to cast off all restraint. Companions hint that he is too much tied to his mother's apron-string. He himself feels that there may be some strange delights which he has never enjoyed; and the curiosity of Mother Eve to taste the fruit of that tree which was good for food, and pleasant to the eyes, and a tree to be desired to make one wise, comes into the young man's mind, and he wishes to put forth his hand, and take the fruit of the tree of the knowledge of good and evil, that he may eat thereof.

He never intends to spend his substance in riotous living, but he would like to have the opportunity of spending it as he likes. He does not mean to be a profligate; still, he would like to have the honour of choosing what is right on his own account. At any rate, he is a man now; he feels his blushing honours full upon him, and he wants now to exercise his own freedom of will, and to feel that he himself is really his own master. Who, indeed, he asks, is Lord over him? Perhaps there are some to whom I am speaking who are just in such a state as that; if so, may the grace of God arrest you before you go any further away from him! May you feel that, to be out of gear with God, to wish to be separated from him and to have other interests than those of him who made you, must be dangerous, and probably will be fatal! Therefore now, even now, may you come to yourself at this earliest stage of your history, and also come to love and rejoice in God as the prodigal returned to his father!

Very soon, however, this young man in the parable entered upon quite another stage. He had received his portion of goods; all that he would have had at his father's death he had turned into ready money, and there it is. It is his own, and he may do what he pleases with it. Having already indulged his independent feeling towards his father and his wish to have a separate establishment altogether from him, he knew that he would be freer to carry out his plans if he was right away. Anywhere near his father there is a check upon him; he feels that the influence of his home somewhat clips his wings. If he could get into a far country, there he should have the opportunity to develop; and all that evolution could do for him he would have the opportunity of enjoying, so he gathers all together and goes into the far country.

It may be that I am addressing some who have reached that stage. Now there is all the delirium of self-indulgence. Now it is all gaiety, "a short life and a merry one," forgetting the long eternity and a woeful one. Now the cup is full, and the red wine sparkles in the bowl. As yet, it has not bitten you like a serpent, nor stung you like an adder, as it will do all too soon; but just now, it is the deadly sweetness that you taste, and the exhilaration of that drugged chalice that deceives you. You are making haste to enjoy yourself. Sin is a dangerous joy, beloved all the more because of the danger; for, where there is a fearful risk, there is often an intense pleasure to a daring heart; and you perhaps are one of that venturous band, spending your days in folly and your nights in riotousness.

Ere long there comes a third stage to the sinner as well as to the prodigal; that is when he has "spent all." We have only a certain amount of spending money after all. He who has gold without limit, yet has not health without limit; or, if health does not fail him in his sinning, yet desire fails, and satiety comes in, as it did with Solomon when he tried this way of seeking happiness. At last, there is no honey left, there is only the sting of the bee. At last, there is no sweetness in the cup, there is only the delirium that follows the intoxication. At last, the meat is eaten to the bone, and there is nothing good to come out of that bone; it contains no marrow, the teeth are broken with it, and the man wishes that he had never sat down to so terrible a feast. He has reached the stage at which the prodigal arrived when he had spent all. Oh, there be some who spend all their character, spend all their health and strength, spend all their hope, spend all their uprightness, spend everything that was worth having! They have spent all. This is another stage in the sinner's history, and it is very apt to lead to despair, and even deeper sin, and sometimes to that worst of sins which drives a man red-handed before the bar of his Maker to account for his own blood.

It is a dreadful state to be in, for there comes at the back of it a terrible hunger. There is a weary labour to get something that may stay the spirit, a descending to the degradation of feeding swine, a willingness to eat of the husks that swine do eat, yet an inability to do so. Many have felt this craving that cannot be satisfied. But, for my part, I am glad when "the rake's progress" has reached this point; for often, in the grace of God, it is the way home for the prodigal; it is a roundabout way, but it is the way home for him. When men have spent all, and poverty has followed on their recklessness, and sickness has come at the call of their vice, then it is that omnipotent grace has stepped in, and there has come another stage in the sinner's history, of which I am now going to speak, as God may help me. That is the point the prodigal had reached "when he came to himself."

Then, first, A SINNER IS BESIDE HIMSELF.

While he is living in his sin, he is out of his mind, he is beside himself. I am sure that it is so. There is nothing more like to madness than sin; and it is a moot point among those who study deep problems how far insanity and the tendency to sin go side by side, and whereabouts it is that great sin and entire loss of responsibility may touch each other. I do not intend to discuss that question at all; but I am going to say that every sinner is morally and responsibly insane, and therefore in a worse condition than if he were only mentally insane.

He is insane, first, because *his judgment is altogether out of order*. He makes fatal mistakes about all-important matters. He reckons a short time of this mortal life to be worth all his thoughts, and he puts eternity into the background. He considers it possible for a creature to be at enmity against the Creator, or indifferent to him, and yet to be happy. He fancies that he knows better what is right for him than the law of God declares. He dreams that the everlasting Gospel, which cost God the life of his own Son, is scarcely worthy of his attention at all, and he passes it by with contempt. He has unshipped the rudder of his judgment and steers towards the rocks with awful deliberation, and seems as if he would wish to know where he can find the surest place to commit eternal shipwreck. His judgment is out of order.

Further, *his actions are those of a madman.* This prodigal son, first of all, had interests apart from his father. He must have been mad to have conceived such an idea as that. For me to have interests apart from him who made me, and keeps me alive—for me, the creature of an hour, to fancy that I can have a will in opposition to the will of God, and that I can so live and prosper—why, I must be a fool! I must be mad to wish any such thing, for it is consistent with the highest reason to believe that he who yields himself up to omnipotent goodness must be in the track of happiness, but that he who sets himself against the almighty grace of God must certainly be kicking against the pricks to his own wounding and hurt. Yet this sinner does not see that it is so, and the reason is that he is beside himself.

Then, next, that young man went away from his home, though it was the best home in all the world. We can judge that from the exceeding tenderness and generosity of the father at the head of it, and from the wonderful way in which all the servants had such entire sympathy with their master. It was a happy home, well stored with all that the son could need; yet he quits it to go he knows not whither, among strangers who did not care a straw for him, and who, when they had drained his purse, would not give him even a penny with which to buy bread to save him from starving. The prodigal must have been mad to act like that; and for any of us to leave him who has been the dwelling-place of his saints in all generations, to quit the warmth and comfort of the Church of God which is the home of joy and peace, is clear insanity. Anyone who does this is acting against his own best interests, he is choosing the path of shame and sorrow, he is casting away all true delight; he must be mad.

You can see that this young man is out of his mind, because, when he gets into the far country, he begins spending his money riotously. He does not lay it out judiciously, he spends his money for that which is not bread, and his labour for that which satisfieth not; and that is just what the sinner does. If he be self-righteous, he is trying to weave a robe out of the worthless material of his own works; and, if he be a voluptuary, given up to sinful indulgence, what vanity it is for him to hope for pleasure in the midst of sin! Should I expect to meet with angels in the sewers, with heavenly light in a dark mine? Nay, these are not places for such things as those; and can I rationally look for joy to my heart from revelling, chambering, wantonness, and such conduct? If I do, I must be mad. Oh, if men were but rational—and they often wrongly suppose that they are—if they were but rational beings, they would see how irrational it is to sin!

Further, the prodigal was a fool, he was mad, for he spent all. He did not even stop half way on the road to penury, but he went on till he had spent all. There is no limit to those who have started in a course of sin. He that stays back from it, by God's grace, may keep from it; but it is with sin as it is with the intoxicating cup. One said to me, "I can drink much, or I can drink none; but I have not the power to drink a little, for if I begin I cannot stop myself, and may go to any length." So is it with sin, God's grace can keep you abstaining from sin; but, if you begin sinning, oh, how one sin draws on another! One sin is the decoy or magnet for another sin, and draws it on; and one cannot tell, when he begins to descend this slippery slide, how quickly and how far he may go. Thus the prodigal spent all in utter recklessness; and, oh, the recklessness of some young sinners whom I know! And, oh, the greater recklessness of some old sinners who seem resolved to be damned, for, having but a little remnant of life left, they waste that last fragment of it in fatal delay!

Then it was, when the prodigal had spent all, that he still further proved his madness. That would have been the time to go home to his father; but, apparently, that thought did not occur to him. "He went and joined himself to a citizen of that country," still overpowered by the fascination that kept him away from the one place where he might have been happy; and that is one of the worst proofs of the madness of some of you who frequent these courts, that, though you know about the great God and his infinite mercy, and know somewhat of how much you need him and his grace, yet you still try to get what you want somewhere else, and do not go back to him.

I shall not have time to say much more upon this point, but I must remind you that, like sinners, *the prodigal had the ways of a madman.* I have had, at times, to deal with those whose reason has failed them, and I have noticed that many of them have been perfectly sane, and even wise and clever, on all points except one. So is it with the sinner. He is a famous politician; just hear him talk. He is a wonderful man of business; see how sharply he looks after every penny. He is very judicious in everything but this, he is mad on one point, he has a fatal monomania, for it concerns his own soul.

A madman will often conceal his madness from those round about him; so will a sinner hide his sin. You may talk with this man about morals, and you may watch him very closely; yet you may be a long time before you can find him out, and be able to say to him, "One thing thou lackest." Perhaps, on a sudden, you touch that weak point, and there he stands fully developed before you, far gone in his insanity. He is right enough elsewhere, but with regard to his soul his reason is gone.

Mad people do not know that they have been mad till they are cured; they think that they alone are wise, and all the rest are fools. Here is another point of their resemblance to sinners, for they also think that everybody is wrong except themselves. Hear how they will abuse a pious wife as "a fool." What hard words they will use towards a gracious daughter! How they will rail at the ministers of the Gospel, and try to tear God's Bible to pieces! Poor mad souls, they think all are mad except themselves! We, with tears, pray God to deliver them from their delusions, and to bring them to sit at the feet of Jesus, clothed, and in their right minds.

Sometimes, the sinner will be seen and known to be mad because he turns on his best friends, as madmen do. Those whom they otherwise would have loved the most they reckon to be their worst enemies. So God, who is man's best Friend, is most despised, and Christ, who is the Friend of sinners, is rejected, and the most earnest Christians are often the most avoided or persecuted by sinners.

Mad people sometimes, too, will rave, and then you know what dreadful things they will say. So is it with sinners when their fits are on them. I dare not speak of what they will do and what they will say. They often pull themselves up, afterwards, and feel ashamed to think that they should have gone so far; yet so it is, for they are beside themselves, even as the prodigal was.

Secondly, IT IS A BLESSED THING WHEN THE SINNER COMES TO HIMSELF: "When he came to himself." This is the first mark of grace working in the sinner as it was the first sign of hope for the prodigal.

Sometimes, *this change occurs suddenly*. I was greatly charmed by meeting with one to whom this happened. It was an old-fashioned sort of conversion, with which I was delighted. There came into this building a man who had not for a long time gone to any place of worship. He despised such things; he could swear, and drink, and do worse things still, he was careless, godless; but he had a mother who often prayed for him, and he had a brother also whose prayer has never ceased for him. He did not come here to worship, he came just to see the preacher whom his brother had been hearing for so many years; but, coming in, somehow he was no sooner in the place than he felt that he was unfit to be here, so he went up into the top gallery, as far back as he could, and, when some friend beckoned him to take a seat, he felt that he could not do so, he must just lean against the wall at the back. Someone else invited him to sit down, but he could not; he felt that he had no right to do so; but when the preacher announced his text— "And the publican, standing afar off, would not lift up so much as his eyes unto heaven, but smote upon his breast, saying, God be merciful to me a sinner;"—and said something like this, "You that stand farthest off in the Tabernacle, and dare not sit down because you feel your guilt to be so great, you are the man to whom God has sent me this morning, and he bids you come to Christ and find mercy," a miracle of love was wrought. Then, "he came to himself," as he will tell us at the Church-Meeting, when he comes forward to confess his faith.

I rejoiced greatly when I heard of it, for in his case there is a change that everybody who knows him can see. He has become full of a desire after everything that is gracious as once he practised everything that was bad. Now that is what sometimes happens, and why should it not happen again now? Why should not some other man, or some woman, come to himself, or to herself now? This is the way home, first to come to yourself, and then to come to your God. "He came to himself."

On the other hand, sometimes *this change is very gradual.* I need not dwell upon that, but there are many who have their eyes opened by degrees. They first see men as trees walking; afterwards, they see all things clearly. So long as they do but come to themselves, and come to the Saviour, I mind not how they come. Some conversions are sudden, some gradual; but in every case, if it be the work of the Holy Spirit, and the man comes to himself, it is well.

Now let us consider *how this change happened.* If you should ask me the outward circumstances of the prodigal's case, I should say that it took a great deal to bring him to himself. "Why, surely!" one says. "He ought to have come to himself when he had spent all, he must have come to himself when he began to be hungry." No; it took a great deal to bring him to himself, and to his father; and it takes a great deal to bring sinners to themselves, and to their God. There are some of you who will have to be beaten with many stripes before you will be saved. I heard one say, who was crushed almost to death in an accident, "If I had not nearly perished, I should have wholly perished." So is it with many sinners; if some had not lost all they had, they would have lost all; but, by strong winds, rough and raging, some are driven into the port of peace.

The occasion of the prodigal's climax was this; he was very hungry, and in great sorrow, and he was alone. It is a grand thing if we can get people to be alone. There was nobody near the poor man, and no sound for him to hear except the grunting of the hogs, and the munching of those husks. Ah, to be alone! I wish that we had more opportunities of being alone in this great city; yet, perhaps the most awful loneliness may be realized while walking a London street. It is a good thing for a sinner sometimes to be alone. The prodigal had nobody to drink with him, nobody to sport with him; he was too far gone for that. He had not a rag to pawn to get another pint, he must therefore just sit still without one of his old companions. They only followed him for what they could get out of him. As long as he could treat them, they would treat him well; but when he had spent all, "no man gave unto him." He was left without a comrade, in misery he could not allay, in hunger he could not satisfy. He pulled that belt up another hole and made it tighter; but it almost seemed as if he would pull himself in two if he drew it any closer. He was reduced almost to a skeleton; emaciation had taken hold of him, and he was ready to lie down there and die. Then it was that he came to himself.

Do you know *why this change occurred in the prodigal's case?* I believe that the real reason was that his father was secretly working for him all the while. His state was known to his father; I am sure it was, because the elder brother knew it; and if the elder brother heard of it, so did the father. The elder brother may have told him; or, if not, the father's greater love would have a readier ear for tidings of his son than the elder brother had. Though the parable cannot tell us—for no parable is meant to teach us everything, yet it was true that the Father was omnipotent, and he was secretly touching the core of this young man's heart and dealing with him by this wondrous surgery of famine and of want to make him at last come to himself.

Perhaps somebody says, "I wish I could come to myself, sir, without going through all that process." Well, you have come to yourself already if you really wish that. Let me suggest to you that, in order to prove that it is so, you should begin seriously to think, to think about who you are, and where you are, and what is to become of you. Take time to think, and think in an orderly, steady, serious manner; and, if you can, jot down your thoughts. It is a wonderful help to some people to put down upon paper an account of their own condition. I believe that there were many who found the Saviour one night when I urged them, when they went home, to write on a piece of paper, "Saved as a believer in Jesus," or else, "Condemned because I believe not on the Son of God." Some who began to write that word "condemned" have never finished it, for they found Christ there and then while seeking him. You keep your account books, do you not? I am sure you do if you are in trade, unless you are going to cheat your creditors. You keep your business books; well, now, keep a record concerning your soul. Really look these matters in the face—the hereafter, death which may come so suddenly, the great eternity, the judgment-seat. Do think about these things; do not shut your eyes to them. I pray you, do not play the fool! If you must play the fool, take some lighter things to trifle with than your souls, and your eternal destinies. Shut yourselves up alone for a while; go through this matter steadily, lay it out in order, make a plan of it. See where you are going. Think over the way of salvation, the story of the Cross, the love of God, the readiness of Christ to save; and I think that, while this process is going on, you will feel your heart melting, and soon you will find your soul believing in the precious blood which sets the sinner free.

I must close with just a few words on this last point, WHEN HE CAME TO HIMSELF, THEN HE CAME TO HIS FATHER.

When a sinner comes to himself, he soon comes to his God. This poor prodigal, soon after he came to himself, said, "I will arise, and go to my father." What led him back to his father? Very briefly let me answer that question.

First, *his memory aroused him.* He recollected his father's house, he remembered the past, his own riotous living. Do not try to forget all that has happened; the terrible recollections of a misspent past may be the means of leading you to a new life. Set memory to work.

Next, *his misery bestirred him.* Every pang of hunger that he felt, the sight of his rags, the degradation of associating with swine—all those things drove him back to his father. Let your very needs, your cravings, your misery, drive you to your God!

Then, *his fears whipped him back.* He said, "I perish with hunger." He had not perished yet, but he was afraid that he soon would do so; he feared that he really would die, for he felt so faint. See what will become of you if you do die in your sins! What awaits you but an endless future of limitless misery? Sin will follow you into eternity and will increase upon you there, and, as you shall go on to sin, so shall you go on to sorrow ever increasing. A deeper degradation and a more tremendous penalty will accompany your sin in the world to come;

therefore, let your fears drive you home, as they drove home the poor prodigal.

Meanwhile, *his hope drew him*. This gentle cord was as powerful as the heavy whip: "In my father's house there is bread enough and to spare; I need not perish with hunger, I may yet be filled." Oh, think of what you may yet be! Poor sinner, think of what God can do and is ready to do for you, to do for you even now! How happy he can make you! How peaceful and how blessed! So let your hope draw you to him.

Then, *his resolve moved him*. He said, "I will arise, and go to my father." All else drove him or drew him, and now he is resolved to return home. He rose up from the earth on which he had been sitting amidst his filthiness, and he said, "I will." Then the man became a man; he had come to himself, the manhood had come back to him, and he said, "I will, I will."

Lastly, there was the real act of going to his father; it was that which brought him home. Nay, let me correct myself; it is said, "*He came to his father*," but there is a higher truth at the back of that, for *his father came to him*. So, when you are moved to return, and the resolution becomes an action, and you arise and go to God, salvation is yours almost before you could have expected it; for, once turn your face that way, and while you are yet a great way off, your Father will outstrip the wind, and come and meet you, and fall upon your neck and kiss you with the kisses of reconciliation. This shall be your portion if you will but trust the Lord Jesus Christ.

As for you, Christian people, who may be saying that there is nothing for you in the sermon, do not turn into a company of grumbling elder brothers; but, on the contrary, go home, and pray God to bless this discourse. "But," you say, "I have not had the fatted calf." "Oh, but, if it was killed for the younger son, it was for you also!" "I did not have the music and dancing." Well, they have had it over the returned prodigal, over some soul that has already believed in Christ now; I know they have, God does not let us preach for nought. He will pay us our wages, and give us our reward; so rejoice with us over all that the Lord has done, and all that he is going to do. The Lord bless you, beloved, all of you, without exception, for Christ's sake!

XVI

THE BRIDGELESS GULF

"Beside all this, between us and you there is a great gulf fixed : so that they which would pass from hence to you cannot; neither can they pass to us, that would come from thence."— Luke 16 : 26.

I HAVE been led to blow the silver trumpet, sounding forth the love and mercy of our God in Christ. Many times I have preached a full Christ for empty sinners, and have set forth the freeness and graciousness of the divine proclamation which in the Gospel is made to the chief of sinners. I have not, concerning that point, shunned to declare unto you the whole counsel of God. But I feel that I must now blow a blast upon the rough ram's horn, for sometimes our congregations need to be reminded of the law and terrors of God, and of the judgment to come; our experience is, that the preaching of judgment is greatly blessed of God; we have remarked that a very large number of conversions have occurred under those sermons in which the declaration of God's wrath against all iniquity has been the most plain and solemn. A thunder-storm clears the air; there are pestilences which would gather beneath the wings of calm which can only be purged away by the lightning flash. When God sends his servant with heavy tidings, his message of alarm cleanses the spiritual atmosphere, and kills the sloth, pride, indifference, and lethargy, which otherwise might fall upon the people. As the sharp needle prepares the way for the thread, so the piercing law makes a way for the bright silver thread of divine grace. The lancet is quite as needful as the healing balm. The law is our pedagogue to bring us to Christ; like the old Greek pedagogue who led the boy to school, so the law leads us to Christ, who teaches and instructs us, and makes us wise unto salvation.

Those who preached the law, as well as the Gospel, in the Puritan times, were the most fruitful soul-winners. We find our blessed Lord and Master, whose heart was overflowing with compassion, and whose very nature was love, often dwelling upon the wrath to come; and indeed, his utterances are more telling and terrible than the most burning threatening from the lips of thundering seers of old. God grant that the effect which so anxiously I desire, may follow from that burden of the Lord which now weighs so heavily upon me. May the Master gather out this day a seed unto himself, who shall be saved from the wrath to come, and be to all eternity the reward of the Redeemer's travail. Lift up your hearts to God, ye that know him and have power with him, and ask that now the divine Spirit may work mightily, that hearts may be broken and sinners led to Jesus.

"Beside all this, between us and you there is a great gulf fixed." Human ingenuity has done very much to bridge great gulfs. Scarcely has the world afforded a river so wide that its floods could not be overleaped; or a torrent so furious that it could not be made to pass under the yoke. High above the foam of America's glorious cataract, man has hung aloft his slender but substantial road of iron, and the shriek of the locomotive is heard above the roar of Niagara. There is, however, one gulf which no human skill or engineering ever shall be able to bridge; there is one chasm which no wing shall ever be able to cross; it is the gulf which divides the world of joy in which the righteous triumph, from that land of sorrow in which the wicked feel the smart of Jehovah's sword. Whatever other arguments there may be why the righteous should have no communion with the wicked in a future state, beside all these other things, any one of which is enough and sufficient of itself, there is a great gulf fixed, so that there can be no passage from the one world to the other.

In trying solemnly to speak upon this matter, I shall commence with this—THERE IS NO PASSAGE FROM HEAVEN TO HELL—"They which would pass from hence to you cannot." Glorified saints cannot visit the prison-house of lost sinners. Long enough were the righteous mingled with the wicked; sufficient was the evil time in which the wheat was choked with the tares; quite long enough was the period in which the chaff laid upon the same floor, side by side with the wheat. Patience had its perfect work. They did both grow together until the time of the harvest; it is not necessary now that harvest has come, that they should lie together any longer. It were inconsistent with the perfect joy and the beatific state of the righteous, with its perfect calm and purity, that sin should be admitted into their midst, or that they should be permitted to find companionships in the abodes of evil.

It follows that *the most earnest and assiduous preacher* must then renounce all hope of converting sinners. God has raised up some apostolic spirits, whose presence in a nation is like the rising of the sun; darkness flies before them, and the light of salvation streams from them to tens of thousands. When they lift up their hands to preach, God gives them power to shake the gates of hell, and when they bend the knee to pray, they unlock the gates of heaven. Men like Baxter with bursting hearts of love, or Joseph Alleine with glowing tongue, or Whitefield with seraph's fire, or Wesley with cherub's zeal; these are the men who bless their age and are most truly great. These men can go to the borders of the earth if they will; their commission is co-extensive with the human race—"Go ye into all the world, and preach the Gospel to every creature;" "Lo, I am with you always, even unto the ends of the world."

These men are never so happy as when they are preaching. Woe is unto them if they preach not the Gospel, and, when they preach it and God helps them, they are like Elihu, refreshed by the effort. They were born to preach the Gospel and to win sinners to Christ, and they are never content except they are fulfilling their high commission. But they must cease from their labours soon, for in heaven they are not needed, and from hell they are excluded. O sinner, even our voice, feeble though it be, may win you to Jesus now; but, if you die impenitent, it can never woo you again to a Saviour. *Now* is my time to preach to you and set open mercy's door before you, but *then* I can never warn you, nor invite you; never again depict the agonies of my Lord and Master and endeavour to attract you by the story of his love, his dying, bleeding love. No, it will be all over then. "That they may rest from their labours; and their works do follow them" (Rev. 14: 13). They must bring their sheaves with them, for they cannot return into another field to sow, nor journey into other broad acres to reap. Burning as their hearts will still be with divine love, they will have to exercise it in another way. Their passionate longings for God's glory will find other channels in which to flow. They will bow their heads and adore him day and night, but they can no longer serve him in Gospel ministry. Poor sinner, fain would I win thee now, for it is now or never with thee and me.

The efforts of the most importunate visitor, the most earnest friend, must cease with death. Some of you have friends who can get nearer to your heart than I can. You can afford sometimes to forget my poor words and go your way to sin again; but you have a sister, and when she pleads with you, you do feel it; you have one loving friend, and when he speaks to you, you cannot be deaf; your conscience has often been impressed by him, and sometimes through him the strivings of the Spirit have been very mighty with your soul. Dost thou hear this? Not only will there be no public congregations, no Sabbaths, no houses of prayer, but there shall be no private messengers, no earnest Christians who shall privately seek thy soul's good. What sayest thou to this? Does not this give an awful value to those tender words of importunate love? Turn thee at the gentle rebuke, for otherwise thou shalt be suddenly destroyed, and that without remedy.

Those who are nearest and dearest must be divided from you, if you perish in your sins. A mother can put her arms about her child's neck and pray for it here; she may affectionately exhort her son to seek peace with God now; she may earnestly and incessantly follow him with her holy entreaties, but she can never come to him from the realms of glory if once he is lost. "They that would come from us to you cannot." Do ye hear it, young man? Those glistening eyes of a mother's love shall never weep again for you. That touching voice which sometimes awoke the echoes of your heart, shall never plead again. O ungodly woman, thou shalt never see thy godly child. Father, is it that daughter you are thinking of who loved and feared God in childhood and was taken from you? Did she say to you when she was dying, "Follow me to heaven, my father"? You have heard her voice for the last time; that child will never see her father more unless he turns from his evil ways. Methinks if she could be in heaven what she was on earth, she would fling her arms about your neck and seek to draw you to the glorious throne of the Most High; but oh! it cannot be. A just

God condemns the impenitent sinner, and just men assent to the Divine sentence.

See then, O ye ungodly ones, you often think our company a great nuisance, and perhaps while I am preaching, my alarming words annoy you. Ah, we shall not annoy you long. When I bring home the judgment to come, is the subject obnoxious to you? I shall not ask your patience long. We shall be separated; if you go your way and follow after sin and wrath, there will come a dividing time, and O let me say to you, you would give worlds if you had them; you would give them if they were solid diamonds, to hear again the voice which now fatigues you, and to listen once more to those plaintive invitations which vex you and spoil your mirth. Ah, how would you bless God if he would let you come back again and have once more those Sabbaths which were so dull and dreary, and permit you to go up once more to the house of God which now perhaps is like a prison-house to your vain and frivolous spirits. I say ye may well have patience with us for a little time and bear with our importunities, for we shall not plague you much longer. We beseech you to come to Jesus; we would pluck you by your garments and beseech you to flee from the wrath to come; forgive us for being thus in earnest, for even if we should fail with you, you will soon escape the importunities of our love.

How earnest this ought to make the people of God to work while it is called to-day. If this is our only time for doing good, let us do good while we can. I hear people sometimes say, "Mr. So-and-so does too much; he works too hard." Oh! we none of us do half enough. Do not talk about working too hard for Jesus Christ. The thing is impossible. Are souls perishing, and shall I sleep? My idle, lazy flesh, shalt thou keep me still while men are dying and hell is filling? Let us be lukewarm no longer. If God makes us lights in the world, let us spend ourselves as a candle does, which consumes itself by shining. As the poor work girl, who has but one light, works with desperate pace because that will soon be burned out, so let us be instant in season and out of season, watching, praying, labouring for the souls of men. If we could but see lost souls, and understand their unutterable woe, we should shake ourselves from the dust, and go forth to work while it is called to-day.

Secondly, as we cannot go from heaven to hell, so the text assures us, "NEITHER CAN THEY COME TO US THAT WOULD COME FROM THENCE." The lost spirits in hell are shut in for ever. The sinner cannot come to heaven for a multitude of reasons. First, *his own character* forbids it. As a man lives and dies, so will he be throughout eternity. The drunkard here will have all a drunkard's thirst there without the means of gratifying it. The swearer here will become a yet more ripe and proficient blasphemer. Death does not change but fixes character; it petrifies it. "He that is unjust let him be unjust still; he that is filthy let him be filthy still" (Rev. 22: 11). The lost man remains a sinner and a growing sinner, and continues to rebel against God. Would you have such a man in heaven? Shall the thief prowl through the streets of the New Jerusalem? Shall the atmosphere of Paradise be polluted by an oath? Shall the songs of angels be disturbed by the ribaldry of licentious conversation? It cannot be. Heaven were no heaven, if the sinner could be permitted to enter it. "Except a man be born again, he cannot see the Kingdom of God" (John 3: 3), and as there is no hope of the finally lost ever being born again, that Kingdom of God they cannot see. Sinner, if you are not fit for heaven now, hast thou any right to hope thou ever wilt be? If you die without God and without hope, where must your portion be? Without a God, can ye dwell in heaven— God's own dominions? Without hope, can ye enter where hope is consummated in full fruition? Never!

Moreover, not only does the man's character shut him out, but also *the sinner's doom*. What was it? "These shall go away into *everlasting* punishment." If it is everlasting, how can they enter heaven? What does the Saviour say, "Where their worm dieth not and their fire is not quenched." If there be any truth in that metaphor, the lost are lost for ever; the worm would die if they entered heaven, and the fire were quenched if they obtained celestial seats. How does the Holy Spirit put it? Does he not describe the wrath to come as a bottomless pit? It were not such if they could get handhold, and afterwards climb upward to the starry thrones of angels.

Moreover, sinner, thou canst not go out of the prison-house because *God's character* and God's word are against thee. Shall

God ever cease to be just? "Holy, Holy, Holy, Lord God of Sabaoth," is the never ceasing cry of cherubim, but as long as he is "Holy, Holy, Holy," thou canst never be acceptable to him. Shall God ever cease to be true? But remember, as long as he is true to his own threatenings, he must and will send his arrows through you, and make his fierce wrath to consume you. Then there stands his decree, "He that believeth not shall be damned;" this is the great gulf, that fixed chasm by which the impenitent sinner is fast as firmest destiny bound like Prometheus to the rock for ever, never to be loosed in time or in eternity.

Nay, yet more, remember sinner, there never was but one bridge between fallen man and a holy God. That bridge you reject. The Person of the Mediator, his substitution, his righteousness, his painful death, these make the only road from sin to righteousness, from wrath to acceptance. But these you reject. If you should ever be lost you will have finally rejected Christ; and inasmuch as you are not saved, O my poor fellow creature, thou art now rejecting Christ; thou art as good as saying, "Christ died, but not for me; Christ shed his blood to save men, but I will not be saved in his way. Let him die. I count his death a trifle, and his blood a vanity; I had sooner perish than be saved by him."

This is what you in effect are saying. I know the words make you shudder; you would not venture to utter them, but that is your feeling. Ye will not have this Man to reign over you; you will not bow the knee and kiss the Son; you will still be an adversary to God, and sooner be destroyed than be saved through the atonement of Christ. Well, now, if you reject the only way, what wonder, if having rejected that, there remains no hope? Besides, remember there is no other sacrifice for sin. Scripture expressly tells us that there remaineth no more sacrifice for sin. Do you think that Jesus will come a second time to die? Shall those divine hands be stretched again to the wood? You reject him now. If he died again you would reject him. Shall the head again be pierced with thorns? Shall the side again be rent with the spear? Why, sinner, if thou refusest to have him now thou wouldest refuse him could he die a second time. But that cannot be. He has offered an atonement once for all, and now for ever he sits down at the right hand of the

Majesty on high. No second atonement—no second redemption shall ever be offered for the sin of men.

Besides, remember, there is no Holy Spirit in the pit. The blessed Spirit is here to-day, and often has he striven with some of you. Do you remember when you trembled like Felix? Do not you remember the time when, like Agrippa, you were almost persuaded? But still all this was put away; conscience was hushed; the Spirit of God was quenched. Well, that Spirit can strive with you again, and if he comes forth in his irresistible strength, if your heart be like a flint, he can break it; and if like iron, he can melt it. But once in the pit, and the Holy Spirit never comes there. If so, then you cannot be born again and cannot enter heaven; ye cannot be sanctified; and unsanctified spirits cannot have a portion in the skies. So then, it is clear enough you cannot possibly pass from hell to heaven. Ah, this will be a judgment upon you, a solemn judgment upon you for many things. You do not like the house of God; you shall be shut out of it. You do not love the Sabbath; you are shut out from the eternal Sabbath. The voice of sacred song had no charm in it for you; you shall not join it. The face of God you never loved; you shall never see it. The name of Jesus Christ was never melodious in your ears; you shall never hear it. Jesus Christ was preached to you, but you rejected him; his blood you trod beneath your feet. The way to heaven was freely set open before you, but you would not come unto him that ye might have life. There is a road from earth to heaven: sinner, though thou hast gone into the depths of sin, if thou hast been the most infamous and most outrageous of offenders, there is a road for thee to heaven yet. The harlot, the thief, the profane, the drunkard, may yet find mercy through the grace of Jesus.

But now, I have to notice in the third place, that while no persons can pass that bridgeless chasm, so NO THINGS CAN. Nothing can come from hell to heaven. Rejoice ye saints in light, triumph in your God for this—no temptation of Satan can ever vex you when once you are landed on the golden strand; you are beyond bowshot of the arch-enemy; he may howl and bite his iron hands, but his howlings cannot terrify and his bitings cannot disturb. No longer shall you be vexed with the filthy conversation of the ungodly. Lot shall never hear another foul word. You shall not have to say, "Woe is me, that I sojourn in Mesech, that I dwell in the tents of Kedar!" (Ps. 120: 5).

> *No light discourse shall reach your heart,*
> *Nor trifles vex your ear.*

You shall be shut out from everything that belongs to hell. And, remember, you shall be in heaven, so secure that the wrath of God which makes hell shall never light on you. Your Saviour carried it; not a drop of it shall fall upon your persons. No present pains shall be in heaven, they are for the lost; no pains of body, no distractions of mind. You shall have no sin; sin cannot pass from them to you; you shall be perfect—like your Lord, without spot or wrinkle, or any such thing.

> *Your inward foes shall all be slain,*
> *Nor Satan vex your peace again.*

You shall have no fears for the future. You shall know that your bliss is eternal. This shall always be the honey of your honeycomb—that it lasts for ever. Millions of years you shall gaze into the face of your beloved; throughout endless ages you shall bask in the sunlight of his smile. This is joy, I say, to the Christian, if he will but think it over; it will reconcile him to the hardest strokes of temporary tribulation, and make him rejoice in the hardest toil of this mortal struggle. Courage, it is but a day or two of wrestling, and then the immortal crown; an hour or two of fighting, and then the everlasting rest. Will ye sheathe your swords? Will ye stop the conflict? No; press on, and let your true Jerusalem blades cut through soul and spirit, and divide joint and marrow, till you reach the summit, and the eternal glory shall be yours.

Again, we change the strain for a fourth point, and this a terrible one. As nothing can come from hell to heaven, so nothing heavenly can ever come to hell. Lazarus is not permitted to dip the tip of his finger in water to administer the cooling drop to the fire-tormented tongue. Not a drop of heavenly water can ever cross that chasm. See then, sinner, heaven is *rest*, perfect rest—but there is no rest in hell. The dreadful music of the eternal *miserere* has not so much as a single stop in it.

Heaven, too, is a place of *joy*; there happy fingers sweep celestial chords; there joyous spirits sing hosannahs day without night; but there is no joy in hell; for music there is the groan; for joy there is the pang; for sweet fellowship there is the binding up in bundles; for everything that is blissful there is everything that is dolorous.

Heaven is the place of *sweet communion* with God—

> *There they behold his face,*
> *And never, never sin;*
> *There from the rivers of his grace,*
> *Drink endless pleasures in.*

There is no communion with God in hell.

Tell me what heaven is if ye will, and I must say of any description that ye give of its joys, that there is none of them in Tophet, for heaven's blessings cannot cross from the celestial regions to the infernal prison-house.

And now, would to God, I could speak with you as my heart desireth; for this is my only opportunity, since, as I have already said, I can do this no more if I be saved and if you be lost. Spare me, then, two or three minutes while I close this poor discourse of mine, by trying to reason with those of you who are unconverted. I will never flatter you by preaching to you as though you were all Christians. The Lord my God knoweth there is many a heart that never was broken; there is many a spirit that never trembled before the majesty of infinite justice, and never kissed the outstretched sceptre of a crucified Redeemer. You know this, some of you; you know you are in the gall of bitterness and in the bonds of iniquity. I do not mean you alone who live in open sin; but I mean you who are amiable, excellent, admirable in your carriage and deportment, but yet the love of God is not in you. There is no fault to be found with your outward character, maybe, but you have not been born again; you have never passed from death unto life. If ye believe not in him, ye shall die in your sins "for there is none other name under heaven given among men, whereby we must be saved" (Acts 4: 12). Come, then, let me plead with you, and I will ask you a question—do you believe all this? Do you believe that there is a hell? Do you believe that there is a heaven to be lost? If you profess that you do not so believe, I have done with you. God bring you to a better mind.

I think I hear many of you say, "Believe it, sir, oh! we never doubted it; we learned it in our earliest childhood, we have heard it always, and we never ventured to doubt." Ah! well then, I ask you—are you in your sober senses to believe that there is a hell, and not seek to escape from it? Do you believe there is a wrath to come, and that it may fall upon you in the next minute, for you may be dead and never leave this house of prayer, and yet do you sit easy in your pews; or are you mad? Has sin so besotted you with its foul intoxication, that you cannot think? For if you can think, and there be an angry God who will punish with the awful force of his omnipotence, how is it that you can be at ease in Zion?

Let me ask you another question: if these things be so, have you used your senses in giving a preference to the pleasures of this life beyond the joys of heaven; in following the pleasures of to-day, when you know they will be followed with the miseries of eternity? Do not mistake, I do not mean to say that a Christian is without pleasures; we have the highest and purest pleasure that mortal or immortal can know; we have not the pleasures of sin, but we have higher, more delightful, and deeper pleasures. But this is what I mean, will you spend yourselves in sinful pleasure? Will you occupy your time with lust, or drunkenness, or with the frivolities of fashionable life, and do you think that these are worth the expense that they will cause? "Oh," said one to me, who holds a high position in society, as I talked with him long, after having preached earnestly the Gospel; he took me by the button, and he said, "It does seem to me to be an awful thing, that I, knowing as I do what will be my lot if I live and die as I am, should still act as I do. When you are with me," said he, "and I listen to a solemn address, I think there shall come a change over me; I will serve God, but, O sir, you do not know the temptations of my life; you do not know how it is when I get into the midst of pomps and vanities, and perhaps mingle with men who ridicule all thoughts of religion, it all goes, and I am such a fool that I sell my soul—sell my soul for it." Oh! there are such fools here to-day, who sell their souls for a little sin—one or two whirls in the world's mad dance, and then the devil is your partner, and your mirth is over. I ask you to use your reason, and judge whether it be worth your while to gain the whole world and lose your own soul.

I shall put it to you in another way. How is it that ye do not lay hold of Christ, since this is the only time when there is a probability that Christ can be laid hold of? I will tell you why it is. You do not love Christ; you love sin. Or else you are too proud to come to Christ; you think yourselves good enough, and you think that Christ is not for such as you are, but only for great sinners and the lowest of the low. Is your pride such a fine thing, that you will be damned in order to maintain its dignity? Throw your pride down, come as a sinner must come, and lay hold of Jesus Christ. Or if it be your sin which hinders, may God the Holy Ghost help you to pluck out the right eye and cast off a right arm sooner than having two eyes and two arms to be cast into hell fire.

"But," saith one, "how may I lay hold on Christ?" May the blessed Spirit enable you to do it. Here it is, trust Jesus Christ and you shall be saved. Conscious that you deserve his wrath, trembling because of his terrible law, look to Jesus. There hangs a bleeding Saviour. Methinks these eyes can see him bleeding there; God eternal, he by whom the heaven of heavens were made, and the earth and the fulness thereof, takes upon himself the form of man and hangs upon the tree of the curse.

See from his head, his hands, his feet,
Sorrow and love flow mingled down!
Did e'er such love and sorrow meet,
Or thorns compose so rich a crown?

"There is life in a look at that crucified One, there is life at this moment for thee." Will you glance at him with a tearful eye, "Jesus, slaughtered, martyred, murdered for my sake, I do believe in thee; here at thy feet I throw myself, all guilty, polluted, foul; let thy blood drop on me; turn thine eye upon me; say to me 'I have loved thee with an everlasting love, therefore with lovingkindness have I drawn thee (Jer. 31: 3). Come and welcome, sinner—come.'"

XVII

THE IMPORTUNATE WIDOW

"And he spake a parable unto them to this end, that men ought always to pray, and not to faint; saying, There was in a city a judge, which feared not God, neither regarded man: and there was a widow in that city; and she came unto him, saying, Avenge me of mine adversary. And he would not for a while: but afterward he said within himself, Though I fear not God, nor regard man; yet because this widow troubleth me, I will avenge her, lest by her continual coming she weary me. And the Lord said, Hear what the unjust judge saith. And shall not God avenge his own elect, which cry day and night unto him, though he bear long with them? I tell you that he will avenge them speedily."—Luke 18: 1–8.

REMEMBER that our Lord did not only inculcate prayer with great earnestness, but he was himself a brilliant example of it. It always gives force to a teacher's words when his hearers well know that he carries out his own instructions. Jesus was a prophet mighty both in deed and in word, and we read of him, "Jesus began both to do and to teach" (Acts 1: 1). In the exercise of prayer, "cold mountains and the midnight air" witnessed that he was as great a doer as a teacher. When he exhorted his disciples to continue in prayer, and to "pray without ceasing," he only bade them follow in his steps. If any one of all the members of the mystical body might have been supposed to need no prayer, it would certainly have been our Covenant Head, but if our Head abounded in supplication, much more ought we, the inferior members. He was never defiled with the sins which have debased and weakened us spiritually; he had no inbred lusts to struggle with. But if the perfectly pure drew near so often unto God, how much more incessant in supplication ought we to be! So mighty, so great, and yet so prayerful! O ye weak ones of the flock, how forcibly does the lesson come home to you! Imagine, therefore, the discourse is not preached to you by me, but comes fresh from the lips of One who was the great master of secret prayer, the highest paragon and pattern of private supplication, and let every word have the force about it as coming from such a One.

First, then, consider OUR LORD'S DESIGN IN THIS PARABLE—"Men ought always to pray, and not to faint."

But can men pray always? There was a sect in the earlier days of Christianity who were foolish enough to read the passage literally, and to attempt praying without ceasing by continual repetition of prayers. They of course separated themselves from all worldly concerns, and in order to fulfil one duty of life neglected every other. Such madmen might well expect to reap the due reward of their follies. Happily there is no need in this age for us to reprobate such an error; there is far more necessity to cry out against those who, under the pretence of praying always, have no settled time for prayer at all, and so run to the opposite extreme. Our Lord meant by saying men ought always to pray, that *they ought to be always in the spirit of prayer*, always ready to pray. Like the old knights, always in warfare, not always on their steeds dashing forward with their lances in rest to unhorse an adversary, but always wearing their weapons where they could readily reach them, and always ready to encounter wounds or death for the sake of the cause which they championed. Those grim warriors often slept in their armour; so even when we sleep, we are still to be in the spirit of prayer, so that if perchance we wake in the night we may still be with God.

Our souls should be in such a condition that ejaculatory prayer should be very frequent with us. No need to pause in business and leave the counter, and fall down upon the knees; the spirit should send up its silent, short, swift petitions to the throne of grace. When Nehemiah would ask a favour of the king, you will remember that he found an opportunity to do so through the king's asking him, "Why art thou sad?" but before he made him an answer he says, "I prayed unto the king of heaven;" instinctively perceiving the occasion, he did not leap forward to embrace it, but he halted just a moment to ask that he might be enabled to embrace it wisely and fulfil his great design therein. So you and I should often feel, "I cannot do this till I have asked a blessing on it." The soul should be not always in the exercise of prayer, but always in the energy of prayer; not always actually praying, but always intentionally praying.

Further, when our Lord says, men ought always to pray, he may also have meant that *the whole life of the Christian should be a life of devotion to God.*

> *Prayer and praise, with sins forgiven,*
> *Bring down to earth the bliss of heaven.*

To praise God for mercies received both with our voices and with our actions, and then to pray to God for the mercies that we need, devoutly acknowledging that they come from him, these two exercises in one form or other should make up the sum total of human life. Our life psalm should be composed of alternating verses of praying and of praising until we get into the next world, where the prayer may cease, and praise may swallow up the whole of our immortality. "But," saith one, "we have our daily business to attend to." I know you have, but there is a way of making business a part of praise and prayer. You say, "Give us this day our daily bread," and that is a prayer as you utter it; you go off to your work, and, as you toil, if you do so in a devout spirit, you are actively praying the same prayer by your lawful labour. You praise God for the mercies received in your morning hymn; and when you go into the duties of life, and there exhibit those graces which reflect honour upon God's name, you are continuing your praises in the best manner. Remember that with Christians to labour is to pray, and that there is much truth in the verse of Coleridge: "He prayeth best who loveth best."

To desire my fellow creatures' good and to seek after it, to desire God's glory, and so to live as to promote it, is the truest of devotion. The devotion of the cloisters is by no means equal to that of the man who is engaged in the battle of life; the devotion of the nunnery and the monastery is at best the heroism of a soldier who shuns the battle; but the devotion of the man in business life, who turns all to the glory of God, is the courage of one who seeks the thickest of the fray, and there bears aloft the grand old standard of Jehovah-nissi ("The Lord is my banner" cp. Exod. 17: 15). You need not be afraid that there is anything in any lawful calling that need make you desist from vital prayer; but, oh! if your calling is such that you cannot pray in it, you had better leave it. If it be a sinful calling, an unholy calling, of course, you cannot present that to God, but any of the ordinary avocations of life are such that if you cannot sanctify them, it is a want of sanctity in yourself, and the fault lies with you. Men ought *always* to pray. Their common garments are to be vestments, their meals are to be sacraments, their ordinary actions are to be sacrifices, and they themselves a royal priesthood, a peculiar people zealous for good works.

A third meaning which I think our Lord intended to convey to us was this: men ought always to pray, that is, *they should persevere in prayer.* This is probably his first meaning. When we ask God for a mercy once, we are not to consider that now we are not further to trouble him with it, but we are to come to him again and again. If we have asked of him seven times, we ought to continue until seventy times seven. In temporal mercies there may be a limit, and the Holy Ghost may bid us ask no more. Then must we say, the "Lord's will be done." If it be anything for our own personal advantage, we must let the Spirit of submission rule us, so that after having sought the Lord thrice, we shall be content with the promise, "My grace is sufficient for thee," and no longer ask that the "thorn in the flesh" should be removed (cp. 2 Cor. 12: 7–9). But in spiritual mercies, and especially in the united prayers of a Church, there is no taking a denial. Here, if we would prevail, we must persist; we must continue incessantly and constantly, and know no pause to our prayer till we win the mercy to the fullest possible extent.

"Men ought always to pray." Week by week, month by month, year by year; the conversion of that dear child is to be the father's main plea. The bringing in of that unconverted husband is to lie upon the wife's heart night and day till she gets it; she is not to take even ten or twenty years of unsuccessful prayer as a reason why she should cease; she is to set God no times nor seasons, but so long as there is life in her and life in the dear object of her solicitude, she is to continue still to plead with the mighty God of Jacob.

The pastor is not to seek a blessing on his people occasionally, and then in receiving a measure of it to desist from further intercession, but he is to continue vehemently without pause, without restraining his energies, to cry aloud and spare not till the windows of heaven be opened and a blessing be given too large for him to house. But how many times we ask of God, and have not because we do not wait long enough at the door! We knock a time or two at the gate of mercy, and as no friendly messenger opens the door, we go our ways. Too many prayers are like boys' runaway knocks, given, and then the giver is away before the door can be opened. O for grace to stand foot to foot with the angel of God, and never, never, never relax our hold; feeling that the cause we plead is one in which we must be successful, for souls depend on it, the glory of God is connected with it, the state of our fellow-men is in jeopardy. If we could have given up in prayer our own lives and the lives of those dearest to us, yet the souls of men we *cannot* give up, we must urge and plead again and again until we obtain the answer.

I cannot leave this part of the subject without observing that our Lord would have us learn that *men should be more frequent in prayer*. Not only should they always have the spirit of prayer, and make their whole lives a prayer, and persevere in any one object which is dear to their souls, but there should be a greater frequency of prayer amongst all the saints. I gather that from the parable, "lest by her continual coming she weary me." Prayerfulness will scarcely be kept up long unless you set apart times and seasons for prayer. There are no times laid down in Scripture except by the example of holy men, for the Lord trusts much to the love of his people and to the spontaneous motions of the inner life. He does not say, "Pray at seven o'clock in the morning every day," or "Pray at night at eight, or nine, or ten, or eleven;" but says, "Pray without ceasing." Yet every Christian will find it exceedingly useful to have his regular times for retirement, and I doubt whether any eminent piety can be maintained without these seasons being very carefully and scrupulously observed.

We read in the old traditions of James the apostle, that he prayed so much that his knees grew hard through his long kneeling: and it is recorded by Fox, that Latimer, during the time of his imprisonment, was so much upon his knees that frequently the poor old man could not rise to his meals and had to be lifted up by his servants. When he could no longer preach, and was immured within stone walls, his prayers went up to heaven for his country, and we in these times are receiving the blessing. Daniel prayed with his windows open daily and at regular intervals. "Seven times a day," saith one, "will I praise thee." David declared that at "Evening, and morning, and at noon," would he wait upon God. O that our intervals of prayer were not so distant one from the other; would God that on the pilgrimage of life the wells at which we drink were more frequent. In this way should we continue in prayer.

Our Lord means, to sum up the whole, that *believers should exercise a universality of supplication*—we ought to pray at all times. There are no canonical hours in the Christian's day or week. We should pray from cockcrowing to midnight, at such times as the Spirit moveth us. We should pray in all estates, in our poverty and in our wealth, in our health and in our sickness, in the bright days of festival and in the dark nights of lamentation. We should pray at the birth and pray at the funeral, we should pray when our soul is glad within us by reason of abundant mercy, and we should pray when our soul draweth nigh unto the gates of death by reason of heaviness.

We should pray in all transactions, whether secular or religious. Prayer should sanctify everything. The Word of God and prayer should come in over and above the common things of daily life. Pray over going into the shop and coming out again. Thou shalt never err by praying too much, thou shalt never make a mistake by asking God's guidance too often.

Secondly, in enforcing this precept, our Lord gives us a parable in which there are TWO ACTORS, the characteristics of the two actors being such as to add strength to his precept.

In the first verse of the parable there is *a judge*. Now, herein is the great advantage to us in prayer. If this poor woman prevailed with a judge whose office is stern, unbending, untender, how much more ought you and I to be instant in prayer and hopeful of success when we have to supplicate a Father! Far other is a father than a judge. The judge must necessarily be impartial, stern, but the father is necessarily partial to his child, compassionate and tender to his own offspring. Doth she prevail over a judge; and shall not we prevail with our Father who is in heaven? And doth she continue in her desperate need to weary him until she wins what she desires; and shall not we continue in the agony of our desires until we get from our heavenly Father whatsoever his word hath promised?

In addition to being a judge, he was *devoid of all good character*. In both branches he failed. He "feared not God." Conscience was seared in him, he had no thoughts of the great judgment-seat before which judges must appear. Though possibly he had taken an oath before God to judge impartially, yet he forgot his oath and trod justice under his foot. "Neither did he regard man." The approbation of his fellow creatures, which is very often a power, even with naturally bad men, either to restrain them from overt evil, or else to constrain them to righteousness, this principle had no effect upon him. Now, if the widow prevailed over such a wretch as this, if the iron of her importunity broke the iron and steel of this man's obduracy, how much more may we expect to be successful with him who is righteous, and just, and good, the Friend of the needy, the Father of the fatherless, and the Avenger of all such as are oppressed! O let the character of God as it rises before you in all its majesty of truthfulness and faithfulness, blended with lovingkindness, and tenderness, and mercy, excite in you an indefatigable ardour of supplication, making you resolve with this poor woman that you will never cease to supplicate until you win your suit.

Note with regard to the character of this judge, that he was one who *consciously cared for nothing but his own ease*. When at last he consented to do justice, the only motive which moved him, was, "lest by her continual coming she weary me." "She *stun* me," might be the Greek word—a kind of slang, I suppose, of that period, meaning lest "she batter me," "she bruise me," and as some translate it, "black my face with her incessant constant batterings." That was the kind of language he used; a short quick sentence of indignation at being bothered, as we should say, by such a case as this. The only thing that moved him was a desire to be at ease and to take things comfortably. If she could prevail over such a one, how much more shall we speed with God whose delight it is to take care of his children, who loves them even as the apple of his eye!

This judge was *practically unkind and cruel* to her; yet the widow continued. For a while he would not listen to her, though her household, her life, her children's comfort, were all hanging upon his will; he left her by a passive injustice to suffer still. But our God has been practically kind and gracious to us; up to this moment he has heard us and granted our requests. Set this against the character of the judge, and surely every loving heart that knows the power of prayer will be moved to incessant importunity.

We must, however, pass on now to notice the other actor in the scene—*the widow*; and here everything tells again the same way, to induce the Church of God to be importunate. She was apparently *a perfect stranger to the judge*. She appeared before him as an individual in whom he took no interest. He had possibly never seen her before; who she was and what she wanted was no concern to him. But when the Church appears before God she comes as Christ's own Bride; she appears before the Father as one whom he has loved with an everlasting love. And shall he not avenge his own elect, his own chosen, his own people? Shall not their prayers prevail with him, when a stranger's importunity won a suit of an unwilling judge?

The widow appeared at the judgment-seat *without a friend*. According to the parable, she had no advocate, no powerful pleader to stand up in the court and say, "I am the patron of this humble woman." If she prevailed, she must prevail by her own ardour and her own intensity of purpose. But when you and I come before our Father, we come not alone, for—

> *He is at the Father's side,*
> *The Man of love, the Crucified.*

We have a Friend who ever liveth to make intercession for us. O Christian, urge thy suit with holy boldness, press thy case, for the blood of Jesus speaks with a voice that must be heard.

This poor woman came *without a promise to encourage her*, nay, with the reverse, with much to discourage; but when you and I come before God, we are commanded to pray by God himself, and we are promised that if we ask it shall be given us; if we seek we shall find. We must not pause nor cease a moment while we have God's promise to back our plea.

The widow, in addition to having no promise whatever, was even *without the right of constant access*. She had, I suppose, a right to clamour to be heard at ordinary times when judgment was administered, but what right had she to dog the judge's footsteps, to waylay him in the streets, to hammer at his private door, to be heard calling at nightfall, so that he, sleeping at the top of his house, was awakened by her cries? She had no permission so to importune, but we may come to God at all times and all seasons. We may cry day and night unto him, for he has bidden us pray without ceasing.

She, poor soul, every time she prayed, *provoked the judge* ; lines of anger were on his face. I doubt not he foamed at the mouth to think he should be wearied by a person so insignificant ; but with Jesus, every time we plead, we please him rather than provoke him. The prayers of the saints are the music of God's ears.

> *To him there's music in a groan,*
> *And beauty in a tear.*

We, speaking after the manner of men, bring a gratification to God when we intercede with him. He is vexed with us if we restrain our supplications ; he is pleased with us when we draw near constantly. Oh, then, as you see the smile upon the Father's face, children of his love, I beseech you faint not, but continue still without ceasing to entreat the blessing.

Once more, this woman had a suit in which *the judge could not be himself personally interested* ; but ours is a case in which the God we plead with is more interested than we are ; for when a Church asks for the conversion of souls, she may justly say, "Arise, O God, plead thine own cause." It is for the honour of Christ that souls should be converted ; it brings glory to the mercy and power of God when great sinners are turned from the error of their ways ; consequently we are pleading for the Judge with the Judge, for God we are pleading with God. Our prayer is virtually *for* Christ as *through* Christ, that his kingdom may come, and his will may be done.

I must not forget to mention that in this woman's case *she was only one.* She prevailed though she was only one, but shall not God avenge his own elect, who are not *one*, but tens of thousands? If there be a promise that if two or three are agreed it shall be done, how much more if in any church hundreds meet together with unanimous souls anxiously desiring that God would fulfil his promise?

The third and last point : THE POWER WHICH, ACCORDING TO THIS PARABLE, TRIUMPHED.

This power was not the woman's eloquence, "I pray thee avenge me of mine adversary." These words are very few. Just eight words. You observe there is no plea, there is nothing about her widowhood, nothing urged about her children, nothing said about the wickedness of her adversary, nothing concerning the judgment of God upon unjust judges, nor about the wrath of God upon unjust men, who devour widows' houses—nothing of the kind. "I pray thee avenge me of mine adversary." Her success, therefore, did not depend upon her power in rhetoric, and we learn from this that the prevalence of a soul or of a Church with God does not rest upon the elocution of its words, or upon the eloquence of its language. The prayer which mounts to heaven may have but very few of the tail feathers of adornment about it, but it must have the strong wing feathers of intense desire ; it must not be as the peacock, gorgeous for beauty, but it must be as the eagle, for soaring aloft, if it would ascend up to the seventh heavens. When you pray in public, as a rule the shorter the better. Verbiage is generally nothing better in prayer than a miserable fig leaf with which to cover the nakedness of an unawakened soul.

Another thing is quite certain, namely, that the woman *did not prevail through the merits of her case.* It may have been a very good case, there is nothing said about that. I do not doubt the rightness of it ; but still, the judge did not know nor care whether it was right or wrong ; all he cared about was, this woman troubled him. He does not say, "She has a good case, and I ought to listen to it." No, he was too bad a man to be moved by such a motive, but "she worries me," that is all, "I will attend to it." So in our suit—in the suit of a sinner with God, it is not the merit of his case that can ever prevail with God. Thou hast no merit. If thou art to win, another's merit must stand instead of thine, and on thy part it must not be merit but misery ; it must not be thy righteousness but thy importunity that is to prevail with God. How this ought to encourage those of you who are labouring under a sense of unworthiness ! However unworthy you may be, continue in prayer.

Note with regard to this woman, that the judge said first, she

troubled him, next he said, she came continually, and then he
added his fear lest "she weary me." I think the case was somewhat after this fashion. The judge was sitting one morning
on his bench, and many were the persons coming before him
asking justice, which he was dealing out with the impartiality
of a villain, giving always his best word to him who brought
the heaviest bribes; when presently a poor woman uttered
her plaint. She had tried to be heard several times, but her
voice had been drowned by others, but this time it was more
shrill and sharp, and she caught the judge's eye. "My lord,
avenge me of mine adversary." He no sooner sees from her
poverty-stricken dress that there are no bribes to be had, than
he replies, "Hold your tongue! I have other business to attend
to." He goes on with another suit in which the fees were more
attractive. Still he hears the cry again, "My lord, I am a
widow, avenge me of mine adversary." Vexed with the
renewed disturbance, he bade the usher put her out, because she
interrupted the silence of the court and stopped the public
business. "Take care she does not get in again to-morrow,"
said he, "she is a troublesome woman."

Long ere the morrow had come, he found out the truth of his
opinion. She waited till he left the court, dogged his footsteps,
and followed him through the streets, until he was glad to get
through his door, and bade the servants fasten it lest that
noisy widow should come in, for she had constantly assailed
him with the cry, "Avenge me of mine adversary." He is now
safely within doors and bids the servants bring in his meal.
They are pouring water on his hands and feet, his lordship is
about to enjoy his repast, when a heavy knock is heard at the
door, followed by a clamour, pushing, and a scuffle. "What
is it?" saith he. "It is a woman outside, a widow woman, who
wants your lordship to see justice done her." "Tell her I cannot
attend to her, she must be gone." He seeks his rest at nightfall
on the housetop, when he hears a heavy knock at the door,
and a voice comes up from the street beneath his residence,
"My lord, avenge me of mine adversary." The next morning
his court is open, and, though she is forbidden to enter, like a
dog that will enter somehow, she finds her way in, and she
interrupts the court continually with her plea, "My lord,
avenge me of mine adversary."

Ask her why she is thus importunate, and she will tell you her husband is dead, and he left a little plot of land—it was all they had, and a cruel neighbour who looked with greedy eyes upon that little plot, has taken it as Ahab took Naboth's vineyard, and now she is without any meal or any oil for the little ones, and they are crying for food. Oh, if their father had been alive, how he would have guarded their interests! But she has no helper, and the case is a glaring one; and what is a judge for if he is not to protect the injured? She has no other chance, for the creditor is about to take away her children to sell them into bondage. She cannot bear that. "No," she says, "I have but one chance; it is that this man should speak up for me and do me justice, and I have made up my mind he shall never rest till he does so. I am resolved that, if I perish, the last words on my lips shall be, 'Avenge me of mine adversary.'"

So the court is continually interrupted. Again the judge shouts, "Put her out; put her out! I cannot conduct the business at all with this crazy woman here continually dinning in my ears a shriek of 'Avenge me of mine adversary.'" But it is sooner said than done. She lays hold of the pillars of the court so as not to be dragged out, and, when at last they get her in the street, she does but wait her chance to enter again, she pursues the judge along the highways, she never lets him have a minute's peace. "Well," says the judge, "I am worried out of my very life. I care not for the widow, nor her property, nor her children; let them starve, what are they to me? But I cannot stand this, it will weary me beyond measure. I will see to it." It is done, and she goes her way. Nothing but her importunity prevails.

Now, you have many other weapons to use with God in prayer, but our Saviour bids you not neglect this master, all-conquering, instrument of importunity. God will be more easily moved than this unjust judge, only be you as importunate as this widow was. If you are sure it is a right thing for which you are asking, plead now, plead at noon, plead at night, plead on; with cries and tears spread out your case, order your arguments, back up your pleas with reasons, urge the precious blood of Jesus, set the wounds of Christ before the Father's eyes, bring out the atoning sacrifice, point to Calvary, enlist the crowned Prince, the Priest who stands at the right hand of God; and resolve in your very soul that, if Zion do not flourish, if souls be not saved, if your family be not blessed, if your own zeal be not revived, yet you will die with the plea upon your lips, and with the importunate wish upon your spirits. Let me tell you that, if any of you should die with your prayers unanswered, you need not conclude that God has disappointed you.

You cannot tell but what, when you are in glory, you should look down from the windows of heaven and receive a double heaven in beholding your dear sons and daughters converted by the words you left behind. I do not say this to make you cease pleading for their immediate conversion, but to encourage you. Never give up prayer, never be tempted to cease from it. So long as there is breath in your body, and breath in their bodies, continue still to pray, for I tell you that he will avenge you speedily though he bear long with you. God bless these words for Jesus' sake.

XVIII

A SERMON FOR THE WORST
MAN ON EARTH

"And the publican, standing afar off, would not lift up so much as his eyes unto heaven, but smote upon his breast, saying, God be merciful to me a sinner."—Luke 18: 13.

IT was the fault of the Pharisee that, though he went up into the temple to pray, he did not pray; there is no prayer in all that he said. It is one excellence of the publican that he went up to the temple to pray, and he did pray: there is nothing but prayer in all that he said. "God be merciful to me a sinner" is a pure, unadulterated prayer throughout. It was the fault of the Pharisee that when he went up to the temple to pray he forgot an essential part of prayer, which is, confession of sin: he spoke as if he had no sins to confess, but many virtues to parade. It was a chief excellence in the devotion of the publican that he did confess his sin, ay, that his utterance was full of confession of sin: from beginning to end it was an acknowledgment of his guilt and an appeal for grace to the merciful God. The prayer of the publican is admirable for its fullness of meaning. An expositor calls it *a holy telegram*; and certainly it is so compact and so condensed, so free from superfluous words, that it is worthy to be called by that name. I do not see how he could have expressed his meaning more fully or more briefly. In the original Greek the words are even fewer than in the English. Oh, that men would learn to pray with less of language and more of meaning! What great things are packed away in this short petition! God, mercy, sin, the propitiation, and forgiveness.

He speaketh of great matters, and trifles are not thought of. He has nothing to do with fastings twice in the week, or the paying of tithes, and such second-rate things; the matters he treats of are of a higher order. His trembling heart moves among sublimities which overcome him, and he speaks in tones consistent therewith. He deals with the greatest things that ever can be: he pleads for his life, his soul. Where could he find themes more weighty, more vital to his eternal interests? He is not playing at prayer, but pleading in awful earnest.

His supplication speeded well with God, and he speedily won his suit with heaven. Mercy granted to him full justification. The prayer so pleased the Lord Jesus Christ, who heard it, that he condescended to become a portrait painter, and took a sketch of the petitioner. I say the prayer in itself was so pleasing to the gracious Saviour, that he tells us how it was offered: "Standing afar off, he would not lift up so much as his eyes unto heaven, but smote upon his breast." Luke, who, according to tradition, was somewhat of an artist as well as a physician, takes great care to place this picture in the national portrait gallery of men saved by sovereign grace. Here we have the portrait of a man who called himself *the* sinner, who may yet be held up as a pattern to saints. I am glad to have the divine sketch of this man, that I may see the bodily form of his devotion. I am gladder still to have his prayer, that we may look into the very soul of his pleading. My heart's desire is that many may seek mercy of the Lord as this publican did, and go down to their houses justified.

In preaching upon the text, I shall endeavour to bring out its innermost spirit. May we be taught of the Spirit, so that we may learn four lessons from it.

The first is this—THE FACT OF SINNERSHIP IS NO REASON FOR DESPAIR. You need none of you say, "I am guilty, and therefore I may not approach to God; I am so greatly guilty that it would be too daring a thing for me to ask for mercy." Dismiss such thoughts at once. My text and a thousand other arguments forbid despair.

For, first, *this man who was a sinner yet dared to approach the Lord.* According to our version, he said, "God be merciful to me *a* sinner," but a more accurate rendering is that which the Revised Version puts in the margin—"*the* sinner." He meant to say that he was emphatically *the* sinner. The Pharisee yonder was *the* saint of his age: but this publican who stood afar off from the holy place was *the* sinner. If there was not another sinner in the world, he was one; and in a world of

sinners he was a prominent offender—the sinner of sinners.
Emphatically he applies to himself the guilty name. He takes
the chief place in condemnation, and yet he cries, "God be
merciful to me *the* sinner." Now if you know yourself to be a
sinner, you may plead with God; but if you mourn that you
are not only a sinner, but *the* sinner with the definite article,
the sinner above all others, you may still hope in the mercy of
the Lord. The worst, the most profane, the most horrible of
sinners may venture, as this man did, to approach the God
of mercy. I know that it looks like a daring action; therefore
you must do it by faith. On any other footing but that of faith
in the mercy of God, you who are a sinner may not dare to
approach the Lord lest you be found guilty of presumption.
But with your eye on mercy you may be bravely trustful.
Believe in the great mercy of God, and though your sins be
abundant, you will find that the Lord will abundantly pardon;
though they blot your character, the Lord will blot them out;
though they be red like crimson, yet the precious blood of Jesus
will make you whiter than snow.

Next, remember that you may not only find encouragement
in looking at the sinner who sought his God, but in the God
whom he sought. Sinner, *there is great mercy in the heart of God.*
How often did that verse ring out as a chorus in the temple
song—

> *For his mercy shall endure*
> *Ever faithful, ever sure!*

Mercy is a specially glorious attribute of Jehovah, the living
God. He is "the Lord God, merciful and gracious." He is
"slow to anger and plenteous in mercy." Do you not see how
this should cheer you? How can the Lord display his mercy
except to the guilty? Goodness is for creatures, but mercy is
for sinners. Angels are not fit recipients of mercy; they do not
require it, for they have not transgressed. Mercy comes into
exercise after law has been broken; not till then. "He delighteth
in mercy." Only to a sinner can God be merciful. Hearest thou
this, thou sinner? Be sure that thou catch at it! If there be
boundless mercy in the heart of God, and it can only exercise
itself towards the guilty, then thou art the man to have it, for
thou art a guilty one.

Moreover, *the conception of salvation implies hope for sinners.*
That salvation which we preach to you every day is glad tidings
for the guilty. Salvation by grace implies that men are guilty.
Salvation means not the reward of the righteous, but the cleansing of the unrighteous. Salvation is meant for the lost, the
ruined, the undone; and the blessings which it brings of par-
doning mercy and cleansing grace must be intended for the
guilty and polluted. "The whole need not a physician;" the
physician has his eye upon the sick. Alms are for the poor,
bread is for the hungry, pardon is for the guilty. O you that
are guilty, you are the men that mercy seeks after! You
were in God's eye when he sent his Son into the world to save
sinners. From the very first inception of redemption to the
completion of it the eyes of the great God were set on the guilty,
and not on the deserving. The very name of Jesus tells us that
he shall save his people from their sins.

Let me further say that, inasmuch as that salvation of God
is a great one, it must have been intended to meet great sins.
Would Christ have shed the blood of his heart for some trifling,
venial sins which your tears could wash away? Think you God
would have given his dear Son to die as a mere superfluity?
If sin had been a small matter, a little sacrifice would have
sufficed. Think you that the divine atonement was made only
for small offences? Did Jesus die for little sins, and leave the
great ones unatoned? No, the Lord God measured the greatness
of our sin, and found it high as heaven, deep as hell, and broad
as the infinite, and therefore he gave so great a Saviour. He
gave his only begotten Son, an infinite sacrifice, an unmeasur-
able atonement. With such throes and pangs of death as never
can be fully described the Lord Jesus poured out his soul in
unknown sufferings, that he might provide a great salvation
for the greatest of sinners. See Jesus on the Cross, and learn
that all manner of sin and of blasphemy shall be forgiven unto
men. Salvation, that is for me, for I am lost. A great salvation,
that is for me, for I am the greatest of sinners. Oh, hear my
word this day! It is God's word of love, and it rings out like a
silver bell. I weep over you, and yet I feel like singing all the
time, for I am sent to proclaim salvation from the Lord for
the very worst of you.

The Gospel is especially, definitely, and distinctly addressed to sinners. Listen to it: "This is a faithful saying, and worthy of all acceptation, that Christ Jesus came into the world to save sinners; of whom I am chief." "I am not come to call the righteous, but sinners to repentance." "The Son of man is come to seek and to save that which was lost." The Gospel is like a letter directed in a clear and legible hand; and if you will read its direction, you will find that it runs thus: "TO THE SINNER." O sinners, to you is the word of this salvation sent. If you are a sinner, you are the very man for whom the Gospel is intended; and I do not mean by this a merely complimentary nominal sinner, but an out-and-out rebel, a transgressor against God and man.

If you will think of it again, there must be hope for sinners, for *the great commands of the Gospel are most suitable to sinners.* Hear, for instance, this word: "Repent ye therefore, and be converted, that your sins may be blotted out" (Acts 3: 19). Who can repent but the guilty? Who can be converted but those who are in the wrong track, and therefore need to be turned? The following text is evidently addressed to those who are good for nothing: "Let the wicked forsake his way, and the unrighteous man his thoughts: and let him return unto the Lord, and he will have mercy upon him; and to our God, for he will abundantly pardon" (Isa. 55: 7). The very word "repent" indicates that it is addressed to those who have sinned; let it beckon you to mercy.

Then you are bidden to believe in the Lord Jesus Christ. Now, salvation by faith must be for guilty men; for the way of life for the innocent is by perseverance in good works. The law saith, "This do, and live." The Gospel talks of salvation by believing, because it is the only way possible for those who have broken the law, and are condemned by it. Salvation is of faith that it might be by grace. Believe and live! Believe and live! Believe and live! This is the jubilee note of the trumpet of free grace. Oh, that you would know the joyful sound, and thus be blessed! "Repent ye, and believe the Gospel."

If you want any other argument—and I hope you do not—I would put it thus: *great sinners have been saved.* All sorts of sinners are being saved to-day. What wonders some of us have seen! What wonders have been wrought in this Tabernacle! A man was heard at a Prayer Meeting pleading in louder tones

than usual; he was a sailor, and his voice was pitched to the
tune of the roaring billows. A lady whispered to her friend,
"Is that Captain F——?" "Yes," said the other, "why do
you ask?" "Because," said she, "the last time I heard that
voice its swearing made my blood run cold; the man's oaths
were beyond measure terrible. Can it be the same man?"
Someone observed, "Go and ask him." The lady timidly said,
"Are you the same Captain F—— that I heard swearing in the
street, outside my house?" "Well," he said, "I am the same
person, and yet, thank God, I am not the same!" Such were
some of us; but we are washed, but we are sanctified! "Wonders of grace to God belong."

I was reading the other day a story of an old shepherd who
had never attended a place of worship; but, when he had
grown grey, and was near to die, he was drawn by curiosity
into the Methodist Chapel, and all was new to him. Hard-
hearted old fellow as he was, he was noticed to shed tears
during the sermon. He had obtained a glimpse of hope. He
saw that there was mercy even for him. He laid hold on eternal
life at once. The surprise was great when he was seen at the
Chapel, and greater still when, on the Monday night, he was
seen at the Prayer Meeting; yes, and heard at the Prayer
Meeting, for he fell down on his knees and praised God that he
had found mercy. Do you wonder that the Methodists shouted,
"Bless the Lord"? Wherever Christ is preached the most
wicked of men and women are made to sit at the Saviour's feet,
"clothed, and in their right minds." Why should it not be so
with you?

I must now advance to my second observation: A SENSE OF
SINNERSHIP CONFERS NO RIGHT TO MERCY. You will wonder
why I mention this self-evident truth; but I must mention it
because of a common error which does great mischief. This
man was very sensible of his sin insomuch that he called himself
THE SINNER; but he did not urge his sense of sin as any reason
why he should find mercy. There is an ingenuity in the heart
of man, nothing less than devilish, by which he will, if he can,
turn the Gospel itself into a yoke of bondage. If we preach to
sinners that they may come to Christ in all their anguish and
misery, one cries—"I do not feel myself to be a sinner as I ought
to feel it. I have not felt those convictions of which you speak,

and, therefore, I cannot come to Jesus." This is a horrible twist of our meaning. We never meant to insinuate that convictions and doubts and despondencies conferred upon men a claim to mercy, and were necessary preparations for grace. I want you, therefore, to learn that a sense of sin gives no man a right to grace.

If a deep sense of sin entitled men to mercy, *it would be a turning of this parable upside down.* Do you dream that this publican was, after all, a Pharisee differently dressed? Do you imagine that he really meant to plead, "God be merciful to me because I am humble and lowly"? Did he say in his heart, "Lord, have mercy upon me because I am not a Pharisee, and am deeply despondent on account of my evil ways"? This would prove that he was in his heart of hearts a Pharisee. If you make a righteousness out of your feelings, you are just as much out of the true way as if you made a righteousness out of your works. Whether it be work or feeling, anything which is relied upon as a claim for grace is an antichrist. You are no more to be saved because of your conscious miseries than because of your conscious merits; there is no virtue either in the one or in the other. If you make a Saviour of convictions you will be lost as surely as if you made a Saviour out of ceremonies. The publican trusted in divine mercy and not in his own convictions, and you must do the same.

To imagine that an awful sense of sin constituted a claim upon mercy would be *like giving a premium to great sin.* Certain seekers think, "I have never been a drunkard, or a swearer, or unchaste, and I almost wish I had been, that I might feel myself to be the chief of sinners, and so might come to Jesus." Do not wish anything so atrocious; there is no good in sin in any shape or way. Thank God if you have been kept from the grosser forms of vice. Do not imagine that repentance is easier when sin is grosser: the reverse is true. Do believe that there is no advantage in having been a horrible offender. You have sins enough; to be worse would not be better. If good works do not help you, certainly bad works would not. You that have been moral and excellent should cry for mercy, and not be so silly as to dream that greater sins would help you to readier repentance. Come as you are, and if your heart be hard, confess it as one of your greatest sins. A deeper sense of sin would not entitle you to the mercy of God; you can have no title to mercy but that which mercy gives you. Could your tears for ever flow, could your grief no respite know, you would have no claim upon the sovereign grace of God, who will have mercy on whom he will have mercy.

Then, remember, if we begin to preach to sinners that they must have a certain sense of sin and a certain measure of conviction, *such teaching would turn the sinner away from God in Christ to himself.* The man begins at once to say, "Have I a broken heart? Do I feel the burden of sin?" This is only another form of looking to self. Man must not look to himself to find reasons for God's grace. The remedy does not lie in the seat of the disease; it lies in the physician's hand. A sense of sin is not a claim, but a gift of that blessed Saviour who is exalted on high to give repentance and remission of sins. Beware of any teaching which makes you look to yourself for help, but cling to that doctrine which makes you look alone to Christ. Whether you know it or not, you are a lost, ruined sinner, only fit to be cast into the flames of hell for ever. Confess this, but do not ask to be driven mad by a sense of it. Come to Jesus just as you are, and do not wait for a preparation made out of your own miseries. Look to Jesus, and to him alone.

If we fall into the notion that a certain sense of sin has a claim upon God, *we shall be putting salvation upon other grounds than that of faith*, and that must be a false ground. Now, the ground of salvation is— "God so loved the world, that he gave his only begotten Son, that whosoever believeth in him should not perish but have everlasting life" (John 3: 16). A simple faith in the Lord Jesus Christ is the way of salvation; but to say, "I shall be saved because I am horribly convicted of sin, and driven to desperation," is not to speak like the Gospel, but to rave out of the pride of an unbelieving heart. The Gospel is that you believe in Christ Jesus; that you get right out of yourself, and depend alone in him. Do you say, "I feel so guilty"? You are certainly guilty, whether you feel it or not; and you are far more guilty than you have any idea of. Come to Christ because you are guilty, not because you have been prepared to come by looking at your guilt. Trust nothing of your own, not even your sense of need. "God be merciful to me a sinner" is the right way to put it, and not, "God be merciful to me because I sufficiently feel my sinnership, and most fittingly bewail it."

My third observation is this: THE KNOWLEDGE OF THEIR SINNERSHIP GUIDES MEN TO RIGHT ACTION. When a man has learned of the Holy Spirit that he is a sinner, then by a kind of instinct of the new life, he does the right thing in the right way. This publican had not often been to the temple, and had not learned the orthodox way of behaving. This publican is out of rank; he does not follow the rubric; he has gestures of his own. First, instead of coming forward he stands afar off. He does not dare to come where that most respectable person, the Pharisee, is displaying himself, for he does not feel worthy. He leaves space between himself and God, an opening for a Mediator, room for an Advocate, place for an Intercessor to interpose between himself and the throne of the Most High. Wise man thus to stand afar off; for by this means he could safely draw near in the person of Jesus.

Furthermore, he would not lift so much as his eyes unto heaven. It seems natural to lift up your hands in prayer, but he would not even lift his eyes. The uplifting of the eyes is very proper, is it not? But it was still more proper for "the sinner" not to lift his eyes. His downcast eyes meant much. Our Lord does not say that he could not lift up his eyes, but he *would* not. He could look up, for he did in spirit look up as he cried, "God be merciful to me"; but he would not, because it seemed indecorous for eyes like his to peer into the heaven where dwells the holy God.

In the meanwhile, the penitent publican kept smiting upon his breast. The original does not say that he smote upon his breast once, but he smote and smote again. It was a continuous act. He seemed to say—Oh, this wicked heart! He would smite it. Again and again he expressed his intense grief by this Oriental gesture, for he did not know how else to set forth his sorrow.

His heart had sinned, and he smote it; his eyes had led him astray, and he made them look down to the earth; and as he himself had sinned by living far off from God, he banished himself far from the manifest Presence. Every gesture and posture is significant, and yet all came spontaneously. He had no book of directions how to behave himself in the house of

God; his sincerity guided him. If you want to know how to behave yourselves as penitents, be penitents. The best rubrics of worship are those which are written on broken hearts. He who prays aright with his heart will not much err with foot, and hand, and head.

Observe that this man, even under the weight of conscious sin, was led aright; for *he went straight away to God.* A sense of sin without faith drives us from God, but a sense of sin with faith draws us immediately to God. He came to God alone; he felt that it would be of no avail to confess his fault to a mortal, or to look for absolution from man. He did not resort to the priest of the temple, but to the God of the temple. He did not ask to speak to the good and learned man, the Pharisee, who stood on the same floor with him. His enquiry-room was the secret of his own soul, and he enquired of the Lord. He ran straight away to God, who alone was able to help; and when he opened his mouth, it was "God be merciful to me a sinner." That is what you have to do, if you would be saved: you must go distinctly and immediately to God in Christ Jesus. No mercy but the mercy of God can serve our turn, and none can give us *that* mercy but the God of mercy.

The publican did not look round on his fellow-worshippers, he was too much absorbed in his own grief of heart. Specially is it noteworthy that he had no remarks to make upon the Pharisee. He did not denounce the pride, or the hypocrisy, or the hard-heartedness of the professor who so offensively looked down upon him. He did not return contempt for contempt, as we are all too apt to do. No; he dealt with the Lord alone in the deep sincerity of his own heart; and it was well. When will you do the same? When will you cease to censure others, and reserve your severity for yourself, your critical observations for your own conduct?

When he came to God it was *with a full confession of sin—* "God be merciful to me a sinner." He poured out his heart before God in the most free and artless manner: his prayer came from the same fountain as that of the prodigal when he said, "Father, I have sinned," and that of David when he cried, "Against thee, thee only have I sinned, and done this evil in thy sight" (Ps. 51: 4).

Then he appealed to mercy only. This was wise. See how

rightly he was guided. What had he to do wil
it could only condemn and destroy him? Like a nak
threatens to sheathe itself in my heart; how can I ap,
justice? Neither power nor wisdom, nor any other quality
the great God could be resorted to; only mercy stretched out
her wing. The prayer, "God be merciful," is the only prayer
that you can pray who have been greatly guilty. If all your
lives you have spurned your Saviour, all you can now do is to
cast yourselves upon the mercy of God.

The original Greek permits us to see that this man had an eye
to the propitiation. I do not say that he fully understood the
doctrine of atonement; but still his prayer was, "God be
propitiated to me the sinner." He had seen the morning and
the evening lamb, and he had heard of the sin-offering; and
though he might not have known all about atonement, expia-
tion, and substitution, yet as far as he did know, his eye was
turned that way. "O God, be propitiated, accept a sacrifice,
and pardon me." If you know your sin, you will be wise to
plead the propitiation which God hath set forth for human sin.
May the Spirit of God constrain you to trust in Jesus now!

I now close with my last head, which is this—THE BELIEVING
CONFESSION OF SINNERSHIP IS THE WAY OF PEACE. "God be
merciful to me a sinner," was the prayer, but what was the
answer? Listen to this: "This man went down to his house
justified rather than the other."

In a few sentences let me sketch this man's progress. He
came to God only as a sinner, nakedly as a sinner. Observe, he
did not say, "God be merciful to me a *penitent* sinner." He
was a penitent sinner, but he did not plead his penitence; and
if you are ever so penitent and convinced of sin, do not mention
it as an argument, lest you be accused of self-righteousness.
Come as you are, as a sinner, and as nothing else. Exhibit
your wounds. Bring your spiritual poverty before God, and
not your supposed wealth. If you have a mouldy crust in the
cupboard of self-righteousness, no bread from heaven will be
yours. You must be nothing and nobody if God is to be your
all in all.

He does not even say, "God be merciful to me the *reformed*
sinner." I have no doubt he did reform and give up his evil
ways, but he does not plead that reformation. Reformation

will not take away your sinnership; therefore do not speak as if it could do so. What you are to be will make no atonement for what you have been. Do not come because you *are* washed, but to be washed!

The publican does not say, "God be merciful to me a *praying* sinner." He was praying, but he does not mention it as a plea, for he thought very little of his own prayers. Do not plead your prayers; you might as well plead your sins. God knows that your prayers have sin in them. Why, your very tears of repentance need washing! Do not trick yourself out in the weeds of your own repentance, much less in the fig-leaves of your own resolutions, but come to God in Christ Jesus in all the nakedness of your sin, and everlasting mercy will cover both you and your sins.

Next, notice that this man did nothing but appeal to mercy: he said, "God be merciful to me." He did not attempt to excuse himself, and say, "Lord, I could not help it. Lord, I was not worse than other publicans. Lord, I was a public servant and only did what every other tax-collector did." No, no, he is too honest to forge excuses. If the Lord should condemn him out of his own mouth, and send him to hell, he cannot help it; his sin is too evident to be denied. He lays his head on the block and humbly pleads, "God be merciful to me a sinner."

Neither does this publican offer any *promises* of future amendment as a set-off. He does not say, "Lord, be merciful for the past, and I will be better in the future." Nothing of the sort; "Be merciful to me the sinner" is his one and only request. So would I have you cry, "O God, be merciful to me! Although I am even now condemned, and deserved to be hopelessly damned by thy justice, yet have mercy upon me, have mercy on me now." He does not offer to *pay* anything; he does not propose any form of self-paid ransom; he does not present to God his tears, his abstinence, his self-denial, his generosity to the Church, his liberality to the poor, or anything else; but simply begs the Lord to be propitiated, and to be merciful to him because of the great sacrifice. Oh, that all of you would at once pray in this fashion!

Now, I want to cheer your hearts by noticing that this man, through this prayer, and through this confession of sin, experienced a remarkable degree of acceptance. He had come up

to the temple condemned; "he went down to his house jus.
fied." A complete change, a sudden change, a happy change
was wrought upon him. Heavy heart and downcast eye were
exchanged for glad heart and hopeful outlook. He came into
that temple with trembling, he left it with rejoicing. I am sure
his wife noticed the difference. What had come over him? The
children began to observe it also. Poor father used to sit alone
and heave many a sigh; but all of a sudden he is so happy; he
even sings psalms of David out of the latter end of the book.

The change was very marked. Before dinner he says, "Children, we must give God thanks before we eat this meal." They
gather round and wonder at dear father's happy face as he
blesses the God of Israel. He says to his friends, "Brethren,
I am comforted; God has had mercy upon me. I went to the
temple guilty, but I have returned justified. My sins are all
forgiven me. God has accepted a propitiation on my behalf."
What good would come of such a happy testimony!

I grant you, life would be very feeble at first; still, there must
be a time in which it was not there at all; and, again, there
must have been an instant in which it begins. There can be no
middle condition between dead and alive. Yet a man may not
know *when* the change took place. If you were going to the
Cape you might cross the equator at dead of night and know
nothing about it, but still you would cross it. Some poor lands-
men have thought that they would see a blue line right across
the waves; but it is not perceptible, although it is truly there;
the equator is quite as real as if we could see a golden belt
around the globe. I want you to cross the line now! Oh, that
you might go out of this house saying, "Glory, glory, hallelujah!
God has had mercy upon me."

Once more, this man went away with a witness such as I pray
we may all have. "He was justified." "But," you add, "how
do I know he was justified?" Listen to these words. Our blessed
Lord says, "*I tell you* that this man went down to his house
justified rather than the other." "*I* tell you." Jesus, our Lord,
can tell. Into our ear he tells it. He tells it to God and the holy
angels, and he tells it to the man himself. The man who has
cried from his heart "God be merciful to me a sinner" is a
justified man.

"*He* went down to his house justified," and why should

not you do the same? Perhaps you have never been to the Tabernacle before. Possibly you are one of those gentlemen who spend Sunday mornings in their shirt-sleeves at home reading the weekly paper. You have come here quite by accident. Blessed be God! I hope you will go home "justified." The Lord grant it! Perhaps you always come here, and have occupied a seat ever since the Tabernacle was built, and yet you have never found mercy. Oh, that you might find mercy to-day. Let us seek this blessing. Come with me to Jesus. I will lead the way; I pray you say with me now: "God be merciful to me *the* sinner." Rest on the great propitiation: trust in Jesus Christ's atoning blood. Cast yourself upon the Saviour's love, and you shall go down to your house justified.